Teacher's Manual

BANKING LAW AND REGULATION

Third Edition

Jonathan R. Macey
J. DuPratt White Professor of Law
Cornell University

Geoffrey P. Miller
Professor of Law
New York University

Richard Scott Carnell
Professor of Law
Fordham University

ASPEN LAW & BUSINESS

ISBN 0 - 7355 - 1997 - 8

This manual is made available as a courtesy to law teachers with the
understanding that it will not be reproduced, quoted or cited, except as where
indicated. In the event that anyone would like to cite the manual for thoughts
drawn from it, a reference to the relevant page number of the materials text
(with the formula "suggested by") may be appropriate.

Copies of this manual are available on computer diskette. Teachers who have
adopted the casebook may obtain a copy of the diskette, free of charge, by calling
the Aspen Law and Business sales assistant at 1 – 800 – 950 – 5259.

Permissions
Aspen Law & Business
A Division of Aspen Publishers, Inc.
1185 Avenue of the Americas
New York, NY 10036

1 2 3 4 5

TABLE OF CONTENTS

Chapter 1.   Introduction and Overview   Page I-1
Chapter 2.   Entry into the Business of Banking   Page II-1
Chapter 3.   Regulation of the Banking Business   Page III-1
Chapter 4.   Safety and Soundness Safeguards   Page IV-1
Chapter 5.   Geographic Limitations   Page V-1
Chapter 6.   Affiliations Between Banks and Other
             Companies   Page VI-1
Chapter 7.   Insurance and Securities Powers of Banking
             Institutions   Page VII-1
Chapter 8.   Investment Companies and the Regulation of
             the Mutual Fund Industry   Page VIII-1
Chapter 9.   Examination and Enforcement   Page IX-1
Chapter 10. Bank Failure   Page X-1
Chapter 11. International Banking   Page XI-1

Chapter 1: Introduction and Overview

We open the course with a broad overview. Here the question arises how to use the historical material—particularly as many students may not have done the reading before the first class. Professor Carnell begins with a PowerPoint presentation combining historical themes with contemporary illustrations such as political cartoons (of which, for example, the Jacksonian Bank War left a rich trove). Professors Macey and Miller begin with the question of defining a bank. They generally find students more receptive to the historical material after first dealing with that question. They may then assign the historical material for the second or third class.

Early on we include a discussion of the state of banking law today to give students a sense of the revolutionary legal and market changes occurring in banking. We encourage students to see from the outset that banking law is one of the most topical courses they will take in law school. The matters we treat in class are regularly discussed on the news and editorial pages of leading newspapers and magazines, and in congressional hearings.

We sometimes find it interesting to ask the class about their own experiences with banking. We might ask where students do their "banking"—thus seeking to draw out the fact that a variety of institutions, including savings and loan institutions, commercial banks, credit unions, and mutual funds all provide services that from students' point of view seem relatively interchangeable. We also sometimes ask whether students or their families have had any money in a bank or savings institution that failed. We might also inquire as to why students chose to put their money in a particular banking institution, especially when the depository institution in question is located far from where the student lives. Of particular interest, in terms of the later topics treated in the course, are students who do their banking with depository institutions located in other states or countries. We find out how these students make deposits, get cash for day-to-day transactions, and so on. The purpose of all these questions is to instill in students a personal curiosity as to why the banking industry is structured as it is.

We might at this point move to a brief description of the major changes that have occurred in the field since 1980. This discussion tracks material on pages 29-39 (which do not, however, need to been assigned).

We discuss some of the implications of these changes for the practice of banking law. The restructuring that has occurred in the industry and its legal regulation has required bank lawyers to spend considerable energy just keeping current with the law as it evolves. We caution students that the legal rules we teach them will almost certainly change during their professional careers (if not by the time they graduate).

We also strongly encourage students to remain aware of the continuing verities of banking regulation. Banks, which we define in Chapter 1 as institutions that offer linked intermediation and transaction services, have been around for centuries upon centuries;

although evolving in form, they are virtually certain to be around far into the future. Even if the rules and techniques used to regulate banks are rapidly changing, the problems of banking regulation are perennial. Moreover, as the historical discussion in Chapter 1 should demonstrate, we strongly believe that the *future* of banking law can hardly be predicted—nor *present* law understood—without a solid grounding in *past* banking regulation. Winston Churchill's adage (quoted on page 2) bears emphasis: "The longer you look back, the farther you can see forward."

HISTORICAL OVERVIEW

The historical material is designed to be read in one or at most two homework assignments. The material should be relatively easy for students to assimilate, although it covers a considerable time span and, in fact, presents a fairly sophisticated picture of how the structure of the banking industry responds to changes in the law and other factors. To the best of our knowledge, there is no single treatment elsewhere in the literature that summarizes the history of banking from this focus.

This historical overview approaches the topic from a methodological perspective on legal-economic history that Professors Macey and Miller have explored elsewhere in individual and jointly authored scholarship. They have called this the "PTML" perspective, for the four great social systems—Politics, Markets, Technology and Law—that interact with one another in various subtle and reciprocal ways and so drive economic history forward. The industry is constantly moving towards establishing an equilibrium among these four systems, but the equilibrium is equally constantly being disrupted by new developments or exogenous changes that affect one or more of the systems. We spare our students detailed meta-historical arguments for (or against) this PTML perspective, although we sometimes illustrate how the systems relate to each other in reciprocal interaction through a concrete example (the history of the NOW account works well for this purpose).

We usually spend a little time drawing out themes that remain important aspects of banking today, such as the following:

First, the history illustrates the enormous importance of politics in the growth and development of banking law. Banks have always been in politics, and the political system has always affected banks. We encourage students to be aware of the powerful and well-entrenched interest groups (discussed on pages 77-78) that help shape contemporary banking politics. We stress that much banking law cannot be fully understood without keeping in mind the underlying political dynamics.

Second, we stress the role that accidents have played in the historical development of banking law. For example, unit banking—in which banks could have one and only one office—did not arise by conscious choice. As described on pages 12-14, unit banking had its roots in antebellum U.S. banking structure, in the disruptions incident to the Civil War, and in early OCC rulings interpreting (or possibly misinterpreting) the National Bank Act. Unit banking was largely an accident. But once established, it took on a life of its own and drew support from powerful interest groups—especially the owners of small banks, who feared competition from big-city rivals.

The dual banking system—with parallel systems of federal and state banking regulation, and in which banks can choose between federal and state charters—similarly has roots in happenstance (page 12). In creating national banks, Congress had no intention of creating a dual banking system. On the contrary, Congress anticipated expected that the state bank charter would wither away as state banks converted to national charters. When most state banks retained their state charters, Congress sought to tax them out of existence by imposing a punitive 10 percent levy on their bank notes. State banks survived by promoting the use of checking accounts. Thus the dual banking system arose by accident. But once established it developed a strong political constituency.

These examples illustrate the kinds of thematic points you can make based on the historical section. You can use other points as well—for example, the deep suspicion of bigness in financial institutions that has pervaded much of the nation's history. We have found that themes like these work well because they provide a structure for understanding the history while also connecting to present-day realities and foreshadowing many of the topics dealt with later in the course (e.g., geographic restrictions and the dual banking system).

WHAT IS A BANK?

Three Definitions *(pages 47-53)*

We sometimes start the discussion with humorous definitions of a "bank": e.g., the building on Main Street that looks like a Greek temple; a place where people wear white shirts and regimental ties (or the feminine equivalent) and go home at 4:00 p.m.; or an institution run by people who believe in never doing anything for the first time.

We briefly discuss the pros and cons of defining a "bank" based on its legal form. Such a definition is clear-cut and easy to identify. But it is also both overinclusive (institutions that have bank charters may do things that don't look much like banking) and underinclusive (institutions that look a lot like banks don't operate with bank charters).

Next we consider a definition based on services. This is essentially the definition applicable under the Bank Holding Company Act from 1970 to 1987 (see pages 432-33): namely, that a bank is an institution that accepts demand deposits and makes commercial loans. We discuss the advantages of this definition (it seems to overcome some of the problems of over-inclusiveness and under-inclusiveness that plague a definition based on legal form) as well as the defects (it doesn't provide any clear guidance as to why a bank is a bank, but merely identifies key features of the business of many banking firms).

Finally, we turn to the definition we prefer, which is one based on economic function. Here we identify two key elements: (1) *banks are financial intermediaries*; and (2) *banks offer transaction services to effect wealth transfers by means of bookkeeping entries.* We spend a fair amount of time in class unpacking these concepts.

It is useful to start by explaining the distinction between intermediated and direct investments. In an intermediated investment the original supplier of capital has a claim only against the intermediary (the firm which takes the capital and in turn invests it in other productive enterprises). In a direct investment the supplier of capital has a claim against the firm that ultimately uses the capital for productive enterprises. We stress that this distinction, although relatively clear in theory, can be murky in practice: an automobile manufacturing firm, for example, isn't usually considered a financial intermediary, even though its corporate treasurer may invest millions of dollars in other enterprises at times when the firm itself does not need the money. And the question of what is a productive enterprise and what is a mere investment can be fraught with difficulty. Nevertheless the distinction is clear enough in principle, and fully sufficient for our purposes.

We find that we can often trigger a good class discussion by asking what advantages the intermediary offers over the direct investment (cf. page 59, question 1). Why don't people *always* eliminate the intermediary by investing their excess money directly in securities markets? Students may respond as follows: The intermediary provides diversification and thus reduces portfolio risk for the average investor. It offers expertise in selecting and monitoring investments. It achieves economies of scale in the making of investments. And it provides liquidity by greatly increasing the borrower's liquidity (a mortgage gives the borrower spendable dollars in place of illiquid land) while not significantly decreasing the liquidity of the investor in the intermediary (the bank customer can still withdraw money on demand).

After exploring the advantages of intermediation, we turn to transaction services. If time permits, we might introduce the subject by noting other mechanisms for transferring wealth to effect economic transactions. We might discuss the defects of barter (no fixed unit of account, and buyer and seller must each want what the other has) and of a system based only on currency (better than barter, but the holder of cash risks being robbed and incurs the opportunity cost of holding idle money without earning interest). We then move on to a system of wealth transfers based on bookkeeping entries. In the U.S., the principal device for transferring wealth through bookkeeping entries (although slips of paper are also used) is the checking account. We discuss the advantages of the checking account over currency—why people would usually prefer to pay for transactions of any significant size by check rather than currency (and why sometimes they might want to use currency despite the advantages of checks). These days, at least, checks offer greater security than cash (although the holder of a checking account is not entirely free from fraud risk), and the checking account may also pay interest.

We sometimes present a series of simple examples of how wealth can be transferred through bookkeeping entries. We might start with a simple transaction between a buyer and a seller, each with accounts at the same bank. Here, the bank effects the transfer of wealth by crediting one account and debiting the other. We then might move to a slightly more complex example in which buyer and seller do business at different banks that have a correspondent relationship with each other: here there is one more step, namely debiting and crediting the accounts that the banks hold at each other. Finally we introduce the concept of a central, clearinghouse bank (in the United States, the Federal Reserve is the prime example), which is necessary if wealth is to be transferred between clearing banks that do not have a correspondent relationship with each other. This can be easily illustrated with simple examples similar to those found in the book. We find that the use of such simple examples keeps students' attention quite well, and provides a good grounding in how banks function.

We then attempt to tie the two parts of the functional definition of a bank—financial intermediary and custodian of the payments system—together. We discuss how there are many financial intermediaries that are not banks (e.g., life insurance firms and pension funds); and how it would be possible to run a payments system by means other than banks (through the use of courier services carrying currency, for example). But we urge students to consider whether it is not the *union* of these two functions that makes a bank a bank.

Of the two, the payments mechanism appears to be fundamental. It turns out that the easiest way to run a payments system is for the bank to maintain customer accounts. This way the bank can effect bookkeeping entries in accounts without actually having to move currency. But if a bank has customers' money on account, it will obviously want to make productive use of that money. So it invests it in enterprises and becomes a financial intermediary.

Demand Deposits and Fractional Reserves *(pages 53-56)*

The book then turns to a brief look at demand deposits and fractional reserves. We emphasize to our students—especially to those with little or no background in finance—that the existence of demand deposits in banking is the fundamental feature underlying much of the regulations we study later in the course. We ask why banks, unlike most other firms, offer demand debt. The answer has to do with banks' role in the payments system: it would not do if buyers and sellers in economic transactions had to wait for the bank's notice period before consummating the transaction.

The idea of demand debt leads naturally to that of fractional reserves. Here we need to correct students' natural misimpression that only banks operate with fractional reserves. All firms operate with fractional reserves, if that term is understood to mean that firms do not keep enough cash on hand to pay off all their liabilities at once. The difference is that other firms, which do not finance themselves with demand debt, can know for certain whether the cash they have on hand will be sufficient to pay off the liabilities that will actually come due. That is because other firms' liabilities have a fixed term. Those firms need to keep only enough cash on hand to pay off the liabilities that will actually come due.

Banks are different. They finance themselves with demand debt; and in theory all depositors could suddenly demand to be repaid at once. Banks never keep enough cash on hand to pay off all depositors at once. They rely instead on the law of large numbers to ensure that depositors do not demand repayment all at once. The law of large numbers is ordinarily very robust: the chance that all depositors at a good sized bank will, *solely by coincidence*, withdraw their money at any one time roughly approximates the chance that through a bizarre quantum-mechanical fluctuation in the structure of space and time you will levitate and conduct your banking law class from the ceiling.

Thus banks need to keep on hand only enough cash to pay out the withdrawals that are to be expected in the ordinary course. This is the principle of fractional reserve banking: banks need not keep on hand enough cash or other assets readily convertible into cash ("reserves") to pay out all the depositors, but only a fraction of depositors.

BANK RUNS, THE MONEY SUPPLY, AND THE PAYMENTS SYSTEM

Fractional reserve banking, in turn, leads to the role of banks in the money supply and to the problem of bank runs and panics.

Bank Runs and Panics *(pages 57-59)*

The problem of runs and panics merits attention as it is the basic evil against which much banking regulation is directed. We emphasize that runs are frightening, panicky phenomena, and we try to make them come alive for students who probably have never seen a run first hand. The movie *It's a Wonderful Life* is good teaching material here; its depiction of a run on Jimmy Stewart's building and loan is excellent. Note that the movie illustrates a panic as well as a run: the problem began at the local commercial bank, and spilled over into the (presumably solvent) building and loan through a contagion effect. We encourage you to think of lively, attention-grabbing ways to illustrate runs, and would much appreciate hearing from you if you devise a way to make this fundamental feature of banking law a vibrant, lived experience.

We ask students the obvious—but difficult—question, "What's so bad about runs?" After all, runs close a bank at a time when it is undergoing stress, and arguably that is all to the good. Without runs banks might continue to operate long after they had become economically insolvent. In fact, something like that occurred during the 1980s among federally insured thrift institutions (and ultimately helped deepen the cost of the thrift debacle). So even though runs appear to be bad, it is not easy to say why they are bad. Usually the discussion here will adduce a number of disadvantages of runs: (1) inconvenience and losses to depositors; (2) discrimination in favor of depositors who run and against those who do not; (3) the costs of forcing banks to liquidate their assets at fire-sale prices to meet depositors' withdrawals; (4) the danger and transaction costs of liquidity runs—runs on banks that are economically solvent but do not have enough cash on hand to meet withdrawals; and (5) the danger that runs on one or a few banks will spread, becoming generalized banking panics of the sort that occurred in 1933, or localized panics of the sort that during the 1980s and early 1990s afflicted Ohio, Maryland and Rhode Island depository institutions that lacked federal deposit insurance.

Questions and Comments (page 59)

1. Given that banks are subject to runs, why would customers (in the absence of deposit insurance) ever put their money in a bank? Banks offered customers sufficient value in the form of transaction services and return on investment to overcome the expected costs of runs.

2. Why were bank buildings once constructed out of beautiful marble in imitation of classical Greek temples? Elegant Greek revival edifices reassured depositors by tangibly displaying a bank's stability and prosperity—a timeless strength very much in the spirit of John Keats' 1819 Ode on a Grecian Urn ("When old age shall this generation waste / Thou shalt remain . . .").

Role of Banks in the Money Supply *(pages 60-63)*

The material on the role of the banks in the money supply and the payments system is best left to background reading unless you as teacher have a special interest in these subjects.

Role of Banks in the Payments System *(pages 63-65)*

Questions and Comments *(page 65)*

Why will a bank probably be reluctant to give cash to a stranger who presents a check drawn on the bank by one of the bank's customers? Such a transaction exposes the bank to a significant risk of fraud, as the check could be stolen or forged. It is safer for the bank to pay checks through the normal clearance process, in which is has recourse against someone it knows and has some reason to trust—either another financial institution or one of its own customers.

Model Bank Balance Sheet *(pages 65-69)*

We use the model bank balance sheet to illustrate the relationship between leverage and bank failure and to discuss the problem of interest rate risk.

Questions and Comments *(page 69)*

1. Why might savings institutions favor making due-on-sale clauses enforceable? Due-on-sale clauses help protect lenders from interest rate risk by allowing them to call in a mortgage loan that has become unprofitable because interest rates have risen since the loan was made. You might use this problem to explore why due on sale clauses are, or are not, economically efficient (they arguably represent a sharing of interest rate risk between borrower and lender).

2. Can you think of any other reasons why banks have higher leverage ratios than do industrial firms? We don't have a definitive answer to the question, but we find that it can spark interesting observations from students.

4. How much of the distinction between banks and industrial firms does the quoted adage capture? The adage suggests that ordinary corporations are sure of when their debts will come due, but are usually uncertain about their future income streams—whereas banks are unsure of when their debts will come due (as they finance themselves with demand debt) but are more certain of their future income streams. This is a debatable proposition: the law of large numbers ordinarily enables banks to anticipate fairly well when their debts will come due; and deregulation has often left banks less sure of their future income streams. This question can facilitate a good review discussion of demand debt and fractional reserves.

STRUCTURE OF BANK REGULATION

The basic material is straightforward. The questions on pages 75-77 can lead to an interesting class discussion of the pros and cons of the current regulatory structure.

Another interesting question, which might be worth exploring in class, is whether the pervasive influence of interest group politics on banking may be an effective method of obtaining socially desirable banking legislation. This question is closely linked with arguments (such as those in the Bush report) for multiple regulators: both invoke concepts of political pluralism as to help justify what otherwise seems like an odd and unwieldy regulatory structure.

BASIC RATIONALES FOR BANK REGULATION

This section presents what amounts to a debate between Gerald Corrigan (then of the Federal Reserve) and Richard Aspinwall (then of Chase Manhattan Bank). This material lends itself fairly well to class discussion, although one could—alternatively—just assign it as background reading.

If you do take up the material in class, it is useful to tease out why the excerpted arguments might serve the interests of the authors' respective institutions. For example, Corrigan's three reasons for the specialness of banks correlate neatly with the core functions of the Federal Reserve. The Fed plays a key role in the nation's payments system (most banks have accounts at the Fed that can be debited or credited to effect wealth transfers, and the Fed also operates wire-transfer and check-clearing systems). The Fed (through its "discount window") provides backup liquidity to the banking system, which Corrigan depicts as the backup liquidity source for the economy as a whole. And the Fed has responsibility for monetary policy. So Corrigan's article arguably depicts banks in a way that maximizes the importance of the Fed's regulatory authority. Note also that Corrigan pays little attention to deposit insurance, which is arguably at least as important as the functions he does mention. Does he downplay deposit insurance because it falls under the jurisdiction of the FDIC?

On the other hand, Aspinwall's response arguably advances the interests of large banks seeking to expand into businesses not traditionally considered part of banking. If banks are special, then that specialness might justify confining banks to more traditional activities—and (as Aspinwall notes) subjecting them to heavy regulation. Aspinwall approaches the issue from a free-market perspective skeptical of the arguments for regulation that might flow from concluding that banks are special.

Chapter 2: Entry into the Business of Banking

INTRODUCTION

The focus of this relatively brief chapter is on the entry controls that exist to screen out inappropriate people and firms who try to enter the business of banking. Obviously a large number of inappropriate people gained entry into the banking and savings and loan businesses during the 1970s and 1980s as evidenced by the high incidence of financial fraud and incompetent management in the banking industry. This suggests that the screening process has not worked as well as it might. One of the issues that we stress when teaching this material is whether it is possible to design a screening process to weed out bad managers without having the process become hopelessly politicized or subjective. In addition we stress three particular aspects of entry controls: (1) the formal legal criteria for obtaining a bank charter; (2) administrative law—the discretion given to governmental actors; (3) the implications of the dual banking system on the shape of bank regulation generally.

We ask students why entrepreneurs should be able to receive a charter for a general corporation as a matter of right, while receiving a charter for a bank is a matter of regulatory discretion. This is the first formal, legal difference between bank chartering and other forms of corporate chartering. The answer to the question is not as obvious as it may at first appear. The most obvious answer is that the government has a lot at stake in the health of the nation's banks due to the presence of federally sponsored deposit insurance. However, deposit insurance simply places the government in the position of being a potential creditor of a federally insured bank. Non-governmental creditors can't prohibit other sorts of businesses from incorporating. Moreover, if the government is worried about the safety and solvency of a particular financial institution, they don't necessarily have to prohibit that institution from receiving a bank charter—the government can protect its financial interests by declining to extend the umbrella of deposit insurance protection.

Thus the existence of a regime of federally sponsored deposit insurance is not a very satisfactory answer to the question of why we allow federal regulators to have discretion over whether bankers will receive a charter or not. Other, more plausible (but not completely plausible) explanations are: (1) that depositors can't adequately protect themselves from unscrupulous bankers both because depositors can't monitor what happens to their deposits and because banks keep a large portion of their liabilities in highly liquid form (cash) which is easy for management to steal; (2) there is a macro-economic need to protect the integrity of the banking system, and chartering serves this need; (3) there is a need to restrict competition in banking but not in other areas; (4) banking is a highly regulated industry and the chartering process is necessary to ensure that all of these regulations will be complied with (thus the bank chartering process can be analogized to the process by which a public utility obtains a certificate of need before establishing a new facility such as a nuclear power plant).

The first major legal difference between the process of obtaining a bank charter and the process of obtaining any other form of corporate charter is that the issuance of bank charters is discretionary with regulators, while the issuance of other forms of charters is not. The second major difference is that there is a dual state/federal system for issuing bank charters; while the issuance of general corporate charters is purely a matter of state law.

THE CHARTERING PROCESS

Practical Problems in the Formation Process *(pages 96-97)*

Like other corporatons, banks are formed by promoters. During the formation process, it is necessary for the promoters to enter into contracts with providers with goods or services. These pre-incorporation contracts present problems of enforcement and the possible personal liability of promoters, that are similar to the problems presented by pre-incorporation contracts for any firm. It is useful to encourage students to think though how a bank is formed as a practical matter, and why this may create problems for the allocation of rights, duties, and risks.

Then, we discuss the special problems that arise when it is a bank that is being formed. Banks present special problems because, unlike most business entities, the formation process can be long and involved, and does not always result in a successful outcome. Corporations can be established as of right, with minimal risk. Banks are much more costly to establish and require affirmative approval by regulators. Thus, preincorporation contracts present special risks to promoters in the banking context.

We also encourage students to imagine the actual process of representing promoters in this context. Much of the job is to establish constructive and helpful working relationships with the staff of the chartering agency. We encouage discussion of the attitudes that regulators are likely to display towards entrepreneurs desiring to establish a bank, and describe the process as one involving important human interactions.

Federal Banking Agencies *(pages 98-106)*

The next issue we discuss is the amount of discretion given to the relevant regulator. The comptrollerof the currency charters national banks. We point out to students that the National Bank Act originally gave the comptroller very little discretion about issuing charters (the relevant statutory language *directs* the comptroller to issue a charter if the prescribed conditions are met). We suggest that this may have made sense at some point in history, but when the FDIC was created the comptroller necessarily got a lot more power because national banks automatically received FDIC insurance. But under FDICIA new national banks must specifically apply to the FDIC for deposit insurance.

The comptroller sees itself as having a lot of discretion in granting bank charters. We spend some time reviewing the criteria that the comptroller considers in deciding whether to issue a charter. On the one hand the comptroller says deficiencies in one area can be overcome by strengths in other areas. On the other hand, the comptroller also says that deficiencies in certain factors tend to reflect negatively on other factors. These statements may not be consistent. We ask students which of these views makes more sense.

We discuss the impact of the Community Reinvestment Act (important) and the need for a comprehensive operating plan. We encourage the students to think through the advice they would give organizers with respect to the types of people they should enlist in the organizing effort (as well as the types they should avoid). In advising bank promotors, counsel face a difficult job of providing legal advice without infringing on the business judgment of the clients, in situations where business factors (the identity of proposed management, the sophistication of the business plan) can play a paramount role in the success of the legal strategy. We encourage students to think through in a realistic way how they might go about walking this fine line.

Questions and Comments (pages 101-02)

1. *In the absence of deposit insurance, what justifications would the OCC or OTS have for denying a charter to a group of entrepreneurs who wished to establish a bank or thrift institution? What if bank charters were granted as a matter of right?* We emphasize that, while the justification for discretionary chartering becomes significantly weaker in the absence of deposit insurance, reasons for discretionary chartering would still exist even in a world without deposit insurance. In the absence of deposit insurance the OCC might still not grant a request for a bank charter if there is a strong possibility that those seeking the charter will engage in fraud. Giving crooks a license to operate a bank is like giving them a license to steal.

2. *What are the pros and cons of vague standards that leave licensing agencies broad case-by-case discretion?* This question offers an opportunity for extended class discussion on an interesting topic. It may be useful to line up arguments offered by students, both pro and con, on the board.

3. *What incentives does a regulator have to grant or deny a charter?* This question is also a potentially fruitful basis for class discussion. Students may come up with the idea that regulators have a strong incentive to grant charters because doing so expands their regulatory turf, but that they have an incentive to deny charters if they fear being criticized *ex post*—say by Congress or the media—if a bank they have chartered subsequently becomes insolvent. These incentives may or may not line up with the public interest.

5. *Why require that a "necessity" exist for any new federal thrift charter?* We don't require that there be a "necessity" when chartering an industrial corporation. Why can't the willingness of entrepreneurs to place substantial capital at risk in the enterprise be a sufficient indication that the proposed institution will serve the public interest and convenience?

6. *How can the OTS determine whether there is a "necessity" for a new institution?* We bring out the fact that the champions of the public interest who come forward to object to

proposed bank charters are often competing banks. One might question their qualifications to protect the public, since these institutions are probably more afraid of competition that will cut into their profits, even while providing services at lower cost for consumers. The question can lead to a discussion of the pros and cons of bank failure, and to thought about whether banks are different from other firms in this respect.

8. What effect would fully and accurately risk-based deposit insurance have on the analysis? If deposit insurance was accurately risk-adjusted and priced, then the government's interest in preventing bank failure would seem to be lower because the federal deposit insurance funds would not be as threatened by the possibility of bank failure. The question raises the issue of the connection between deposit insurance and the chartering decision, which is one of the most fundamental issues in the area.

Camp v. Pitts (pages 102-05)

This case addresses the question of what standard reviewing courts should use when the comptroller denies a request for a bank charter and the applicant protests.

We first ask why the comptroller denied this request for a bank charter. His vague conclusion was that "factors in support of the establishment of a new National bank in the area are not favorable." This indicates that the comptroller seemed to think that the problem was that there were already too many banks in the area. In other words, the bank did not meet the convenience and needs factor.

With regard to the standard of review issue, we note that a key fact in the case is that the relevant statutes do not require formal hearings. We then spend some time comparing the various decisions of the district court, the court of appeals, and the Supreme Court.

The district court concluded that de novo review was not warranted in the circumstances and found that the comptroller had not acted in an arbitrary or capricious manner. On the basis of this finding, the court upheld the comptroller's determination.

The court of appeals decided that the comptroller's ruling was "unacceptable" because its basis was not stated with sufficient clarity to permit judicial review. And the court of appeals said that the case should be remanded for a trial de novo before the district court because the comptroller had not adequately responded to the applicants' presentation after having two opportunities to do so internally.

In the litigation before the Supreme Court, the comptroller did not challenge the appellate court's conclusion that the comptroller's decision was not sufficiently specific. Rather, the comptroller only challenged the court's ruling that the case should be remanded for a trial de novo before the district court.

The Supreme Court held that: (a) the comptroller's action is subject to judicial review under the Administrative Procedure Act; and (b) there is no requirement that the comptroller hold a hearing or make formal findings when passing on applications for new banking authorities.

For the Court the critical point was that there could not be de novo review without a formal hearing to create a record at the trial court level. To the Court it simply made no sense as a matter of statutory interpretation to create a legal regime in which an administrative agency could be compelled to submit to a hearing before a trial court when the relevant statute did not compel the agency to conduct a hearing within the agency itself. Put another way, unlike situations where the APA or other statutes require a hearing record, the court reasoned that it would make no sense to require parties to prepare a record in a judicial proceeding more substantial than required by the comptroller under the statute. The Court declared that, as a general matter, judicial review should focus on an administrative record. Where there is no administrative record, then there is no basis for de novo review.

Clearly, the Court's decision is not without logic. But what, we ask, is the implication of this decision? The court finds that the "focal point for judicial review of the comptroller's determination should be the administrative record already in existence, and no some new record made initially in the reviewing court." And, the Court reasons, if the comptroller has not created a record that is sufficient to provide a reviewing court with a basis for evaluating the decision, the reviewing court should simply obtain from the comptroller either through affidavits or testimony, whatever additional information it may need.

This suggests that the comptroller never has to do anything to justify its decisions. One might even ask whether the comptroller can do nothing until its (arbitrary) decision is challenged and then justify its decision *ex post*. The point seems reinforced by the fact that the Court does not require there to be a contemporaneous explanation of the agency's decision. But, the Court says, where there is a contemporary explanation of that decision, "the validity of the comptroller's action must . . . stand or fall on the propriety of that finding." Thus, the comptroller seems to be discouraged from providing a contemporaneous explanation of its decision!

Finally, after acknowledging the logic of the Court's decision (which, as noted above, rests on the fact that it doesn't seem right for the courts to create a requirement that an administrative agency grant a hearing when the statute did not compel one), we go back to the court of appeals' decision and ask whether that was really as nonsensical as the Court suggests. The court of appeals was not suggesting that frustrated applicants for bank charters have a general right to a de novo judicial hearing. Rather, the court of appeals would only have required a new trial where the comptroller's earlier actions had been inadequate. This doesn't seem to do nearly as much violence to Congress's intentions as the Court was suggesting.

Chartering Process for State Banks *(pages 106-09)*

If for some reason a would-be entrant into the banking industry can't get—or doesn't want—a charter from the comptroller, it can consider applying for a charter from a state regulator. In this sub-section we devote some time to the significance of this fact.

Here there still is a large federal role because the FDIC considers the same factors as the comptroller when determining whether to give a state chartered bank deposit insurance. As noted above, the role of the FDIC has been strengthened as a result of FDICIA since now separate application must be made even by national banks for deposit insurance.

For us the key question in this sub-section is what is the state interest in controlling entry into the chartering business. We briefly describe the relevant state statutes. The case we have selected provides a way of addressing this question.

In *State Banking Board v. Allied Bank, Marble Falls*, the Supreme Court of Texas reversed the lower court and allowed the bank charter. The point is to make sure students understand that there is a different, but by no means less complex, set of administrative rules and standards that apply when decisions by state banking regulators are being challenged. Another, equally important point is to observe that the lower court was probably right that the agency was very vague; but to point out that since the regulator's decision about whether to grant a charter application is inherently subjective, there may be no way to reach the kind of objectivity in fact finding that the court of appeals is seeking in its opinion. Thus some form of deference to the decisions by administrative agencies may be inevitable in the chartering context.

THE DUAL BANKING SYSTEM

This section continues with the theme introduced in the preceding section about the proper scope of state law in the context of bank chartering in light of the fact that the federal stake is so large due to the presence of federally sponsored deposit insurance. In light of the fact that deposit insurance raises the federal interest in sound banking regulation and reduces the interests of state regulators, is the competition among regulators really such a good thing? That is the basic issue evaluated in this section.

The dual banking system means that, at various points in history banks could choose the regulations to which they are subjected with respect to such things as: (1) reserve requirements; (2) capitalization rates; and (3) branching rules. Over time, the states' persistent efforts to permit banks to operate under a more liberal regulatory environment has led the federal government to preempt state authority in each of these areas.

Professor Miller's article (pages 110-15) observes that the dual banking system is a political sacred cow. We ask why this is the case. One reason is that the state bureaucrats have organized into a powerful political coalition to ensure their own survival. The banks they regulate also have a strong interest in maintaining the present system.

Professor Miller favors a system of chartering for banks just like the system for chartering nonbanking corporations. But if there is a conflict of interest between state and federal regulators that has led to a "race to the bottom" because the states get all of the benefits from a loose system of regulation while all of the costs are borne by the federal government, wouldn't this situation be even worse under the regime Professor Miller describes? On the other hand, if these reforms were coupled with risk-based deposit insurance that really coupled deposit insurance premiums to bank riskiness, this problem would disappear, and the benefits of federalism and jurisdictional competition for bank chartering described by Professor Miller and Professor Scott could still exist.

We spend a bit of time describing Professor Miller's basic points, and then relating them to the arguments of Professors Butler and Macey described in Question and Comment 5 (pages 115-16).

Questions and Comments (pages 115-17)

2. How does competition in bank chartering differ from competition in corporate chartering? The differences are (1) banks have historically been forced to charter in the state where they have their principal depository business, whereas general corporations can charter in any state, even if their offices or plants are elsewhere; and (2) banks have a choice between state and federal chartering authorities (and actually a choice of types of charter at both levels), whereas corporations must obtain a charter from a state agency. Note that as a result of interstate banking, it is becoming easier for banks to obtain charters in states even when much of their business is conducted in other states.

9. In light of the analysis presented in this chapter, what, if anything, do you think is accomplished by the dual banking system? This question sometimes sparks heated, and interesting, disagreements among students.

This material provides a nice introduction to chapter 3, which deals with the regulation of the business of banking, because they suggest that the nature of the regulations that are likely to be promulgated in a particular area depend on many factors such as historical factors, the identity of the relevant regulators, and the nature of their incentives.

Chapter 3: Regulation of the Banking Business

The book now turns to an investigation of the sorts of things a depository institution may do once it has obtained the necessary regulatory approvals to commence business, as discussed in Chapter 2. This chapter discusses regulation of banks themselves, not that of bank holding companies. Also, certain major substantive issues are deferred for later treatment: geographic expansion (deferred until Chapter 5) and securities and insurance activities (largely deferred until Chapter 7).

The chapter begins with a discussion of state and federal power, thus extending the treatment of the dual banking system in a more applied context. The remainder of the material in this chapter is structured around a bank's balance sheet (recall the simple model balance sheet in Chapter 1). After a note about the respective powers of the state and federal governments over banking institutions chartered by the other sovereign, we look at the limits on various fee-generating activities by banks, which are off-balance sheet. We then look at the asset side of the balance sheet, and examine the various limitations on bank investments. We move to the liability side of the balance sheet and ask about various restrictions and programs affecting the liabilities that a bank can take on. We look at the topic of capital adequacy, which ties capital (on the right side of the balance sheet) with assets (on the left). Finally, we go off the balance sheet again with a brief nod towards the corporate law regulation of banking firms.

THE DUAL BANKING SYSTEM: A REPRISE

The material in Chapter 3 starts with another look at the dual banking system, this time focusing on the specific question of the powers of state or federal regulators to control the business of depository institutions chartered by the other sovereign.

There are two aspects to the problem here: (1) state regulation of federally chartered institutions; and (2) federal regulation of state chartered institutions. Both are treated under the heading of pre-emption. An interesting discussion can sometimes be triggered by asking whether the pre-emption analysis should be the same or different in these two settings. This can get us to fairly deep questions about the (anomalous) nature of a federally-chartered private enterprise.

As to state regulation of national banks, is there is a special federal interest in national banks that could support a stronger-than-normal pre-emption rule? Or perhaps, given the oddity of federal chartering, perhaps the pre-emption rule should be weaker than normal? Or should the strength of federal pre-emption of state regulation depend on the nature of the regulation in question?

As to federal pre-emption of state laws regulating state-chartered institutions, we can deal here with issues already discussed in Chapter 2, regarding the competition in regulation and the rationales for the dual banking system. We also can ask whether there is a special federal interest in the banking industry (as illustrated, in fact, by the presence of federal bank chartering), that might justify a stronger-than-normal set of pre-emption standards in the banking context. The presence of federal common law in this area, notwithstanding the *Erie RR v. Tompkins* decision, adds another interesting wrinkle. The courts continue to recognize the presence of federal common law in the banking area, notwithstanding its anomalous character. Should this common law be pre-emptive of state regulations? To the same extent as statutes or regulations? Should the fact that common law is judge-made make a difference for the pre-emption analysis?

ACTIVITIES RESTRICTIONS

National Banks *(pages 123-47)*

This topic requires close attention to the statutory language of 12 U.S.C. § 24(Seventh). The textual description of the statute is sufficient for discussion purposes, although students would profit from carefully reading the actual text in the statutory supplement (ask why the clause has become so long and complicated; the answer is that political interests have obtained many special deals which have been successively added to the original, short clause). The key here is the incidental powers clause, which provides that national banks shall have "all such incidental powers as shall be necessary to carry on the business of banking."

We start by noting the analogy between this clause and the necessary and proper clause of the constitution, which most students have studied. We ask whether the standards for interpreting the clauses should be the same, or different. We try to draw out the argument that the interpretation of the Constitution might be much broader than that of the statute, since the Constitution was designed to endure for the ages and was made intentionally hard to amend, while Congress can easily amend the banking law if some provision is no longer adequate. This suggests that the powers given to national banks under § 24(7) might be narrower than the corresponding powers of the Congress under the necessary and proper clause.

It is interesting to discuss whether § 24(7) expands or contracts the powers that national banks would enjoy in the absence of the provision. It might seem obvious that the clause expands the powers of national banks, but on careful consideration the answer is not clear-cut. If the clause had not been included in the banking law, national banks would almost certainly have been given incidental powers in any event under the general principle that the grant of a power carries with it incidental powers necessary to make the powers transferred in the grant effective. The explicit adoption of an incidental powers provision thus might possibly be taken to indicate a congressional intent that the powers of national banks not be extended too far by interpretation.

Section 24(7) apparently establishes two zones of powers: (1) the "business of banking" strictly construed, and (2) powers "necessary" to carry on the business of banking. The latter is logically broader than the former. One of the consequences of this logic is that it is very difficult to get a handle on what the "business of banking" is because it is never necessary for courts to actually decide that issue. This is a problem that haunts the cases. Congress has provided some guidance by specifying a number of powers as falling expressly in § 24(7), including discounting and negotiating promissory notes, receiving deposits, etc. You might ask students how helpful this is (it looks helpful at first, but if you analyze the specific powers set forth in § 24(7) you realize that they are not incidental powers but the essence of banking). If these are the incidental powers, then perhaps § 24(7) means very little. On the other hand, if they represent (counter to the apparent terms of the statute) the "business of banking" *per se*, then what is incidental to them is completely a matter of interpretation.

Another fundamental problem of interpretation with this statute is whether the powers granted therein are "fixed" in their Nineteenth Century form, or whether the statute adopts an evolving standard for the business of banking. And, if the standard is an evolving one, how is it to be administered in a particular case where applying the statute would apparently stop a course of evolution that would otherwise occur? This too is an issue that will haunt the cases.

Arnold Tours (pages 124-29), involving travel agency services, provides the test adopted by all major decisions until *VALIC* (page 129-30): whether the activity in question is "convenient or useful in connection with the performance of one of the bank's established activities pursuant to its express powers under the National Bank Act." We start by asking whether this isn't too generous a test, even though as applied to the facts it invalidated the activity in question. After all, § 24(7) speaks of powers "necessary" to carry on the business of banking, while the court here speaks of powers that are "convenient or useful." Many things that are convenient or useful are not necessary.

You can use this case to highlight the problem of statutory evolution. The court here finds it important that national banks have not traditionally been in the travel agency business except for very minor services undertaken as accommodations to customers. This implies that the case might have come out differently if banks had in fact been in the travel agency business for a long time. You can also ask whether the court's test carries a dynamic or evolutionary element. Note that the court expands on the statute by establishing three zones, not two as in the statute: (1) a bank's "express powers" under the National Bank Act; (2) a bank's "established activities" pursuant to those express powers; and (3) activities which are "convenient or useful" in connection with the performance of one of those established activities. The second element of this test suggests a dynamic interpretation: the court will show deference to established activities if they are pursuant to the express powers under the statute.

We find it useful to ask what social policy is fulfilled by keeping banks out of the travel agency business. This usually provokes an interesting discussion. Some students suggest the potential for conflicts of interest in one form or another—banks, for example, might steer customers to organizations that borrow from the bank, etc. Other students are likely to adopt a more cynical posture and suggest that the major social policy served by keeping banks out of the travel business is the policy of protecting the travel agency business from competition. These students argue that consumers of travel services would likely be well served if banks were allowed to operate travel agencies.

One other point that might be worth bringing out about this case is the notable lack of deference shown by the court to the comptroller of the currency, even though the comptroller as the officer charged with the administration of the National Bank Act would ordinarily be entitled to great judicial deference. The same thing happens in a number of later cases in the book. We ask students why the court did not defer to the comptroller in this case, and return to that theme in later cases.

Questions and Comments (*pages 129-31*)

1. Note that the *VALIC* case is the authoritative word on the subject. We have included the case in the note because the discussion in *Arnold Tours* strikes us as more thoughtful (and thought-provoking). It is useful to have students articulate what, exactly, the Supreme Court is saying as a matter of doctrine. It is including certain activities within the "core" of the "business of banking," right? But, if this is the rule, are there any limits to the kinds of things the comptroller can authorize, either as part of this core authority, or as "incidental" to it? You might explore with students whether the qualification in the footnote provides a sufficient brake on a comptroller anxious to authorize new powers.

2. Doesn't Judge Hamley egregiously mangle the statutory language? Where does a court get the discretion to re-write a statute like this? You can use this question as an entrée into a jurisprudential discussion about the respective roles of courts, legislatures, and agencies in the regulation of banking institutions.

5. What is suggested is that an "established activity" might be brought within the ambit of "express powers." This would allow the statute to evolve with changing technologies and markets. History then becomes relevant as a means for determining whether such evolution has occurred. Of course, the formulation in the case begs the question of whether such evolution was contemplated by Congress, or what the limits on its speed should be.

M&M Leasing (pages 131-38), treats personal property leasing. We use this case to explore whether the statute adopts an evolving standard for the business of banking. Judge Sneed says that he doesn't want to repeat Justice Holt's mistake—which was to think that he could stop commercial development by judicial fiat. But Sneed himself might fall prey to the same mistake, in that he refuses to accept as within the powers of a national bank a personal property lease in which the bank incurs substantial residual risk of fluctuations in value at lease-end. If the industry was evolving in this direction, doesn't it stop progress to deny banks this power?

You might also use the case to illustrate how what is essentially a loan transaction can be structured as a lease. This raises basic questions about the nature of business law. There's a tension throughout this course, and in many other business law courses as well, between the goals of (a) allowing entrepreneurs to do business in a flexible manner, with confidence that their arrangements will result in predictable legal consequences; and (2) preventing people from evading important legal restrictions and regulations by carrying on the substance of a transaction through a different legal form. There are important arguments in favor of preferring form, and equally important arguments favoring looking through the form to the substance. This is a useful discussion to have with the class at some point during the course, and the *M&M Leasing* case is a good opportunity to broach the subject.

Note the discussion after the case indicating that the actual business problem dealt with by bank leasing transactions is no longer very important, as a result of changes in the tax code and the banking law. This does not however detract from the importance of the case insofar as it engages in a general discussion of the incidental powers of national banks, or the interpretation of § 24(7).

National Retailers Corp. (pages 141-43). At issue is a service offered by a national bank that takes transaction data as recorded in cash registers and performs computation operations on them that permit the customer retailing firm to obtain information about various aspects of its business. The bank undercuts the price of a nearly identical service offered by National Retailers Corp. and takes away customers. National Retailers sues claiming the activity was not authorized for national banks. The district court applies the *Arnold Tours* test to conclude that the activity in question was not convenient or useful to any of a bank's express powers under the National Bank Act.

Once again the comptroller has tried to allow national banks into a new line of business and once again the courts have stopped him. Why don't the courts pay deference to the administrative interpretation? It almost appears as if the opposite is happening. We ask students what is wrong as a matter of policy with allowing banks to offer this service to retailers. Perhaps it is that banks will get too much information from their customers, or that the banks will use the information for improper purposes. But the same information was available to other data processing service organizations, and the retailer didn't have to use the bank's service if it didn't want to. In any event what is wrong with giving banks lots of information about the business affairs of their customers? Arguably this information would improve the bank's credit decisions by providing useful information about the customer's default risk. Some banking economists have suggested that the practice of compensating balances (bank borrowers were expected to keep substantial funds at the lending bank in checking accounts) fulfilled this purpose: it allowed banks to obtain information about their loan customers and thus make the credit decision more accurately.

The OCC Interpretative Letter (pages143-46) illustrates how far the law has evolved from the restrictive standard of *National Retailers*, even though the case itself has not been repudiated. You can go through the letter and try to identify what sorts of activities are considered by the comptroller to be in the "core" of the banking business, and what sorts are incidental to the core. You can ask whether there are any real limits to the sorts of activities that could be justified for national banks, given the analytical style adopted by the OCC staff. The letter also provides a good introduction to the Internet, and to the kinds of Internet-based services that banks today are providing to their customers.

Questions and Comments *(page 147)*

1. We repeatedly ask our students to identify the public policy rationale for denying particular powers to banking institutions. Typically, the answers bring us back to the presence of deposit insurance. This helps illustrate why the presence of demand debt in a bank's balance sheet, and the government provision of deposit insurance as a means for coping with the structural problems incident to this demand debt, is one of the most fundamental issues for bank regulation. Students are also likely to identify political influence and desire for protection from competition as relevant factors. This can lead to interesting policy discussions.

2. Try challenging students to reconcile the comptroller's letter with the *National Retailers* case. Some typically try to do it. You can poll students to see if the class views the two as consistent.

LIMITATIONS ON INVESTMENTS

The text now jumps on to the balance sheet and looks at the regulatory limitations on the bank's assets. First the book treats limitations on the kinds of investments a bank can make.

Impermissible Investments *(pages 150-56)*

Real Estate (pages 150-53)

We start with investments that are categorically prohibited to national banks. Most real estate investments fall in this category, other than real estate acquired through foreclosure of mortgages and the bank's premises. We discuss why banks might be limited in their ownership of real estate. Real estate may have highly volatile values and thus present significant investment risk. Real estate is illiquid and cannot be sold easily to meet depositor demands to withdraw funds. Real estate may require substantial management and oversight for which a bank may not be competent. There may be conflicts of interest if a bank takes an equity or ownership interest in real estate when it is also a lender, although this requires some analysis and thought.

On the other hand, is real estate more volatile than other investments a bank makes—for example, unsecured loans? The value of these investments depends both on current interest rates, which fluctuate, and on the probability that the loan will be paid off. At least if a bank purchases real estate, it will always have the property, and therefore will have some value (unless the property happens to be encumbered by environmental liabilities such as toxic wastes). And real estate may not fluctuate in value in tandem with other bank investments, thus providing an opportunity for a more diversified investment portfolio. So how clear is the case against bank real estate investment?

You should probably note the exceptions to bank real estate investment powers. Obviously if real estate is to be collateral for loans, banks have to have power to foreclose and own the property, at least for a while. Banks can also own their own premises (why?).

Questions and Comments (pages 152-53)

2. Banks' authority to own their own premises creates the potential for abuse, as noted in this problem. Here you might return to a question posed on page 59: why were bank buildings once constructed out of beautiful marble in imitation of classical Greek temples? The explanation we look for is that if a bank can permanently own only one piece of real estate, it is likely to overspend on it relative to other investments.

3. The case of *murabaha* financing is interesting, especially if you have someone in the class with personal experience in Islamic finance. This issue can raise interesting—if somewhat

sensitive—questions about cultural differences in banking, and about the sorts of problems that U.S. bank face as they do increasing business overseas.

Securities (pages 153-56)

Next we turn to securities investments. It is worth spending some time on the rules in this area. In light of the savings and loan debacle, we find it stimulating to invite discussion of whether the regulators were correct in barring banks and savings and loans from the junk bond market (was it a matter of locking the barn door after the horse was out; did it aggravate the problem by impairing the market for the massive portfolios of junk bonds that banks and savings and loans held; are junk bonds clearly such bad investments?).

We ask students to explain the rationale underlying the general rule that depository institutions may not hold equity securities. The theory appears to be that equities are more risky than debt securities, but query whether a blue chip stock is more risky than a typical corporate bond. Further, equities, although more risky, have historically offered higher rates of return. And by the application of modern portfolio theory banks could, if they were permitted to do so, obtain a diversified portfolio of equities that was no more risky than the market as a whole. The prohibition against banks owning stocks dates from a period before portfolio theory; should it be modified to allow banks to hold diversified portfolios?

We also discuss the exceptions to the rule against national banks owning equities. Obviously, a bank can hold stock in its subsidiaries. Otherwise banks could not have subsidiaries. The service corporation subsidiary is also pretty easy to justify; most larger banks could just as easily perform the activities in question though a subsidiary of a bank holding company, but smaller banks can take advantage of the power to invest in service corporation stock in order to perform the services in question without having to go through the expense of forming a banking holding company.

The small business investment company exception is harder to explain on public policy grounds. The principal rationale for keeping banks out of general equity securities is a concern for risk; yet here banks are permitted to invest in highly risky venture capital operations, subject to fairly generous maximum investment limits. We ask our students to explain this rule; they usually come up with the explanation that the exception is due to the political influence of the small business lobby.

You might also make reference at this point to the topic of merchant banking and portfolio investments by banking institutions. These are treated in chapters 6 and 7.

Restrictions on the Extension of Credit (pages 156-233)

The book now turns to the function of making loans. We start this section by observing that banking regulation strongly encourages banks to make loans rather than to invest their assets in other ways. We ask why this might be so, given that there is no guarantee that loans are safer than securities investments of various sorts. Loans, indeed, may often be less safe in the sense that there is usually less of a developed market for them—especially for the commercial loans that have long formed the core of the commercial bank's loan portfolio. If the concern is to preserve bank safety and soundness, isn't it rather odd to force banks into a market that is less efficient and often more risky than alternative investments? This question should lead to a brief reprise of the nature of a bank as a financial intermediary. Banks may be efficient suppliers of capital to loan markets because of their expertise about such markets and their superior information about the borrower's condition. Even so, why should the law enter the picture to push the banks in the direction of making loans? If banks have a comparative advantage in making loans, why can't they be expected to serve loan markets on their own, without special encouragement from the government?

Usury *(pages 156-72)*

We start with an exploration of usury. We discuss the economic pros and cons. Most economists, at least, believe that the cons outweigh the pros, since the usury statutes, where they have any bite, tend to choke off the supply of credit to those who need it most—poor people and those with questionable credit. These people, if they need loans, may be forced to go to less reputable sources such as loan sharks. They may thereby lose the protections that the law affords to other borrowers (such as protection against harassment in bill collection), and they will have to pay an interest rate that reflects, not only their own default risk, but also the surcharge the loan shark demands to compensate himself or herself against the risk of being apprehended and invited to become a guest at a government-operated correctional facility.

Nevertheless the laws on usury have an undeniably ancient pedigree. This raises the puzzle as to why they may have endured for so long. We encourage you to throw this question out for class discussion. It's adventurous, but students seem to like to speculate about the topic and they often have interesting things to say.

Questions and Comments *(pages 157-59)*

1. This raises the question whether choice of law provisions can provide a means for avoiding usury ceilings. You might ask whether it makes sense to deny parties the ability to freely contract for high-interest loans, but to allow them to freely contract for an applicable law that allows such loans.

2. The time-price differential rule seems to give merchants an advantage over banks with respect to the supply of store credit. We ask briefly what might explain this rule. One answer is that a paternalist government might be less worried about merchant credit because there is built-in assurance that the customer is using the credit to purchase the sorts of useful things you can get in a department store rather than socially wasteful things such as liquor or drugs. Another is that merchants have high costs of enforcement because it is difficult for them to obtain an enforceable security interest in the items they sell—although this doesn't distinguish merchants from unsecured lenders who are subject to the usury prohibition. Yet another answer is political: merchants have enough political influence to protect this practice in which they have been engaging for hundreds of years.

6. If usury laws have a good purpose, isn't it limited to cases where the debtor is poor or unsophisticated? Does it make any sense to apply these laws with full force to situations where both parties are solvent and/or sophisticated?

We examine usury limits on national banks, beginning on page 159. The relevant statute is 12 U.S.C. § 85, and the most important (and most interesting) issue concerns the provision relating national bank interest to the interest allowed under state law. Here we contrast two notions: (1) competitive equality between national and state banks—under which national banks would be treated the same as state banks for all purposes, and (2) most favored lender status—under which national banks enjoy special treatment and are entitled to charge the highest interest rate allowed by state law to lenders of any sort, even if state-chartered banks are limited to a lower rate (as will be seen, the competitive equality rule plays a major role in the jurisprudence over branching restrictions on national banks, discussed in Chapter 5).

The *Tiffany* case (pages 159-61) established that national banks enjoyed most favored lender status for purposes of the usury statute. We ask students to describe the scenario the court probably had in mind when it decided the case. After several tries, they usually note that the case was decided in 1874, at a time when the national government was trying to force the state-chartered banks to convert over to national charter (recall the history discussion on pages 11-12).

Question 3 (page 161). The scenario is that some former state bankers, or other business interests in the state, prevail on the state legislature to adopt a statute limiting state banks to a rate, say, of 3 percent while permitting other lenders in the state to charge 8 percent. This would not hurt state banks because by hypothesis no state banks would be left if the National Bank Act had succeeded in driving them out of business. The result might be discrimination against national banks, and this was something that the National Bank Act was designed, in part, to prevent.

The *Marquette* case (pages 162-66) involves the important question of the territorial application of § 85. We encourage students to engage in careful statutory analysis by asking them to identify the word on which the outcome of this case turned (it is "located"). As will be seen, many of the cases elsewhere in this book turn on one or another key words. We will frequently encounter examples of the craft of the business lawyer in reading a statute carefully on behalf of a client to discover ways of interpreting the statute to allow the client to do what the client wants to do. Here, if the Omaha bank was "located" in Minnesota for purposes of § 85, the Minnesota state rate would govern. The Supreme Court ruled, probably on public policy grounds, that the Nebraska statute applied; this opened the national market to the exportation of state usury ceilings.

We ask what would have happened if the Minnesota-based Marquette bank had retaliated by entering the Nebraska market and attempting to charge Nebraska customers at the higher Nebraska usury rate. The simple answer is that since the Court ruled that a bank is "located" where it has its home office, the Minnesota bank could not adopt the usury rate of the state where its customers were located. But a careful reading of the statute suggests a way around this difficulty; the "except" clause of the statute suggests that a national bank might be able to charge the rate allowed by a state where it serves customers if it "exists" in that state, even if it is not "located" there; and the wording of the statute seems to imply that a bank can "exist" in a state other than the one where it is "organized". This might what the obscure note 19 in the Court's opinion is all about.

Smiley v. Citibank (pages 167-71) tests the limits of the *Marquette* ruling. The issue here is whether § 85 authorizes a national bank to charge late-payment fees that are lawful in the bank's home State but prohibited in the states where the cardholders reside. As the Supreme Court observes, the case turns on the definition of "interest" under the federal statute. If late-payment fees are interest, then § 85 applies; otherwise, no.

Once again, the case implicates the comptroller's discretion under *Chevron*. In what might be viewed as a blatant attempt to influence the outcome of pending litigation, the comptroller noticed for public comment a proposed regulation declaring that late fees and certain other charges were "interest" under § 85. This regulation was proposed more than a hundred years after the enactment of the original § 85. For the deference-minded Supreme Court, this made no difference: "we accord deference to agencies under *Chevron* . . . because of a presumption that Congress, when it left ambiguity in a statute, meant for implementation by an agency, understood that the ambiguity would be resolved, first and foremost, by the agency, and desired the agency (rather than the courts) to possess whatever degree of discretion the ambiguity allows."

Given such a test, it is hardly surprising that the Court upheld the comptroller's interpretation as reasonable. You might ask your students if they agree. Isn't "interest" compensation for the advance of money? Late fees sound more like a penalty for breaching a promise—a sort of liquidated damages. Further, have you ever heard of interest that didn't depend on the amount of time credit was extended? Yet late fees didn't usually depend on the amount of time the credit was outstanding; they applied as soon as the repayment was late. Given the result in *Smiley*, are there any legally enforceable limits to the comptroller's powers? Or, is this too shortsighted an approach: are the limits political rather than legal?

Questions and Comments (pages 171-72)

1. The question suggests that states will follow suit in order that their own institutions not be at a competitive disadvantage. This again illustrates some of the dynamic features of the dual banking system.

2. Credit card banks are important parts of the national financial landscape. They are not a central focus of this book, although it should be noted that they can obtain federal deposit insurance and can obtain national bank charters. Students can be assigned the statute if the instructor thinks these are worth more extended discussion.

Modern Consumer Protection Rules (pages 172-82)

One interesting feature of borrower-protection regulation, worth raising with students, is why we survived so long under a regime where the only borrower-protection rule was the hoary prohibition of usury, whereas since the mid-1970s there has been a plethora of new legislation enacted for this purpose.

The material should be self-explanatory for the most part, and we do not give it extended class discussion. We do ask why bank lobbyists didn't derail the juggernaut of consumer protection statutes since the 1970s. The reasons appear to include the fact that the statutes were not thought to be that costly to banks, that they were seen as the price banks had to pay to avoid more burdensome regulations, and that because they applied to all the relevant interest groups in the banking industry no single group had a major incentive to fight them.

Note on financial privacy (pages 175-78): You might mention the tension between the goals of law enforcement and economic efficiency, and the concern for maintaining privacy in customer financial records, which has recently emerged on the front burner of public debate. Different laws go in different directions. For example, the Bank Secrecy Act and the Anti-Drug Abuse Act both require disclosure of customer information, whereas the Financial Privacy Act and the Gramm-Leach-Bliley Act protect customer privacy. It is interesting to have students identify the competing policy considerations and suggest appropriate methods for reconciling them, which may or may not align with the course actually taken by Congress. Students may be inclined to favor stringent protections of privacy, but the instructor might illustrate ways in which the law enforcement and economic efficiency rationales could suggest an interest in more restricted privacy rights for financial institution customers. In the course of discussion, you might ask whether there is a difference between financial privacy, on the one hand, and other types of privacy, on the other (e.g., the interests in privacy protected by the Constitution).

Question 6 (page 178). This question suggests that the privacy protections favor large financial conglomerates which can share information internally. Is it sensible for Congress to provide a built-in benefit for large institutions? Is privacy any less threatened when a customer's information is shared within a large financial conglomerate than when it is sold to a third party?

Predatory lending (page 179): As the book went to press, the issue of predatory lending had not been squarely addressed by either Congress or the regulatory agencies, although it was clear that enhanced regulation was imminent. Here, the instructor might bring out the tension between protecting homeowners and other vulnerable borrowers, on the one hand, and enhancing the credit available to low income communities on the other. The tension might seem easy to resolve, but this is not necessarily so: unless the category of "predatory" loans is carefully defined and circumscribed, lending institutions might balk at increasing their loans to low-income borrowers out of fear that their actions could be classed as "predatory" even if they merely reflect justifiable business needs. Lending institutions may complain that they are caught between the rock of the CRA, which requires them to make loans in low income communities, and the hard place of rules on predatory lending, which may require that any loans they make be uneconomical. However, such complaints should be reviewed skeptically because they may reflect the institutions' self-interest. It may be useful to encourage a relatively free-floating discussion of these issues, although the instructor must be aware that they can be emotionally charged and that the topics need to be handled with sensitivity and with respect for all reasonable points of view.
The Seidman testimony can be a jumping off place for discussion, both for what it says about predatory lending, and for the relatively amorphous definition she provides.

Regulations Intended to Ensure Credit Availability (pages 182-99)

The ECOA is an important statute. We discuss a principal enforcement problem, namely how to treat the use of apparently bona fide credit risk information that has the effect of screening out disproportionate numbers of persons in one or another of the protected classes. The banking agencies accept that the ECOA adopts an effects test; this seems reasonable since it would be extremely difficult in most cases to prove intent. On the other hand, the statute would hardly make sense if it required banks to make credit equally available to all applicants regardless of their credit risk. The Fed attempts to resolve the difficulty by allowing banks to take income—the principal credit risk variable—into account in allocating credit so long as there is a "demonstrable relationship" between an income requirement and creditworthiness for the level of credit involved. Query, however, whether this represents an adequate disposition of the problem.

Possible avenues for discussion are suggested in the questions and comments on pages 182-84. Question 2 raises an issue whether there can be a bona fide business defense to an apparent violation of the ECOA, as well as an issue as to the definition of "credit" in that statute. Question 3 raises the question of discrimination based on citizenship, which is permitted: should it be? What about "reverse" discrimination based on age (question 4) or socioeconomic status (question 5)? Are these valid exceptions to the general rule of nondiscrimination? Should they be?

The consent decree in *Chevy Chase Federal Savings Bank* (page 184-85) is an important event in the evolution of fair credit law. Here, the Justice Department extended the theory of the ECOA to go after a depository institution for alleged "red-lining" (refusing to make loans in predominantly poor, minority areas). You might ask your students whether this is a proper extension of the law, given that it doesn't depend on proof that the institution actually discriminated against any particular individual. You might also consider why, if Chevy Chase was so adamant that it had done nothing wrong, it elected to settle with the government? Was the government so strong that the institution had no choice but to capitulate, even if it believed itself in the right—or do you think it actually had something to hide?

The CRA material (page 186-99) merits discussion in light of the increasing importance of this statute in banking regulation. We start by noting that although the CRA was not considered to be very significant when it was enacted, it has become a major stumbling block in the path of bank expansion and consolidation. CRA challenges have derailed or delayed a number of mergers over the past few years, and the threat of such challenges has generated a flood of publicity by banks regarding their community reinvestment policies. The CRA has also become exceptionally controversial from a political point of view: it is dear to many community activists, and deeply troubling to many conservatives. This political aspect has given the CRA a symbolic significance even beyond its practical importance. As the book notes, in 1999 conflict over whether the CRA should be pruned back or expanded nearly derailed the Gramm-Leach-Bliley Act, the most fundamental bank reform legislation of a generation. In the end, however, Congress left the CRA more or less alone.

We try to get students to evaluate the pros and cons of the CRA. Among the pros, consider: (1) it supplements the antidiscrimination rules of the ECOA by requiring depository institutions to demonstrate affirmative efforts to serve some of the same groups that are protected by the ECOA; (2) it encourages economic development in low and moderate income neighborhoods, and thus contributes to "self-help" efforts from within these communities to combat problems such as poverty, drug abuse, unemployment, illiteracy etc.; (3) it helps preserve distinctive communities within the United States, thus sustaining a "gene pool", as it were, of cultural resources that otherwise might be lost; (4) it encourages banks to commit their resources in local communities where those resources can best (most efficiently?) be invested.

Among the cons: (1) the CRA discourages the supply of credit to the very people whom the act is designed to help—people living in low and moderate income neighborhoods—since depository institutions will be loath to serve these neighborhoods in the first place if they know that they will be required to make extensive uneconomical investments if they do; (2) the CRA contributes to an inefficient allocation of credit in the society by requiring financial institutions to make uneconomic loans in their local communities; (3) the CRA discourages the diversification of loan portfolios by encouraging nondiversified concentration of loans in local neighborhoods; (4) the CRA reduces the profitability of banks despite the fact that bank failures have cost taxpayers hundreds of billions of dollars; (5) the CRA is prone to capricious or biased administration by regulators, who might use ostensible CRA noncompliance as a means of punishing institutions for thwarting the regulatory will in other respects; (6) the CRA is a potentially fertile breeding ground for extortion by local community leaders who might use the threat of a CRA challenge as a means for obtaining low cost credit for themselves or their friends; (7) the CRA treats depository institutions as public utilities, when in fact they are private institutions; (8) the CRA requires a great deal of costly paperwork and administrative expense, yet can be relatively easily circumvented by depository institutions which utilize sophisticated public relations firms to present a positive picture of their commitments to local communities.

The fact that more cons are listed than pros does not necessarily mean that they are weightier; the pros may be more important than the cons. The readings on the CRA are provocative and interesting, and can generate excellent class discussion. Emotions can run high in this area, and it is important for the professor to maintain an atmosphere of respect for differing points of view. Moderate positions, such as Swire's "safe harbor" approach or Klausner's tradable CRA credit proposal, are worth serious consideration.

It can also be very interesting to explore the idea of community development lending as an alternative to the CRA that might accomplish some of its goals while avoiding some of what critics see as the CRA's costs. If the government makes grants to community development lenders, who then re-allocate credit to minority or low-income neighborhoods on the basis of a profit motive rather than bureaucratic guidelines or political influence, wouldn't this be a potentially constructive way to enlist the operation of the price system in the service of valuable social goals?

Questions and Comments (pages 191-92)

3. This can be used as a vehicle to bring out the policy issues of whether the regulations should, or could, be clarified.

4. This raises the issue whether the community reinvestment act is really about communities any more, or rather about something else, such as the politics of race or redistribution.

Questions and Comments *(pages 197-98)*

5. The question of the scope of the CRA—limited to insured depository institutions other than credit unions—can be the basis for an interesting discussion. If the purpose is to direct credit to low-income or minority communities, shouldn't other lenders be included? What about firms whose lending is limited to making investments in securities?

Note on community development lending (pages 198-99). Instructors might bring out a difference between CRA and community development banks. The latter enlist the private sector as a means for allocating credit to low-income communities in ways that might be more economically efficient than could be achieved by the government. This can be the basis for an interesting discussion about the use of the private sector, and the profit motive, as a mechanism for allocating government subsidies and benefits.

Instructors can also use this material to discuss other means for facilitating and enhancing economic development in low-income communities. These might include the Korean revolving credit system discussed in the Macey-Miller article, or other proposals floated by students in class. It is sometimes possible to stimulate a genuinely creative, thoughtful dialog among students about the best means for achieving what most would agree is a desirable public policy goal of enhancing economic development in depressed communities.

Lender Liability *(pages 199-33)*

This material introduces the important topic of lender liability. There are two main types of lender liability: first, liability to borrowers for actions taken by the lender during the course of the lending relationship that are found not to be in good faith; and second, liability to third parties for harms caused by the borrower that are related in some way to the extension of credit by the lender. In the second case, the question is whether the lender participated sufficiently in the borrower's affairs to be liable for harms the borrower may have caused.

Brown v. Avemco (pages 200-04) introduces the first topic. Borrower purchases an airplane with borrowed funds and gives the lender a security interest in the aircraft. The loan contract contains a standard acceleration clause giving the lender an explicit right to accelerate the note if the airplane is sold, leased, transferred or otherwise encumbered without the prior permission of the lender. Borrower enters a lease agreement with three others, without providing formal notice to the lender, under which the others will contribute to debt service and when the loan is paid off will have an option to purchase a one fourth interest in the plane each for a nominal sum. After a while the group attempts to prepay the loan by tendering the outstanding principal and interest, but the lender rejects the tender on the ground that the ownership change obligated the lender to purchase additional insurance. Lender says it is accelerating the loan and demands full payment including payment for the additional insurance (around $200). The borrower refuses to pay for the additional insurance, whereupon the lender repossesses the airplane and sells it at auction to satisfy the debt. Borrower sues for conversion of the aircraft. The trial court rules that the lender can accelerate the loan at will provided there was a breach of the acceleration clause, but the appeals court says that the lender had a duty to be reasonable in its acceleration of the loan and remands for a new trial.

We start by establishing that the lender had exercised rights that were at least ostensibly given in the contract to which the borrower had freely agreed. The question at issue in the case is not whether the lender had the right to accelerate the loan under the contract, but whether the lender's decision to accelerate the loan and then repossess the collateral was within the bounds of good faith.

We ask whether there is evidence that the lender was behaving opportunistically on the facts as recited in the case. The lender did appear to be more than a bit stiff-necked about the insurance, since the borrower was at the lender's doorstep tendering full payment of the principal and interest. It is somewhat difficult to see why the lender was demanding insurance since the loan was going to be repaid imminently.

There is little evidence, however, that the lender was behaving in a classically opportunistic manner—that is, by seeking to obtain an unbargained-for advantage during the course of contractual performance. If, as Professor Fischel believes, the purpose behind the good faith requirement is to police against opportunism, then perhaps lender liability would not be appropriate on these facts.

We ask students to recommend what the lender should have done in this case. The obvious solution, after cases like *Brown v. Avemco*, is for lenders to negotiate with borrowers before acting against the collateral. Much apparently depends on creating a good paper record showing efforts to be reasonable. Thus, rather than precipitously sending an agent out to repossess the airplane, perhaps the lender should have attempted further negotiations. Note, however, that there are costs of further negotiations. If the borrower receives notice that the lender is likely to go after the collateral, the borrower might hide the collateral or move it somewhere where the lender cannot get at it, thus increasing the lender's costs and reducing the lender's security. This danger is obviously present when the collateral is an airplane.

Even more importantly, attempts to negotiate with borrowers pose the danger that the lender will be held to have waived rights under the loan contract. This happened in the interesting note case, *Alaska State Bank v. Fairco* (page 205, note 7), where the lender repeatedly extended a loan to a borrower that defaulted on its obligations from the very start. When the lender did finally proceed against the collateral, the borrower sued for damages and won. The trial court held that the course of dealing between the parties effected a modification of the loan agreement under which the bank would not go after the collateral for a reasonable period. Another case illustrating the same sort of danger is *First National Bank v. Twombly* (note 8), where a bank was mulcted in punitive damages for allegedly acting fraudulently or maliciously in its dealings with a defaulting debtor.

State National Bank v. Farah Manufacturing Co. (pages 206-13) is a famous lender liability case involving FMC Corp., a clothing manufacturing concern in El Paso, Texas. The essence of the case is the management change clause, which the lenders had inserted into the loan in order to prevent the return to management of William Farah, the former dominating figure in the company who had been forced out during an earlier period of financial distress. The management change clause gave the banks the right to call the loan if there was any change in top management which any two of the banks in the lending consortium considered to be adverse to their interests.

William Farah attempted to get back into the management, and apparently had the votes on the board of directors to get himself reinstated as CEO. This presented the banks with a dilemma. They didn't want Farah back, but they also didn't want to call the loan because doing so would bankrupt the company. Acting through attorney Donohoe, the banks elected to bluff: they threatened to call the loan if William Farah returned to management, even though they didn't have any firm intention to do so (and in fact probably intended not to do so). The threats were believed, and Farah didn't return. Things continued to slide downhill under the management approved by the banks, however, and eventually Farah did return. Miraculously, under his management the company made a turnaround. And Farah exacted his revenge on the banks by suing them and obtaining a judgment for nearly $19 million. The Texas Supreme Court affirmed the judgment, concluding that the evidence was sufficient to support liability on any of three theories: (1) fraud, (2) duress, and (3) tortious interference with contract.

Students generally find this case quite interesting, despite (or perhaps because of) its rather complex factual setting. We ask whether it was realistic for the court to expect that the banks would not threaten to exercise their rights under the acceleration clause even though they had no fixed intention of actually carrying out the threat. In ordinary negotiations people threaten to exercise legal rights all the time even though they don't intend to carry out the threats. Why should banks be different? What else were the banks supposed to do to protect their security?

We ask what the attorney should have done in this case to avoid liability. Students often come up with excellent answers, to the effect that the attorney could have achieved much of his purpose by indicating that the lenders would seriously consider calling the loan if William Farah returned, without bluntly saying that he intended to padlock the building. These answers suggest that the opinion may not have as much effect on banking practice as might be believed on first glance.

We ask whether the banks were behaving opportunistically here. It doesn't look like they were: they were trying to protect their security, and to do so in a way that was perhaps impolitic, but probably not opportunistic. Indeed, as Professor Fischel observes, Farah's return to management was the very eventuality against which the management change clause was inserted in the loan agreement. Given the probable absence of opportunism, was the court right to impose liability on the lenders for their actions in this case?

Kham and Nate's Shoes (pages 215-19) introduces the possibility that a lender's claim will be equitably subordinated by a bankruptcy trustee. The simplified facts of this case, as presented by the court of appeals, are that the bank, which had substantial unsecured loans outstanding to the debtor, opened a $300,000 line of credit for the debtor in reorganization under chapter 11 of the bankruptcy code under a judge's order giving this loan super-secured status, senior even to the expenses of the reorganization. The contract establishing the line of credit provided that it could be canceled on 5 days notice and that the bank retained the right to terminate financing at any time.

The borrower drew down $75,000 line of credit ($10,000 of which was repaid), after which the bank gave notice of termination. Later the bankruptcy judge approved a plan of reorganization which subordinated the bank's claims under the line of credit, thus converting this loan from super-secured statutes to the status of an ordinary unsecured credit.

We start by establishing the facts and calling students' attention to § 510(c) of the bankruptcy code which authorizes subordination under equitable principles. We then ask what the bank did to justify the subordination, in the bankruptcy judge's view. There were three principal actions: (1) the bank forced the debtor into bankruptcy in the first place by refusing to extend further credit on earlier loans unless bankruptcy was declared (the bank wanted the debtor to go into bankruptcy in order to obtain super-secured status for additional advances); (2) the bank terminated the line of credit without just cause, since its claim on the line of credit was super-secured and never was in realistic danger of not being paid off; (3) the bank allegedly terminated the line of credit in an attempt to increase the priority of draws under its earlier, unsecured letter of credit, thus attempting to gain an unfair advantage over other creditors; (4) the bank unreasonably terminated the line of credit without giving the borrower a fair opportunity to seek additional lenders.

Judge Easterbrook's opinion is noteworthy, not only because it rejects these arguments, but also because of the rhetoric it uses to do so. It is very difficult, in our view, to reconcile the rhetoric of Judge Easterbrook's opinion in the present case with the views expressed in the earlier lender liability cases excerpted in this book. Judge Easterbrook takes the position that a contract is a contract, and that in the absence of fraud or opportunism the lender is entitled to enforce the contract according to its terms.

In discussing this case, you might ask students why the lender abruptly terminated the line of credit. There appears to have been no evidence that the lender believed that advances under the line of credit were insecure. It is quite possible that the lender actually hoped, as the bankruptcy judge found, that the termination of the line of credit would somehow enhance draws on the unsecured letters of credit and promote them to super-secured status. This may have been a quixotic hope, and the lender abandoned any claim to super-security for the earlier loans in its appellate briefs, but assuming that the lender did intend to get the better of other creditors by this strategy, wasn't this a good reason to conclude that it was behaving inequitably and to subordinate its claim?

We now move to a discussion of lender liability rules protecting third parties. The key to these cases is the extent of the lender's control over the borrower's operations. Clearly if the lender does no more than advance funds and insist on repayment when due, the lender faces no serious threat of liability to any third party with whom the borrower may have dealt (or whom the borrower may have otherwise injured). But when the lender's activities go beyond this, it may face a risk of potential liability. The problem, of course, is that lenders as a practical matter must monitor borrowers and must retain an array of sanctions to assure that the borrower does not act so as to place the lender's security in jeopardy.

The classic case is *Connor v. Great Western Savings & Loan* (pages 221-26). The essential facts are these: the developer goes to a bank for financing for tract housing. The bank supplies the funds to enable the developer to purchase the land and construct the houses. In addition to the interest the bank gets for the land purchase funds and the construction loan, it has the right of first refusal to make long term mortgage loans to the buyers of the homes. The loan for the purchase of the land is structured as an arrangement under which the bank takes title to the real estate in order to avoid state law limitations on the percent of appraised valuation that a bank could loan (note by the way that California savings and loans are shown here as being allowed to invest directly in real estate).

Pursuant to this arrangement the bank requires the developer to submit plans of the homes to be built but does not examine the plans. It does suggest increases in selling prices, and does make first mortgage loans to home buyers under the right of first refusal. During construction the bank's inspectors visit the site weekly to verify that the plans are being followed and money is being disbursed only for work done. The homes are eventually sold, and later it turns out that the slab foundations are poorly designed and crack due to the soil conditions at the site, causing financial harm to the homeowners. We can assume that the developer is out of the picture—bankrupt—and we have a suit against the lender to make good the harm. Chief Justice Traynor of the California Supreme Court concludes that the complaints state a cause of action and that the suit should go forward.

We start by asking students what, specifically, the bank *did* to subject itself to liability in this case. Was it the fact that the bank requested plans but didn't look at them? Isn't it standard practice for a construction lender to request copies of the construction plans—in fact, wouldn't it be irresponsible if a construction lender didn't get copies of the plans? Was it the fact that the bank's inspectors visited the site weekly but didn't discover the problem with the slabs? Again, however, weren't the bank's site visits for the purpose of making sure that the funds were being spent as called for under the construction loan—not to check out on soil conditions? Would the bank have escaped liability if its inspectors had not visited the site? Was liability based on the fact that the bank had a right of first refusal for first mortgages on the homes to be sold? But why should this make a difference?

We examine some of the economic arguments. Justice Traynor dismisses as "conjectural" the argument that imposing liability on lenders in this kind of situation would drive marginal builders out of existence, increase housing costs, and decrease the total housing stock. Conjectural, maybe, but isn't the conjecture pretty persuasive? Isn't the probable result of this decision to impose a new set of costs on banks making loans for home construction, and that those costs are going to be passed on to the builder, and ultimately the consumer, in the form of higher prices? And isn't it plausible that some homes would not be built because the cost of financing would be too high with this liability in place?

Justice Traynor offers some conjectures of his own. He says that if reliable construction is the norm, the recognition of a duty on the part of tract financiers to home buyers should not materially increase the cost of housing or drive small builders out of existence. But doesn't this assume that reliable construction is costless? There's always a risk that even the best-laid plans—or house foundations—will "gang aglee," right?

What about Justice Traynor's suggestion that if existing sanctions are inadequate, imposition of a duty at the point of effective financial control of tract building will insure responsible building practices? This assumes that financial institutions are good monitors of quality in new housing construction, doesn't it? Is this clearly correct? Is the construction lender the most efficient bearer of the risk that the homes will not be soundly constructed?

What about Justice Traynor's apparent slam-dunk that "there is no enduring social utility in fostering the construction of seriously defective homes." Who could argue with this? But doesn't Justice Traynor mis-state the issue here? In pointing to the benefits of imposing a duty on construction lenders, doesn't he ignore some of the potential costs?

On the other hand, there is much to be said for Justice Traynor's concern, is there not? After all, who is in a better position than the construction lender to monitor the builder, or to exercise leverage over the builder to ensure that adequate quality is provided to home buyers? And it's true, isn't it, that the housing market is one in which there are significant information asymmetries—the defects are often hidden or latent, and in such situations it often makes sense for the law to impose an implied warranty of habitability and merchantability. Given that home builders often operate with very small capital, and so are likely to be judgment proof in the event of a serious defect of the sort discovered in this case, doesn't it make good sense to insert the construction lender as a de facto insurer for the construction lender's ability to stand behind the quality of his or her work?

You should emphasize to your students that the *Connor* case is unusual; no other state has gone this far by way of imposing liability on the lender for defects in the construction, and even California has cut back on the rule. This reception might suggest that *Connor* is bad law. On the other hand, the class should consider the possibility that the home building industry might exercise political clout sufficient to prevent a rule like this from spreading even if it represents very sound social policy.

CERCLA liability (page 227-33): *Fleet Factors* and *Bergsoe Metal* involved potentially devastating liability for the costs of cleaning up toxic waste disposal sites under the Comprehensive Environmental Response, Compensation and Liability Act (CERCLA). At issue was whether a lender is an "owner or operator" of a facility; if so, CERCLA's strict cleanup liability attaches. The statute provides little guidance as to the meaning of the terms "owner" or "operator". It does provide, however, that the phrase "owner or operator" does not include "any person who, without participation in the management of a . . . facility, holds indicia of ownership primarily to protect his security interest in the . . . facility." 42 U.S.C. § 9601(20)(A).

The subsequent history of the controversy is also quite fascinating. The EPA issued a rule to govern the problem after extensive consultation with banks, environmental groups, and other affected parties (excerpted starting on page 228). Perhaps adopting an overly zealous approach to agency powers, the D.C. Circuit rejected the rule as being beyond EPA's statutory authority. The Justice Department and the EPA thumbed their noses at the D.C. Circuit, saying that they were going to follow the EPA rule anyway as a matter of their enforcement discretion. This odd and somewhat unsatisfactory compromise was finally resolved—or so it appears— when Congress, as part of a Defense Department Appropriations measure (!), reincarnated the

EPA's rule and forbade further judicial review. So, constitutional challenge aside, it appears that the EPA rule is, indeed, the authoritative interpretation of the secured lender exception to the Superfund statute.

You can use questions 1-2 (pages 232-232) to identify the relevant policies.

We have not included specific problem sets about CERCLA, but as an exercise, it might not be a bad idea for the instructor to prepare such a problem set in order to test the student's ability to understand the detailed provisions of the EPA rule which are excerpted in the book.

Regulation of Deposit Taking *(pages 233-63)*

Issues Under the Federal Deposit Insurance Act *(pages 234-46)*

The book now leaves the asset side of the balance sheet and moves to the liability side. The text sets forth the basic deposit insurance program. The things to remember are (1) there are now two programs, the Bank Insurance Fund (known by the jocular acronym "BIF") and the Savings Association Insurance Fund (referred to ironically as "SAIF"), each administered by the FDIC; (2) the FDIC charges insured institutions assessments—insurance premiums—to cover its losses and administrative expenses in carrying out its insurance function (but may waive these assessments if the fund is well-capitalized); (3) these assessments are based on the amounts of deposits and were not traditionally adjusted for risk; (4) the 1991 FDICIA statute required risk-adjusted premiums, although it provided no guidance as to how risk is to be calculated. We start with some technical issues under the deposit insurance program, before moving to the policy issues.

Philadelphia Gear (pages 235-42) concerns the question of what is a "deposit" subject to the deposit insurance program. This case deals with a standby letter of credit. Here the question is not whether national banks can offer standby letters of credit, but rather whether the standby letter of credit represents a deposit within the meaning of the Federal Deposit Insurance Act. If it is a deposit then it will be insured up to $100,000 in the event of bank failure. Thus if a bank fails while a standby letter of credit it issues is outstanding, and if thereafter the beneficiary seeks to recover on the letter of credit on the ground that the account party has defaulted, the FDIC must determine whether to pay out the first $100,000 on the letter of credit under the federal deposit insurance system.

This is what happened in *Philadelphia Gear*. Orion is a customer of Philadelphia Gear. As account party Orion obtains a letter of credit from the now-infamous Penn Square Bank for the benefit of Philadelphia Gear in the amount of $145,000, the letter to be payable only upon presentation to the bank of documents by Philadelphia Gear indicating that Orion had failed to pay its debt to Philadelphia Gear. In connection with the letter of credit Orion gives the bank a promissory note in the amount of $145,000. The promissory note evidenced the bank's rights against Orion in the event that the bank had to pay on the letter of credit.

Now Penn Square bank goes broke, spectacularly broke. Later Orion doesn't pay Philadelphia Gear. Philadelphia Gear presents the letter of credit and supporting documentation to the FDIC as receiver of the Penn Square bank; the FDIC refuses to pay anything. So the question is clearly framed: is a standby letter of credit a "deposit" protected by the federal deposit insurance system.

After establishing what the court's holding was—that the standby letter of credit was not a deposit—we ask students if they agree with the decision. We start with the plain language; again part of the purpose of this exercise is to drill students in the careful reading of a statute, a skill that we find often needs remedial attention.

The statute defines "deposit" to mean "the *unpaid balance of* money [that's not at issue here] *or its equivalent* [put that on hold] *received* or held *by the bank in the usual course of business* for *which it has given or is obligated to give credit, either conditionally or unconditionally, to a commercial . . . account* [that's satisfied here] *which is evidenced by a letter of credit . . . on which the bank is primarily liable* [that's satisfied—the bank issued a letter of credit on which it was primarily liable]". So the only issue under the statute seems to be whether there is present here the unpaid balance of the equivalent of money. All the other elements of the definition seem to be satisfied.

The statute provides guidance on this question. An account is regarded as evidencing the receipt of the "equivalent" of money when issued in exchange for a "promissory note upon which the person obtaining any such credit . . . is primarily or secondarily liable." Is that present here? Certainly: Orion gave the bank a promissory note on which Orion was primarily liable. So it looks, does it not, as if every element of the plain language of the statute is entirely satisfied. Why isn't this enough to end the case right there, especially given the Court's repeated assertions in other cases that if the language is plain that is the end of the matter?

How does the Court escape this statutory language? Its theory is that "while the note here may have been labeled a promissory note on its face and may have been a promissory note under state law, it was not a promissory note for purposes of . . . federal law". So the court here creates a new category of oxymoron: the non-note note. It's called a note, looks like a note, smells like a note: but it's not a note, at least not for purposes of the FDI Act.

Now where does the Court get off saying this is not a note? After all, it seems to satisfy all the prerequisites for a note commonly understood, right? O'Connor's theory is that to be a note for purposes of the Federal Deposit Insurance Act, it must represent the "hard earnings" of individuals. She draws this "hard earnings" theory from the remarks of Rep. Steagall on the floor of the House of Representatives where he says that we need a banking system in which citizens can place their "hard earnings" without fear of bank failure. So, says O'Connor, Congress wanted to ensure that someone who put tangible assets into a bank could always get those assets back.

We press our students as to whether this theory makes any sense. Wasn't this language about "hard earnings" more or less a way of giving a populist flavor to the proposed legislation, rather than a clear statement that something that was not hard earnings was not to be protected even if it fell within the plain language of the statute? Shouldn't something clearer than that be offered if the Court is to trump the plain language of the statute?

Anyway, even granting the hard earnings theory, does this theory stand up? Is it really true that Orion's note didn't represent hard earnings? What happens if Orion defaults as it did: isn't the bank going to go after it on the note, and isn't the bank going to get at Orion's assets—its other bank accounts, its plant and equipment, its accounts receivable? Aren't these "hard earnings"?

Moreover, isn't the theory grossly overinclusive? When someone borrows money from a bank the loan doesn't represent their hard earnings until it is paid off. Yet the loan proceeds would certainly be protected by the FDIC in the event that the bank failed after they were credited to the borrower's account. Can this be distinguished easily from the facts of *Philadelphia Gear*?

We ask about this case from the standpoint of social policy: whether the student agrees with it or not; what its likely effect will be on the competitive positions of big and small banks (it might help big banks which don't have to pay insurance premiums on the standby letters of credit they issue); and whether the FDIC was wise in the first place to treat standby letters of credit as not being deposits (it lost billions of deposit insurance premiums over the years).

Note that the precedential effect of the ruling in this case may not be that great because the Penn Square bank failure was unusual. The FDIC liquidated the Penn Square bank rather than selling its assets and arranging for the transfer of its liabilities to another bank. In the more usual bank failure situation the FDIC arranges for the assets and liabilities to be transferred to another institution, so that the standby letter of credit would be honored by the assuming institution.

Note on brokered deposits (page 245). This is important for providing a key element in the history of the banking crisis of the 1980s. The deregulation of deposit interest rates at the beginning sparked the development of a new industry of deposit brokerage—firms that for a fee would direct investors to the banks or savings associations paying the highest interest rates. Sophisticated investors were happy to utilize deposit brokers since the investments were risk-free (so long as they were less than or equal to $100,000). Banks and especially savings and loan institutions found that they could obtain virtually limitless funds simply by bidding the highest in the brokered deposit market. And the institutions that bid the most for funds in this market were usually the shakiest firms that were relying on rapid growth to disguise fundamental weaknesses in their operations. Thus, perversely, the deposit brokerage industry directed capital to firms that were likely to be among the worst users, not the highest and best users as we would wish in a well-functioning price system (note that the problem was not due to a defect in the price system so much as to a government program that had been partially deregulated).

The FSLIC and the FDIC became aware of the threat posed by deposit brokerage relatively early in the decade and acted to stop the practice by regulation. In the *FAIC Securities* case, however, the court of appeals (*per* Judge Scalia) rejected the regulatory initiative as inconsistent with the plain language of the statute. Arguably, in retrospect at least, the decision was disastrously misguided as a matter of social policy, since deposit brokers continued to distort the flow of capital in the banking industry for several more years, thus greatly increasing the costs of the federal bailout that was eventually required for the thrift industry in 1989.

Congress has now brought deposit brokerage under significant regulation. As discussed in the section, FDICIA provided that insured depository institutions may not pay rates of interest significantly in excess of market interest rates if they use deposit brokers, and that institutions that are undercapitalized may not solicit deposits through means other than deposit brokers if the rates of interest they offer are significantly higher than prevailing market rates.

Policy Issues in the Federal Deposit Insurance Programs (pages246-63)

This discussion leads us to the question of the structure of deposit insurance, since the deposit brokerage industry was almost wholly an artifact of this particular regulatory program. The book now turns to an express treatment of the pressing public policy issues involved in the design of federal deposit insurance. In many respects this is the core, central policy concern of the entire course.

We begin this module by remarking that until about 1980 deposit insurance was nearly completely unproblematic. It seemed like such a huge success that no one really questioned its underlying premises. Even Milton Friedman raved about it, and Friedman is (to say the least) not known as being well-inclined towards government regulation.

But that was then. Now, although politicians continue to support deposit insurance, it is difficult to find anyone who will offer unmodified praise of the program. The general consensus among policy-makers is that the deposit insurance system in effect during the 1980s was a significant contributing cause of the debacles in the banking industry, and that reform of a more or less fundamental sort is required. Congress made a significant step in the direction of reform in the 1991 FDICIA law, although it did not do as much as the more radical reformers had proposed. As the Third Edition goes to press, Congress, the regulatory agencies, and the academic community are once again involved in a spirited debate about the justifications for, and proper design of, the federal deposit insurance program.

We teach this material by comparing deposit insurance with standard insurance of other sorts—a subject with which our students always have some familiarity in their own personal lives. A basic problem in the design of any insurance contract is moral hazard—the problem that in insuring an actor against the costs of a certain risk, the insurance itself may reduce the incentives the actor might otherwise have to avoid the risk. We talk about whether our students drive as safely when they are behind the wheel of a rental car with comprehensive collision coverage; most admit that they will take more risks in such conditions.

This leads to the general point that moral hazard is pervasive in private insurance markets. We then explore the ways private insurers have developed for coping with moral hazard—coinsurance through deductibles and policy limits, risk-adjusted premiums, exclusions for certain types of risks (e.g., suicide), etc. Although these contractual mechanisms are not perfect by any means, they are sufficiently efficacious as to allow private insurance markets to function relatively well despite the pervasive presence of moral hazard.

Then we introduce the comparison to the federal deposit insurance system. We see that, until recently at least, the deposit insurance system was singularly bad at controlling moral hazard, for a number of reasons.

First, however, we identify a difference between deposit insurance and ordinary insurance contracts that might be seen as a reason for thinking that moral hazard is not so much of a problem in deposit insurance. The difference is that in deposit insurance risk is transferred away from a *creditor* of the actor (depositors are creditors of banks) rather than the actor in question. This fact this might be said to mitigate moral hazard as compared with a private insurance setup, except that it removes an important source of discipline on the activities of bank managers (suppliers of credit no longer monitor the bank's management carefully to ensure that they do not take on undue risks) and therefore encourages such managers to act in unduly risky ways.

Second, we identify the devices for controlling moral hazard in private insurance markets that have historically been lacking in deposit insurance. There are no deductibles (depositors are not required to bear a first increment of loss). There is an insurance ceiling, as in private insurance markets, but unlike private insurance markets the ceiling can be avoided by splitting the risk among a number of different risk-bearers; in private markets you need to get supplemental insurance over the ceiling which is often quite expensive. Any depositor who does not need to keep funds at a central location for transaction purposes (such as making payroll) can easily avoid the $100,000 ceiling by splitting deposits among depository institutions. Traditionally premiums were not adjusted for risk, but this has been changed by the FDICIA which requires risk-adjusted deposit insurance premiums although it provides no real guidance as to how risk is to be calculated.

We generally encourage a relatively free-floating discussion about optimal design of deposit insurance systems at this point—keeping alive as one option the abandonment of the whole system. The points we try to cover include the following:

Market Discipline (pages 250-57): We discuss depositor discipline, and some of the problems with using relatively unsophisticated and poorly informed depositors as monitors of bank management. The problems with depositor discipline are lack of information and the fact that discipline when felt might take the form of destabilizing runs. We probe further, however, by asking whether, if depositors were at risk, information might not be made more available in the form of newsletters, commercially available reports, rating systems, or the like. Also, we ask whether runs are all that bad. Arguably they have an *in terrorem* effect on bank management that might be quite effective at inducing prudent management practices.

We also discuss the potential use of subordinated debt to achieve market discipline. This approach has been highly touted in policy circles, and represents the most widely favored form of market discipline for banks. Sub debt has an advantage over deposits in that it is regularly traded on markets and thus the risk premium demanded by the market might be used as a pricing mechanism for government insurance. Further, the trustee of a trust indenture may be a much more effective monitor than the mass of depositors. However, a problem with the use of sub debt is that it works only for larger financial institutions; the thousands of smaller banks and thrifts could not find a ready market for their subordinated debt, and the costs of issuing such debt can be large.

The Federal Deposit Insurance Act requires risk-based premiums (pages 257-61). We ask whether such premiums are a good idea. We try to get students to identify the major problem with risk-adjusted premiums, which is the calculation of the level of risk. The brute fact is that no one has yet come up with a foolproof measure of bank risk. Accounting measures of risk are not very good, and tend to lag behind the actual condition of the bank. Banks often go downhill very quickly, so that the accounting measures may not catch the riskiness in time. The results of bank examinations fare little better; although bank regulators don't like to admit it, their examination programs are little better at identifying problem institutions than analysis that can be done by computer on publicly available data. So the regulators are now in the position of having to devise a system for calculating risk premiums when they have no really effective methodology for determine how risky an institution is in fact.

The FDICIA encourages experimentation with private sector pricing of federal deposit insurance premiums. A small sliver of the risk of bank failure could be carved out and sold on private reinsurance markets. The risk premium charged in these private markets could be used as the basis for pricing the government risk premium. Whether or not such private sector pricing schemes will work is yet to be seen

Narrow bank proposals (pages 261-63) envision splitting banking into two kinds of banks—narrow banks with insured deposits, and all other banks with uninsured deposits. Narrow banks would offer insured transaction accounts and would be severely limited in their assets to extremely safe, liquid investments. Because of this stringent asset regulation, deposit insurance would become a vestigial regulatory system: it would be around, but the cases where the FDIC would need to pay off would be very few. And as Professor Scott points out, there could easily be a single institution operating both as a "narrow" bank and as an uninsured bank: the only requirement would be that all insured accounts be fully collateralized by suitably safe and liquid assets. The danger of the narrow bank proposal is that because narrow banks would not pay high interest rates, most banking functions would occur in the uninsured sector, and here the banking system might get right back into the danger of runs and contagions that deposit insurance was designed to overcome.

The instructor should also at this point call students' attention to the system for prompt corrective action, which we discuss in Chapter 4. If prompt corrective action works as intended, banks will not fail and therefore no draw on the deposit insurance funds will be required. Thus, the prompt corrective action regime can be understood as another mechanism for dealing with the moral hazard problem implicit in federal deposit insurance.

CORPORATE LAW REGULATION

The material on corporate regulation is worth treating briefly. The instructor can use this material as a way of emphasizing to students that banks, although special in many respects, are still business corporations. As such, they like other business corporations may merge, consolidate, liquidate, or engage in other fundamental corporate change. The material starting on page 263 discusses the special rules that apply when banks undertake such actions.

Reorganization Under the National Bank Act (pages 263-66)

A major problem for national banks has been the absence of a "freeze-out" provision analogous to that available for business corporations under state corporate laws. The instructor may want to bring out the reasons why a majority shareholder may want to get 100 percent ownership (principally, in order to avoid having fiduciary duties to minority shareholders). The book describes the problems created by the Eighth Circuit in *Lewis v. Clark*, which not only undermined the ability of national banks to conduct freeze-out mergers, but more fundamentally, raised questions about the power of national banks to engage in any corporate action not expressly contemplated by the National Bank Act. The comptroller's response to this decision, allowing national banks to elect to be governed by the corporate governance rules of the state where they are located, is creative and raises a number of interesting legal questions.

Question 2, page 266. This is a general thought experiment for students. Utilizing the comptroller's election option is the most obvious way to avoid the decision.

Issues of Management and Control (pages 266-71)

The most interesting such issues involve the extraordinary powers that the banking agencies enjoy over personnel. You can use Question 1, page 270, as a doorway into the policy questions. Question 2 can be the basis for an interesting discussion about whether we should license bankers the way we license lawyers. Why not?

This material also raises the question of employment at will for bank managers. The National Bank Act seems to provide for employment at will, but the distinct trend in some states is to provide greater protections against dismissal than would be accorded by an at-will regime. What if a state attempts to provide such protections to an officer of a national bank located in the state? The *Peatros* case, cited on page 267, is probably the first of many that raise this issue, which eventually may wind up in the Supreme Court.

Problems of Mutual Organization (pages 271-73)

You might use this material as the basis for either (or both) of two discussions. First, why have some banks been organized in mutual form? What are the advantages and disadvantages of this form of ownership? (If you know your movies, you will know that Jimmy Stewart's building and loan association in *It's a Wonderful Life* was held in mutual ownership). From the standpoint of bank officers, the mutual form can be great because it makes hostile takeovers nearly impossible and virtually eliminates meaningful monitoring by shareholders; but these may not be particularly desirable from the standpoint of public policy. Even economists don't have a clear answer to this puzzle, but the discussion can be challenging.

The most important practical problem of mutual form these days is the treatment of the value realized in a mutual-to-stock conversion. In theory, but only in theory, the mutual institution is owned by its depositors, so one might imagine that the depositors should receive their pro rate share of any increased value realized on conversion to stock form. This has not proved to be the case, however. In the early conversions, the lion's share of the gain went to management insiders who subscribed to large amounts of stock which was being sold at prices—or so it was claimed—that were well below actual market value. These days, the banking agencies have tightened up the rules on conversions, so that insiders are not quite as well rewarded in conversions as heretofore, but the issue has not been definitively resolved and, from time to time, politicians object to the appearance of unfairness.

It is interesting to explore with students the question posed on page273: who, in fact, *are* the owners of the surplus value of a mutual institution? Perhaps the right answer is that no one is the true owner, so that the value should escheat to the state? How should we think about this problem? Perhaps the better approach is to consider the incentive effects of different compensation schemes: what allocation of the resource would best serve social goals?

Credit Union Membership (pages 273-74)

This brief note addresses the aftermath of the *National Credit Union Administration v. First National Bank and Trust Co.* case. You can use it as a basis for asking whether the "common bond" requirement, as it exists under current law, really is much of a restraint. If not, what is the basis for a separate regulatory regime, and for the somewhat more favorable regulatory treatment (e.g., exemption from the CRA) enjoyed by credit unions today?

Chapter 4: Safety and Soundness Safeguards

CAPITAL

Capital is crucial to modern safety-and-soundness regulation. Yet many students initially find the topic difficult, particularly students with little background in accounting, finance, or microeconomics. We have sought to make the chapter accessible even to students who lack such backgrounds.

To make the material further accessible (and less intimidating), we deal with capital in class in three stages. First, we briefly introduce and explain the basic concept of capital during the class *before* students tackle the main reading assignment (i.e., during a class still mainly devoted to topics from Chapter 3). This helps demystify the topic and also gives students a chance to ask questions. As background for the explanation, we assign pages 275-79. Second, for the first class devoted to capital, we assign pages 275-90 plus the problems on pages 297-99. Third, only after dealing with that material do we turn to the additional complexities involved in regulators' efforts to refine the risk-based capital standards (pages 290-96).

Meaning of Capital *(pages 275-77 and 278-79)*

For purposes of banking regulation, a bank's "capital" is—in basic concept—the amount by which the bank's assets exceed the bank's liabilities. Thus the bank's "capital" approximates its "net worth" or its shareholders' "equity." In fact, regulatory capital rules are more complicated than that: some types of equity (e.g., short-term preferred stock) do not qualify as capital for any purpose; other types of equity (e.g., cumulative or intermediate-term preferred) count only for some purposes; and for some purposes qualifying subordinated debt counts as capital even though it is a liability. But these refinements are still just variations on the basic theme of capital as the amount by which assets exceed liabilities.

In the book we seek to explain capital—and head off common misunderstandings—in several ways.

First, we point out how "capital" has several very different meanings (some of which, quite inconveniently for present purposes, appear in federal banking statutes). Awareness of these different meanings helps students disentangle the concept used here from the other meanings (e.g., legal capital for purposes of corporate law dividend restrictions).

Second, we illustrate the concept of capital with the bar chart on page 279, which depicts four hypothetical banks—identical in every respect except the amount of their total liabilities. We ask students at which bank they would prefer to make an uninsured deposit.

Even students with no financial background quickly recognize that the more a bank's assets exceed the bank's liabilities, the safer their money would be.

Importance of Capital *(pages 277-79)*

This brings us to the importance of capital—well summarized (albeit with some redundancy) in the 1991 Treasury report quoted on pages 277-78.

First, capital *reduces the risk of failure*. Other things being equal, the more a bank's assets exceed its liabilities, the greater the probability that the bank can (even in the face of financial setbacks) meet its liabilities as they come due and thus avoid default.

Second, capital *reduces incentives to take excessive risk*. Bank shareholders stand to gain from greater risk-taking: they get whatever profits remain after the bank has satisfied its creditors, and yet the bank's limited liability protects the shareholders from losing more than they invested. This asymmetry between limited downside risk and potentially unlimited upside gain creates a bias toward greater risk-taking. Capital helps counteract this bias: the larger a bank's capital, the more its shareholders stand to lose if the bank fails.

Third, capital *acts as a buffer in front of the deposit insurance fund and the taxpayer*. This buffering function reflects the priority depositors' claims have in any bank receivership: deposits must get paid in full before other claims (those of general creditors, subordinated debtholders, and shareholders—in that order) can get paid at all.

Fourth, capital *reduces misallocation of credit caused by any safety net subsidy*. If the federal government subsidizes deposit insurance and the Federal Reserve discount window, weak banks will tend to grow at the expense of nondepository financial institutions and strong banks. Weak banks are likely to make worse credit judgments than strong banks. Moreover, insofar as the subsidy favors banks over nondepository institutions, it will tend to promote overinvestment in the kinds of assets banks can hold (e.g., real-estate loans) and corresponding underinvestment in other kinds of assets.

The fifth and sixths stated benefits of capital (which reflect hot political topics of the early 1990s) follow from benefits already discussed. Capital helps *avoid credit crunches* (in which even creditworthy borrowers cannot obtain credit) by: reducing the risk of failure, and thus better enabling banks to lend even during hard times; and reducing incentives to take excessive risks, and thus dampening the speculative booms, busts, and overreactions that can engender credit crunches. Capital *increases long-term competitiveness* insofar as it promotes economic efficiency.

Regulatory Capital Requirements *(pages 279-88)*

Having discussed the meaning and importance of capital, we introduce the key regulatory capital requirements: the leverage limit and the risk-based capital standards. We explain—step by step, using concrete examples—how to calculate a bank's leverage ratio and total risk-based capital ratio. We use the 1980s origins of the risk-based standards to highlight the policy rationale for those standards and some aspects of the business and accounting context in which they operate (e.g., securitization and the substitution of off-balance-sheet items for balance-sheet assets).

Questions and Comments (page 288)

1. Do the risk-based capital standards effectively prevent a risk-preferring bank from taking on a great deal of risk? Certainly not. The risk-based standards avoid some of the leverage limit's blind spots, but have major blind spots of their own. Regulators acknowledge that a bank can operate in a risky manner and still meet the current standards.

2. Does the Modigliani-Miller theorem cast doubt on the wisdom of relegating subordinated debt to tier 2 capital? Independent economists have argued that it does—and that subordinated debt has advantages (e.g., creating a class of creditors with strong incentives to monitor the issuing bank's risk-taking; see pages IV-8 to -9 below) that far outweigh any disadvantages (e.g., the bank must pay interest on its subordinated debt even if the bank's financial condition deteriorates).

Capital Problems (pages 297-99)

These problems—like the other problems in this chapter—are designed to help students better understand the concepts in question by applying the relevant rules to specific facts. The three capital problems are of gradually increasing complexity. We encourage students to do the problems on their own before class, and we then work through the problems in class.

Problem 1—Beta Bank

This problem is quite simple. It involves a short list of assets, no off-balance-sheet items, and no tier 2 capital.

Leverage Ratio: Beta Bank has $5 million in common shareholders' equity, which qualifies as tier 1 capital, and $100 million in total assets. Leverage ratio = $5 million ÷ $100 million = 5 percent.

Total Risk-Based Capital Ratio: To calculate the bank's total risk-based capital ratio, we follow the eight-step process set forth on pages 281-88. First, we sort each of the bank's assets into one of four risk-weight categories (millions of dollars):

0 percent:
Cash	$ 7
Treasury securities	18
	$25

20 percent:
     Not applicable

50 percent:
     First mortgages on 1-4 family housing   <u>30</u>

                                                          30

100 percent:
     Consumer loan   20
     Commercial loans   <u>25</u>

                                                           45

The bank has no off-balance sheet liabilities, so we skip the second and third steps.

Fourth, we multiply the dollar total for each of the risk-weight categories by the relevant percentage:

0% category:	$25 million	x	0%	= $0
50 % category:	$30 million	x	50%	= $15 million
100 % category:	$45 million	x	100%	= $45 million

Fifth, we add the totals for these risk-weight categories: $0 + $15 million +$45 million = $60 million in risk-weighted assets.

Sixth, the bank has $5 million in tier 1 capital and no tier 2 capital, making the bank's total capital $5 million (seventh step).

Eighth, $5 million in total capital ÷ $60 million in risk-weighted assets = 8.3 percent total risk-based capital ratio.

Problem 2—Gamma Bank

This problem involves a wider range of assets, some off-balance-sheet items, and some tier 2 capital.

Leverage Ratio: Gamma Bank's balance sheet shows two types of tier 1 capital: $110 million in common shareholders' equity + $50 million in noncumulative perpetual preferred stock = $160 million in total tier 1 capital. Leverage ratio = $160 million ÷ $1,600 million in total assets = 10 percent.

Total Risk-Based Capital Ratio: First, we sort each of Gamma Bank's assets into one of four risk-weight categories (millions of dollars):

0 percent:
     Cash $ 80
     U.S. Treasury securities   <u>15</u>

$ 95

20 percent:
    New Mexico state general obligation bonds   30
    City of Farmington general obligation bonds   20
    Mortgage-backed securities
        guaranteed by Freddie Mac   200
                                                    250

50 percent:
    First mortgages on 1-4 family housing   100
                                                  100

100 percent:
    Secured loans to individuals   100
    Unsecured loans to individuals   180
    Commercial loans   280
    Commercial real-estate loans   150
    Bank premises and equipment   40
                                                  750

Second, we take the off-balance sheet liabilities and multiply them by the appropriate credit-conversion factor to calculate the credit-equivalent amount. As the $10 million in standby letters of credit involve financial guarantees, and thus have a 100 percent credit-conversion factor, we multiply $10 million by 100 percent to arrive at a credit-equivalent amount of $10 million. As the bank can at any time cancel the $150 million in unused credit card lines of credit, those lines of credit have a 0 percent credit-conversion factor and a credit-equivalent amount of $0.

Third, we sort the $10 million credit-equivalent amount for the standby letters of credit into the appropriate risk-weight category. The letters guarantee obligations of commercial companies. If the bank made loans to those companies, the loans would go into the 100 percent risk-weight category. Thus the $10 million credit-equivalent amount also goes into that category.

Fourth, we multiply the dollar total for each of the four risk-weight categories by the relevant percentage.

0% category: $95 million   x 0%   = $0
20% category: $250   x 20%   = $50 million
50% category: $100 million   x 50%   = $50 million
100% category: $750 million   x 100%= $750 million

Fifth, we add the totals for the four risk-weight categories: $0 + $50 million + $50 million + $750 million = $850 million in risk-weighted assets.

Sixth, we ascertain how much of the bank's capital is tier 1 and how much is tier 2. In calculating the leverage limit, we already ascertained that the bank has $160 million in tier 1 capital. Further inspection of the bank's balance sheet shows two items qualifying as tier 2 capital: $30 million in qualifying subordinated debt + $20 million in cumulative preferred stock = $50 million in tier 2 capital.

Seventh, $160 million in tier 1 capital + $50 million in tier 2 capital = $210 million in total capital. As the bank's tier 1 capital exceeds its tier 2 capital, we include the entire $50 million of tier 2 capital.

Eighth, $210 million in total capital ÷ $850 million in risk-weighted assets = 24.7 percent total risk-based capital ratio.

Problem 3—Delta Bank

This problem brings into play the limits on tier 2 capital.

Leverage Ratio: Delta Bank has only one kind of tier 1 capital: $160 million in common shareholders' equity. The long-term preferred stock is not perpetual and therefore does not qualify as tier 1 capital. Leverage ratio = $160 million in tier 1 capital ÷ $5 billion in total assets = 3.2 percent.

Total Risk-Based Capital Ratio: First, we sort each of Delta Bank's assets into one of the 4 risk-weight categories (millions of dollars):

0 percent:		
Cash	$250	
U.S. Treasury securities	400	
		$ 650
20 percent:		
California state general obligation bonds		100
		100
50 percent:		
First mortgages on 1-4 family housing	600	
		600
100 percent:		
Secured loans to individuals	650	
Unsecured loans to individuals	900	
Commercial loans	1100	
Commercial real-estate loans	750	
Real estate owned	130	
Bank premises and equipment	120	
		3,650

Second, we take the off-balance sheet liabilities and multiply them by the appropriate credit-conversion factor to calculate the credit-equivalent amount. $100 million in standby letters of credit involving financial guarantees x 100 percent credit-conversion factor = $100 million credit-equivalent amount. $6 million in standby letters of credit backing performance of construction subcontractors and suppliers x 50 percent credit-conversion factor = $3 million.

Third, we sort the credit-equivalent amounts calculated during the second step into the appropriate risk-weight category. If the bank made loans to the commercial companies, subcontractors, and suppliers whose obligations the standby letters of credit guarantee, the loans would go into the 100 percent risk-weight category. Thus the $100 million and $3 million credit-equivalent amounts also go into that category.

Fourth, we multiply the dollar total for each of the four risk-weight categories by the relevant percentage.

0% category:	$650 million	x 0%	=	$0
20% category:	$100 million	x 20%	=	$20 million
50% category:	$600 million	x 50%	=	$300 million
100% category:	$3,650 million	x 100%	=	$3,650 million

Fifth, we add the totals for the four risk-weight categories: $0 + $20 million + $300 million + $3,650 million = $3,970 million in risk-weighted assets.

Sixth, we ascertain how much of the bank's capital is tier 1 and how much is tier 2. In calculating the leverage limit, we already ascertained that the bank has $160 million in tier 1 capital. Further inspection of the bank's balance sheet shows two items qualifying as tier 2 capital: $130 million in qualifying subordinated debt + $180 million in long-term preferred stock. But the subordinated debt we include in tier 2 capital cannot exceed 50 percent of tier 1 capital, or $80 million. So we add $80 million in subordinated debt + $180 million in long-term preferred stock = $260 million in tier 2 capital.

Seventh, we add tier 1 capital and tier 2 capital. As the bank has less tier 1 capital ($160 million) than tier 2 capital ($260 million), we include only the first $160 million of tier 2 capital. So total capital = $160 million in tier 1 + $160 million in tier 2 = $320 million.

Eighth, $320 million in total capital ÷ $4,073 million in risk-weighted assets = 7.86 percent total risk-based capital ratio. Delta Bank is undercapitalized.

Refining the Risk-Based Capital Requirement *(pages 290-96)*

This may well be the most difficult part of the capital section. As previously noted, we suggest dealing with it after the problems on pages 297-99.

Meyer, Financial Globalization and Efficient Banking Regulation (pages 291-94)

This important speech provides a cogent critique of the risk-based capital requirement. But the prose is dense and a bit heavy on jargon like "banking book" and "regulatory capital arbitrage"; some students will find it difficult to read. One way to render it less intimidating is to stress that students should focus on the main ideas and not fret about the details.

Governor Meyer criticizes the current risk-based capital requirement for (inter alia) lumping most assets into the 100 percent risk-weight category, requiring excessive capital for many assets, and thus encouraging banks to find ways to conduct the activity in question at a lower capital charge. This "regulatory capital arbitrage" masks banks' true riskiness. At least in the case of big banks, Meyer proposes eventually replacing the risk-based capital requirement with a capital charge derived from banks' own internal risk-management models.

Notice of Proposed Rulemaking on Recourse and Direct Credit Substitutes (pages 294-95)

This proposed regulation would implement the Basel Committee's proposal to use credit ratings by such independent rating agencies as Moody's and Standard and Poor's to establish the risk-weightings for recourse, direct credit substitutes, and asset securitizations.

Questions and Comments (pages 295-96)

3. Shadow Financial Regulatory Committee: This group would agree with Meyer's criticisms of the risk-based capital requirement. But instead of seeking to refine that requirement, the group would discard it altogether—in favor of strengthening the leverage limit, eliminating the distinction between tier 1 and tier 2 capital, and requiring big banks to have subordinated debt outstanding.

The Shadow group's proposal provides an opportunity to revisit bank-issued subordinated debt as a means of protecting the deposit insurance funds (page 251). Because subordinated debtholders will at most receive their principal back with interest, they have nothing to gain from the bank taking excessive risks. And because subordinated debt has a low priority in receivership, subordinated debtholders have strong incentives to monitor the bank's risk-taking and overall financial health. Indeed, such debtholders are much like a canary in a coal mine. Just as lethal subterranean gases overcome the canary before they affect the miners, financial problems in the bank affect the subordinated debtholders before they affect depositors and other creditors. The market price of the subordinated debt falls—and the current yield on the debt (the annual interest paid divided by market price of the debt) correspondingly rises. The current yield on subordinated debt reflects the market's judgment about the bank's financial health and can serve as a useful signal to regulators and creditors. To avoid having to pay higher interest rates on new or adjustable-rate obligations, the bank has incentives to manage risk carefully, maintain adequate capital, and fully disclose its financial condition.

4. What would be the advantages and disadvantages of basing a bank's risk-based capital requirement on the bank's internal risk-management model? Advantages: A well-run bank knows its own business better than any regulator. Thus its internal model can be more precise and sophisticated than any set of regulatory rules. Consistent with portfolio theory, the model can take account of interactions within the bank's portfolio of assets and liabilities. And as Governor Meyer argues, more accurately measuring risk is tantamount to reducing risk.

Disadvantages: Because a bank has superior knowledge of own model, reliance on that model may in practice accord the bank excessive deference and thus promote capital forbearance. Regulators, mindful of the bank's superior knowledge, may not challenge the model until they accumulate evidence of its faults—by which time the bank may already be headed for trouble. Moreover, the near-failure of Long-Term Capital Management in 1998 highlights "model risk"—the risk that even the most sophisticated models can end up erring badly.

FIRREA's Reform of Thrift Capital Requirements; Goodwill Litigation *(pages 299-307)*

Meaning of Goodwill (pages 299-300)

We include a plain-language explanation of "goodwill" (pages 299-300) as background for the Supreme Court's decision in *United States v. Winstar Corporation* (pages 300-06).

Winstar involved the "purchase method" of accounting for mergers under generally accepted accounting principles (GAAP)—a legitimate, well-recognized accounting technique. (Indeed, as expected, if the Financial Accounting Standards Board makes the "pooling method" unavailable, the purchase method will become even more important.)

Consider an acquired firm with the following radically simplified balance sheet:

Assets	*Liabilities and Net Worth*
$100 tangible assets	$85 debt
	$15 net worth

This balance sheet may or may not accurately reflect the firm's market value. Now let's say the firm is acquired in a merger in which the buyer pays $40 in cash and assumes the existing debt of $85, making the total purchase price $125. If the firm's identifiable assets are worth only $100, how is the buyer to account for the purchase? The buyer may conceivably have overpaid. But the acquired firm was probably worth more than its book value (e.g., because of loyal customers or talented employees). Under the purchase method, the buyer books as a new asset—"goodwill"—the amount by which the $125 purchase price exceeded the $100 in identifiable assets:

Assets	*Liabilities and Net Worth*
$100 tangible assets	$85 debt
$25 goodwill	$40 net worth

Yet the value reflected in goodwill may deteriorate over time. Accordingly, GAAP required the buyer to amortize (i.e., gradually write off) goodwill.

Thus far we have discussed goodwill under GAAP. But in dealing with the thrift industry during the 1980s, FSLIC adopted regulatory accounting principles (RAP) that served to inflate the net worth of open thrift institutions and encourage the acquisition of failed thrifts. RAP extended to the accounting treatment of "supervisory mergers," in which FSLIC arranged for a solvent (or nominally solvent) thrift to acquire the assets and assume the liabilities of a failed thrift. (Chapter 10 discusses "purchase and assumption" transactions.) In keeping with the purchase method, FSLIC treated the goodwill arising from such mergers as an asset of the acquiring thrift for purposes of calculating capital.

RAP also substantially deviated from GAAP. RAP allowed acquirers to double-count any cash that FSLIC had contributed to make the acquisition more attractive. An even more important deviation involved the interaction between amortization of goodwill and "accretion of discount"—an abstruse point discussed in *Winstar* (see pages 302-03) but, in the interest of simplicity, omitted from our introduction to goodwill on pages 299-300. A failed thrift's assets consisted largely of loans. These loans were typically worth much less than their face value because they bore low interest rates. But the loans also increased in value as they approached maturity. RAP allowed the acquirer to write *down* goodwill much more slowly than it wrote *up* the value of the failed thrift's loans. These two items—the decrease in value of the goodwill and the increase in the value of the loan portfolio—would ultimately offset each other. But the difference between the write-down and write-up rates enabled the acquirer to show artificially inflated earnings during the initial years after the acquisition (although the acquirer would have to show artificially depressed earnings later on).

United States v. Winstar Corporation (pages 300-06)

Winstar considered whether the thrift capital standards of FIRREA—in overriding FSLIC's agreement to treat goodwill as capital—rendered the government liable for damages. The Court held the government liable but left open the crucial question of how to measure damages.

This case recounts the history of FSLIC's handling (or mishandling) of the thrift debacle. The shift to RAP was part of FSLIC's strategy to defer or avoid the day of reckoning for FSLIC itself and much of the thrift industry.

Questions and Comments *(pages 306-07)*

6. How would the waiver provision in the Senate-passed version of FDICIA affect the potential for Winstar-type litigation based on future changes in safety-and-soundness regulation? The waiver provision should help the government make pointed arguments about the tradeoffs between continued federal deposit insurance and improved safety-and-soundness regulation. No one would dispute that Congress can: limit the dollar amount of FDIC insurance coverage; increase FDIC premiums; empower the FDIC to terminate the insurance of banks that operate unsafely and unsoundly; and prospectively reform bank regulation to limit or reduce the FDIC's risk exposure. Similarly, Congress may in effect require banks dissatisfied with such reforms to choose whether or not to remain insured—and if not, to terminate their deposit insurance promptly. If the plaintiffs elect to remain insured, one could reasonably infer that on balance the plaintiffs still find federal deposit insurance more attractive than all other available alternatives. Indeed, but for such insurance, market discipline (in the form of a run by depositors) would probably have closed the plaintiffs' doors permanently.

7. Does Winstar have any adverse implications for prompt corrective action? Prompt corrective action is distinguishable in that it does not alter the government's *contractual* relations with insured depository institutions. Moreover, since the enactment of FDICIA in 1991, all such institutions have had notice of the potential consequences of capital deficiencies—and have been free to manage their affairs so as to avoid such deficiencies.

PROMPT CORRECTIVE ACTION

Basics of Prompt Corrective Action

Carnell, A Partial Antidote to Perverse Incentives *(pages 309-22)*

This article argues that prompt corrective action and other key reforms in FDICIA represent a systematic attempt to counteract perverse incentives in the pre-FDICIA system of deposit insurance and depository institution regulation—incentives that had led insured depository institutions to take excessive risks and led their regulators to practice imprudent forbearance and overextend the federal safety net. The article discusses these perverse incentives and then explains how the various provisions of the prompt corrective action statute seek to give depository institutions' owners, managers, and regulators incentives better aligned with the interests of the deposit insurance funds.

In so doing, the article responds to critics who saw in FDICIA only a vengeful overreaction to the thrift debacle and the banking crisis of the early 1990s. According to Professor Carnell, FDICIA's core reforms (notably prompt corrective action, risk-based premiums, and least-cost resolution) have a strong free-market orientation. These reforms sought to require risky institutions to internalize more of the costs of their risk-taking and require sick institutions to take timely action to replenish capital and correct other problems. In so doing, the reforms sought to curtail the wasteful and ultimately unsustainable practice of forcing healthy, well-managed institutions to subsidize their mismanaged, risk-preferring, or chronically sick competitors.

Questions and Comments *(pages 322-24)*

3. How many provisions of the prompt corrective action statute allow no regulatory discretion? According to Professor Carnell,

> Only a few [prompt corrective action] rules are categorical. No institution can pay dividends or management fees if it is, or would become, undercapitalized. Asset growth by an undercapitalized institution depends on having an approved capital restoration plan and an improving capital ratio. An institution lacking an approved plan cannot increase its top officials' compensation. Regulators must subject a significantly undercapitalized institution to at least one safeguard chosen from a long list. But these categorical rules are themselves the exceptions in section 38 [i.e., 12 U.S.C. § 1831o].
>
> Most of section 38's rules involve some degree of regulatory discretion. Presumptive rules—coupling a mandatory requirement or prohibition with limited regulatory authority to make exceptions—outnumber categorical rules. . . . Regulators can generally make exceptions if the prescribed action would not help avoid or minimize loss to the insurance fund.
>
> Many other rules are purely discretionary . . . .

12 Ann. Rev. Banking L. 317, 349-50 (1993).

5. Which set of perverse incentives do you think the prompt corrective action statute deals with more effectively: those of owners and managers or those of regulators? The statute does a much better job of changing owners' and managers' incentives than changing regulators' incentives. But the statute is unusual for even attempting to change regulators' incentives.

6. How could recalcitrant regulators subvert the prompt corrective action statute? As prompt corrective action is keyed to capital, regulators could readily subvert it by allowing banks to overstate the value of their assets (and thus overstate their capital). Regulators could also subvert the statute by setting overly low required capital levels and by taking only the most minimal action required against capital-deficient banks.

7. How could prompt corrective action go wrong? What unintended consequences could it end up having? Prompt corrective action will work best insofar as it changes banks' incentives and behavior while banks still have time to avoid failure. Under an extreme scenario, many insured banks might nonetheless persist past the point of no return in having capital insufficient for the risks they faced—and prompt corrective action (coupled with abrupt changes in how regulators exercised their considerable discretion) might arguably contribute to catalyzing the failure of those banks, imposing needless losses on the FDIC, and exacerbating a cyclical economic downturn. Of course, nothing in the prompt corrective action statute would compel outcomes that increased costs to the FDIC: minimizing such costs is the lodestone of the statute. Moreover, the record of the Japanese banking system during the 1990s underscores how protracted capital forbearance (achieved by letting banks overstate the value of their assets) can not only increase resolution costs but take a more general toll on public confidence in the financial system and the economy).

9. *Could the federal banking agencies impose a subordinated debt requirement using their authority under 12 U.S.C. § 1831o(c)(1)(B)(i) to prescribe additional relevant capital measures for purposes of prompt corrective action?* The federal banking agencies have solicited public comment on exempting small banks from the risk-based capital requirement. 65 Fed. Reg. 66,193 (2000). Under § 1831o(c)(1)(A)(ii), the risk-based requirement must be a required capital measure for purposes of prompt corrective action unless regulators determine under § 1831o(c)(1)(B)(i) that the risk-based requirement "is no longer an appropriate means for carrying out the purpose" of prompt corrective action. Regulators have not proposed eliminating the risk-based requirement for large banks. Accordingly, exempting small banks would evidently involve making the risk-based requirement a required capital measure for large banks but not small banks. If regulators could do that, then they should also be able (as suggested in Question 9) to make subordinated debt a required capital measure for large banks but not small banks.

Prompt Corrective Action Problems *(pages 324-326)*

Problem 1—Epsilon Bank

> Epsilon Bank has a leverage ratio of 11 percent and a total risk-based capital ratio of 15 percent. The appropriate federal banking agency most recently examined Epsilon Bank three months ago. The examiner-in-charge, Susan Sharp, found the bank's loan committee gathered around a roulette wheel. After further investigation Sharp concluded that the loan committee had been using the roulette wheel for the past six months to make decisions in close cases. Based upon the examination the agency has rated the bank's management unsatisfactory but has given the highest possible rating to the bank's asset quality, earnings, and liquidity. Can the agency take any action against the bank under the prompt corrective action statute?

Even if Epsilon Bank is well-capitalized, the unsatisfactory management rating permits the agency to take action against the bank under the prompt corrective action statute, 12 U.S.C. § 1831o. If an insured depository institution receives an unsatisfactory rating for asset quality, management, earnings, or liquidity, the agency may (if the deficiency is not corrected) deem the institution to be engaging in an unsafe or unsound practice for purposes of 12 U.S.C. § 1818(b)(8). (This is known as an "AMEL downgrade," after the noncapital components of the CAMEL rating system in effect at the time of FDICIA.) If the bank is well-capitalized, the agency may reclassify it as adequately capitalized; if the bank is adequately capitalized or undercapitalized, the agency may treat it as if it were in the next-lower capital category. Id. § 1831o(g)(1).

Why should a bank care whether regulators reclassify it from well-capitalized to adequately capitalized? Such a reclassification could increase the bank's deposit insurance premiums and constrain the bank's ability to affiliate with nonbanking companies, merge with other depository institutions across state lines, accept brokered deposits, and take advantage of various streamlined procedures.

Problem 2—Zeta Bank

Zeta Bank has $500 million in total assets, $475 million in total liabilities, and $25 million in common shareholders' equity. May Zeta Bank pay a dividend of $7 million?

The bank cannot pay a $7 million dividend, as such a dividend would render the bank undercapitalized. The bank's leverage ratio would fall from 5.0 percent ($25 million in tier 1 capital ÷ $500 million in total assets) to 3.65 percent ($18 million in capital ÷ $493 million in total assets). An insured depository institution can make no capital distribution if, after making the distribution, the institution would be undercapitalized. 12 U.S.C. § 1831o(d)(1)(A).

Problem 3—Eta Bank

Shortly after Pegasus Financial Corporation acquires Eta Bank, serious problems come to light in the bank's large portfolio of commercial real estate loans. Eta Bank's leverage ratio falls to 3.5 percent and its total risk-based capital ratio to 6.4 percent. The bank submits to the appropriate federal banking agency a capital restoration plan envisioning that the bank will cease new commercial real estate lending and become a specialist in financing timeshare executive jet aircraft.

(a) *May the agency accept Eta Bank's capital restoration plan, which contemplates aggressive expansion into timeshare aircraft financing?* Probably not. Under 12 U.S.C. §1831o(e)(2)(C), a capital restoration plan must rest on realistic assumptions, be likely to succeed in restoring the bank's capital, and not appreciably increase the risk to which the bank is exposed. This plan seems iffy at best. The bank would get out of one risky area and try to become a leader in an altogether new area. Such a repositioning can be difficult even for a bank that has none of Eta Bank's troubles. Moreover, the plan contemplates that Eta Bank would go for three years with only "modest profits," in hopes of making big profits later on. During those three years, the bank's capital ratios would tend to decline—as the bank increased its total assets by 50 percent even as it built capital only through retained earnings. And it is uncertain whether the big profits would ever materialize.

(b) *May the agency accept Eta Bank's capital restoration plan without Pegasus Financial Corporation guaranteeing the bank's compliance with the plan?* No. The agency can accept the plan only if every company having control of Eta Bank guarantees the bank's compliance with the plan. See id. § 1831o(e)(2)(C)(ii).

(c) *If the agency does not accept Eta Bank's capital restoration plan, what restrictions apply to the bank?* The bank cannot increase its total assets, make acquisitions, open branches, or commence new lines of business. Id. § 1831o(e)(3)-(4).

May the bank begin implementing the plan while discussions with the agency continue? No. In so doing, the bank would violate the prohibition against increasing its total assets without an approved plan and the prohibition against commencing a new line of business without the agency's prior approval. Id.

What are the most serious actions that the agency could take toward the bank? The agency could place the bank in receivership: an undercapitalized bank's failure to submit a timely and acceptable capital restoration plan is, in itself, grounds for receivership or conservatorship. Id. § 1811(c)(5)(K)(iii). Even if the agency did not appoint a receiver, it could—indeed, would have to—treat the bank as significantly undercapitalized. See id. § 1831o(f)(1)(B)(i).

Problem 4—Theta Bank

Over the past 25 years, Theta Bank has grown from a two-branch suburban bank into a regional banking powerhouse under the leadership of Gus Growel, the bank's hard-charging CEO. But a deep regional recession depletes Theta Bank's capital and leaves Growel at loose ends. Struggling vainly to stem the bank's losses, he becomes belligerent and insufferable. The bank's leverage ratio falls to 3 percent and its total risk-based capital ratio to 5.8 percent.

(a) Can the appropriate federal banking agency compel Theta Bank to accept VoraciCorp's offer to acquire Theta Bank? If so, how? The agency can compel Theta Bank to accept VoraciCorp's offer. Theta Bank is significantly undercapitalized. The agency can therefore require the bank to sell enough shares or subordinated debt to become adequately capitalized—thus overcoming management's natural reluctance to dilute the interests of existing shareholders. 12 U.S.C. § 1831o(f)(2)(A)(i). If the bank then fails to recapitalize, that failure is in itself grounds for appointing a receiver. Id. § 1811(c)(5)(K)(ii). As such grounds exist, the agency can require Theta Bank to merge with, or be acquired by, another institution. Id. § 1831o(f)(2)(A)(iii).

The agency might also seek to use its authority to dismiss officers and directors of a significantly undercapitalized bank under 12 U.S.C. § 1831o(f)(2)(F)(ii)—at issue in part (b) of this problem—to secure Theta Bank's acceptance of VoraciCorp's offer. But would that be a proper use of the summary dismissal authority? Would directors breach their fiduciary duties if they accepted the offer only because of agency pressure backed up by the threat of summary dismissal? Can we distinguish assenting to a lawful order to merge or be acquired under§ 1831o(f)(2)(A)(iii) from bowing to pressure exerted simply by agency threats of summary dismissal?

(b) Can the agency take any action against Growel, whose rudeness is driving the bank's other executives to leave? If so, what action? As Theta Bank is significantly undercapitalized and Growel had held office for more than 180 days before bank became undercapitalized, the agency can require the bank to summarily dismiss Growel from office. Id. § 1831o(f)(2)(F)(ii).

If Growel resists the agency, who will have the burden of proving what? Growel will have a right to a post-dismissal hearing at which he will have the burden of proving that his continued employment would materially strengthen Theta Bank's ability to become adequately capitalized. Id. § 1831o(n).

Problem 5—Iota Bank

Iota Bank is the leading bank in Iotaburg. Hammered by loan losses, the bank's capital has declined precipitously over the past two years. Nearly three months ago, that capital fell below 2 percent of the bank's total assets. The FDIC has sought without success to interest other financial institutions in acquiring Iota Bank. Caitlin Ventana, an Iotaburg native who had made a fortune starting her own computer software firm, expresses interest in acquiring and recapitalizing Iota Bank.

(a) Given Caitlin Ventana's interest in recapitalizing Iota Bank, what action does the prompt corrective action statute require the agency to take toward the bank? Iota Bank is critically undercapitalized. Thus the agency must, within 90 days, either (1) place bank in conservatorship or receivership; or (2) take other action that would better achieve the purpose of the prompt corrective action statute (i.e., avoiding or minimizing loss to the deposit insurance fund). 12 U.S.C. § 1831o(h)(3)(A). Here the agency should keep the bank open—under appropriate operating safeguards—and let the FDIC pursue a possible recapitalization by Ventana.

(b) Given the breakdown of negotiations between Ventana and the FDIC and the lack of other prospective acquirers, what action does the prompt corrective action statute require? There is now evidently little alternative to appointing a conservator or receiver. Regulators are out of options and out of time.

Problem 6—Lacey Faher

Lacey Faher heads one of the four federal banking agencies. She believes that the leverage limit serves no useful purpose. She accordingly has her agency publish in the Federal Register a notice of proposed rulemaking to eliminate the leverage limit for depository institutions regulated by her agency. The FDIC strongly disagrees, arguing that the leverage limit still plays an important role in helping keep depository institutions safe and sound. Can the FDIC do anything to prevent Faher's agency from implementing its proposal?

The FDIC can prevent Faher's agency from eliminating the leverage limit. For any federal banking agency to eliminate the leverage limit, the other three agencies must concur that the limit is no longer an appropriate means for carrying out the purpose of prompt corrective action (i.e., avoiding or minimizing loss to the deposit insurance funds). 12 U.S.C. § 1831o(c)(1)(B).

Since FDICIA, the banking agencies have acted unanimously in setting capital requirements. Unilateral action such as that contemplated by Faher would represent a serious breach of interagency comity.

We briefly bring out in class the rationale for the lending limit: to promote portfolio diversification and thus reduce the risk of bank failure. We then ask how effective the lending limit is likely to be in ensuring portfolio diversification. The limit is a crude device: although constraining loans to any one borrower (or set of related borrowers), it in no way precludes a bank from filling its portfolio with loans to unrelated borrowers with highly correlated default risks. Thus the statute would not preclude a bank from making 100 percent of its loans to wheat farmers who might default if confronted with a disastrous harvest or a sharp and sudden drop in prices. Indeed, many small agricultural banks faced problems like these during the early 1980s. Similarly undiversified loan portfolios in the "oilpatch" of Texas, Oklahoma, and Louisiana destabilized local banks when oil prices dropped precipitously during the 1980s. Accordingly, one needs to bear in mind that the lending limit represents only a partial solution to the challenge of ensuring adequate portfolio diversification.

We also emphasize that the additional 10 percent limit is available only for loans fully secured by qualifying "readily marketable collateral." This it does not apply to loans by such valuable but illiquid collateral as real estate or fine art. Such rigidity may be the price that the regulatory system must pay to achieve reasonable certainty in administering the lending limit.

Lending Limit Problems *(pages 331-33)*

Problem 1—Kappa Bank

(a) What is the largest unsecured loan that Kappa Bank can make to Herbivore? Kappa Bank has $9 million in capital ($7 million in tier 1 plus $2 million in tier 2). Lending limit = 15 percent of $9 million = $1.35 million.

(b) How much, if any, additional money (i.e., beyond the $1.35 million permissible under the basic 15-percent-of-capital limit) can the bank lend Herbivore if Herbivore gives the bank a security interest in the following collateral:

(1) Prime real estate having a current market value of $1.2 million: Nothing. Real estate does not qualify as readily marketable collateral. Nor does the transaction fall within any other exception to the 15 percent limit. (But note the OCC's September 2000 proposal, discussed on page 330, to permit some healthy small national banks—when making loans to small businesses and first-mortgage loans on one-to-four-family housing—to lend an additional amount up to the lesser of $10 million or 10 percent of the bank's capital if state law permitted state banks to do so.)

(2) Silver bullion having a current market value of $500,000: The OCC classifies "bullion" as readily marketable collateral if it is "salable under ordinary market conditions with reasonable promptness at a fair market value determined by quotations based upon actual transactions on an auction or similarly available daily bid and ask price markets." 12 C.F.R. § 32.2(m). Silver bullion meets these criteria.

Accordingly, the bank can lend up to the full $500,000 value of the collateral (as that sum falls within the 10-percent-of-capital limit for loans secured by readily marketable collateral).

(3) Common stock of Sparkle Software currently worth $700,000: The stock is traded on the NASDAQ, and its price is very volatile. Is it readily marketable collateral? Yes. NASDAQ listing meets the readily marketable standard. So here the bank can lend up to the full $700,000 value of the collateral (since that's less than 10 percent of capital).

(4) Stock of Casamance Corporation currently worth at least $1.5 million: Nothing. There is no reason to believe the stock (held by a total of 17 shareholders) is traded on a national securities exchange. Hence it is not readily marketable collateral.

(c) Did the bank's $2 million loan to Herbivore, secured by $700,000 worth of Sparkle Software stock, comply with the bank's lending limit? Yes. The bank's basic 15-percent-of-capital lending limit is $1.35 million. It can also lend an additional $900,000—10 percent of capital—if fully secured by readily marketable collateral. The Sparkle Software stock constitutes readily marketable collateral. So the bank can lend $1.35 million plus $700,000 secured by the Sparkle Software stock, for a total of $2.05 million. Thus the $2 million loan complies with the bank's lending limit.

What must the bank do if the price of Sparkle Software stock falls from $7 per share to $5 per share? With the value of the collateral having fallen to $500,000, the loan has become nonconforming. As the loan is for $2 million and the bank has a basic 15-percent-of-capital lending limit of $1.35 million, the bank should have readily marketable collateral worth at least $650,000 ($2 million minus $1.35 million). The bank must correct the collateral deficiency within 30 days. 12 C.F.R. § 32.6(c). It can do that by getting Herbivore to repay part of the loan or to post additional collateral. (Note that, in order to be able to get Herbivore to take such action, the bank needs to have thought ahead and specified in the loan agreement that Herbivore would have such duties if the value of the collateral declined below a specified level.)

Problem 2—Lambda Bank

(a) How large an unsecured loan can Lambda Bank make to one borrower? For lending-limit purposes, we look to the tier 1 and tier 2 capital included in calculating a bank's total risk-based capital ratio. We must thus follow the rule that a bank can count tier 2 capital only to the extent that the bank has tier 1 capital. Accordingly, we add the full $20 million in tier 1 capital to the first $20 million in tier 2 capital (thus disregarding the other $5 million in tier 2 capital), for a total of $40 million. Unsecured lending limit = 15 percent of $40 million = $6 million.

(b) If the bank has a $9 million general loan-loss reserve and the bank's $25 million in tier 2 capital includes $6 million of that reserve, how large an unsecured loan can the

bank make to one borrower? To calculate the bank's capital for lending-limit purposes, we add together the following three items: $20 million in tier 1 capital + $20 million in tier 2 capital (same reasoning as above) + $3 million amount by which the general loan-loss reserve exceeds 1.25 percent of total assets (and is therefore excluded from tier 2 capital) = $43 million in capital. Unsecured lending limit = 15 percent of $43 million = $6.45 million.

Problem 3—Mu Bank

(a) *May the bank make loan OCI an additional $5 million to cover construction cost overruns?* No. The bank has $205 million in capital and thus a lending limit of $30.75 million. Lending an additional $5 million would exceed that limit. The loan would evidently not fall within any exception. The bank has no legal obligation to lend the additional $5 million. Real estate does not qualify as readily marketable collateral for purposes of the additional 10 percent lending limit.

(b) *May the bank loan a total of $1 million to finance leasehold improvements by tenants of the Oinkin Center shopping mall?* No, not the full $1 million. If a common enterprise exists between OCI and the tenants, then for purposes of the lending limit one would aggregate the $1 million loan to the tenants with all outstanding loans to OCI. A common enterprise exists if the borrowers have the same expected source of repayment. All $31 million in loans would rely on the future success of Oinkin Center: OCI has few other assets, and the three tenants are start-up businesses.

(c) *May the bank advance the money needed for the taxes, insurance, and waterproofing?* Yes. The bank can advance additional money—beyond its lending limit—to pay taxes, insurance, utilities, security, and maintenance and operating expenses necessary to preserve the value of real property securing a loan, but only if bank makes the advance to protect its own interest in the collateral. 12 C.F.R. § 32.2(j)(2)(i).

(d) *Can the bank restructure the loan to reduce OCI's monthly payments?* Yes. A bank can restructure a loan—without advancing new money—if it has made reasonable efforts to bring the loan into conformity with lending limit. 12 C.F.R. § 32.2(j)(2)(iv).

(e) *Can the bank make an $8.5 million nonrecourse loan to Fran Fischer to finance her purchase of Oinkin Center?* Yes. The lending limit does not apply when a bank finances the sale of its own assets, including property acquired by foreclosure, if the financing leaves the bank no worse off than when the bank owned the assets. 12 C.F.R. § 32.2(j)(2)(iii). This transaction leaves the bank better off in at least two ways: (1) Fischer pays the bank $500,000; and (2) Fischer takes the property off the bank's hands, sparing the bank the bother and expense of maintaining it. The transaction is certainly not ideal for the bank, which finances almost 95 percent of the sales price and has no recourse against Fischer. But the applicable legal standard is quite low: merely that the financing leaves the bank no worse off than when it owned the property.

Problem 4—Nu Bank

The $10 million unsecured loan to Crabapple Delights violates Nu Bank's $9 million lending limit (15 percent of $60 million). As Nu Bank already has $2 million in unsecured loans outstanding to Crabapple, it can make no more than $7 million in additional unsecured loans. Nu Bank sought to avoid lending limit problems by having Xi Bank put up $4 million of the $10 million. But because Nu Bank bears the first 3 percent of any loss on the loan, Xi Bank does not share proportionately in bearing the credit risk and the entire $10 million counts against Nu Bank's lending limit. See 12 C.F.R. § 32.2(j)(2)(vi)(A) (loan participations sold without recourse do not count against the originating bank's lending limit if the participation "results in a pro rate sharing of credit risk proportionate to the respective interests of the originating and participating lenders").

Del Junco v. Conover *(pages 333-35)*

An obvious way to circumvent the lending limit would be to make loans nominally to different borrowers but actually for the same borrower. Aggregation rules such as 12 C.F.R. § 32.5 seek to prevent such evasion. *Del Junco v. Conover* presents a strong case for aggregation.

Del Junco also raises the more difficult issue of how to treat repayments when a bank has violated the lending limit. The bank had made a legal unsecured loan and then two over-limit secured loans. The OCC sought to hold the directors liable for any losses the bank incurred until all three loans were repaid. The directors argued that their liability exposure should end once the two over-limit loans were repaid. Yet the legal loan—lacking collateral—posed the greatest risk of loss. Thus accepting the directors' argument would have unfairly shifted risk from the directors to the bank. It could also have encouraged future lending-limit violations by directors with the foresight to allocate all available collateral to the over-limit loans—and thus minimize their liability for the violation. Accordingly, *Del Junco* let the OCC require the bank to attribute repayments first to the legal loan and then to the over-limit loans.

Query how to treat the following situation:

- On January 5 Bank makes a $1 million loan to A, due on December 5.

- On January 10 Bank makes a $500,000 loan to A, due October 1. As Bank's lending limit is only $1 million, this loan is illegal.

- On October 1 A repays the $500,000 illegal loan in accordance with its terms.

- On December 20 A defaults on the original $1 million loan.

Bank's directors could argue that they should not be liable for losses on the $1 million loan because A repaid the over-limit $500,000 loan in accordance with its terms at a time when the legal loan was not in default. Yet the over-limit loan did increase the risk to Bank. The policies underlying the lending limit may favor holding the directors liable here if in making the over-limit loan they acted with the requisite mental culpability.

Del Junco involved a cease-and-desist proceeding. In connection with class discussion of the case, the professor may wish to provide a capsule description of such a proceeding: (1) The agency issues a notice of charges alleging that the bank or someone connected to the bank engaged, is engaged, or is about to engage in an unsafe or unsound practice or a violation of law. (2) The respondent has the right to a hearing before an administrative law judge, who gives the agency proposed factual findings and legal conclusions. (3) The agency then decides whether to issue a cease-and-desist order and, if so, what the order should contain.

Questions & Comments *(pages 335-36)*

4. Do lending limits impose any efficiency costs? Why not let banks decide for themselves how much to lend particular borrowers? What incentives do bank managers have to make excessively undiversified loans? The lending limit can impose efficiency costs. It may prevent a bank from making additional sound, profitable loans to its best customers—loans that might well constitute the best investment available to the bank. The lending limit may even prompt good customers to change banks. But the lending limit also serves a useful purpose by constraining the natural human tendency to overinvest in whatever seems most promising at the time (e.g., to make more and more loans to a particular oil-related business at a time when oil prices have risen sharply and continue to defy gravity).

The lending limit in the National Bank Act is simplistic—a relic of slower, simpler times. Policymakers could certainly devise a more sophisticated approach to limiting concentration of credit risk. (Indeed, § 305(b)(1)(A)(ii) of FDICIA required the federal banking agencies to incorporate such a reform into the risk-based capital requirement.) But several obstacles stand in the way of such a reform. Bankers would argue, "If it ain't broke, don't fix it." State bank advocates would argue that only the states should set lending limits for federally insured state banks. And insofar as the new limit were more restrictive than § 84 (e.g., by tending to constrain lending to different firms in the same business), the OCC would fear that applying the limit only to national banks might precipitate an unacceptable number of charter-changes.

5. How do lending limits affect the structure of the banking industry? A large bank can more easily make large loans. But through loan syndication (discussed on pages 329-30) a bank can, albeit with increased transaction costs, lawfully meet its customer's needs for a loan exceeding the bank's lending limit.

INTERBANK LIABILITIES

Of the prudential restrictions we discuss, the limit on interbank liabilities is the newest—and, as implemented, also the least quantitative and the most judgmental and process-oriented. Is this combination of recency and subjectivity mere coincidence—or does it reflect regulators' unease about the arbitrariness of more objective constraints? If the latter, then what does that suggest about the future of such quantitative constraints as the lending limit, the limits on insider lending, or even the current capital standards? In connection with these questions, the following points regarding the limit on interbank liabilities may be of interest:

- The Federal Reserve Board—the agency charged by statute with implementing the limit—never really supported the limit during the legislative process. The Fed privately dismissed as outdated congressional concern that banks' exposure to an unhealthy large bank might create pressure for too-big-to-fail treatment. (Public-choice theorists might note that insofar as objective safeguards succeeded in containing systemic risk, those safeguards might also diminish the crisis-management opportunities available to the Fed as lender of last resort.)

- The Fed initially proposed applying the 25-percent-of-capital limit to exposure to any depository institution that was not *well-capitalized*. 57 Fed. Reg. 31,974 (1992). But the Fed retreated in the face of banking industry complaints—including complaints from Citibank, which was then only adequately capitalized.

- Changes in banking practices and differences in subject-matter may distinguish the limit on interbank liabilities from the limits on loans to one borrower or insider lending. Modern banking has better internal controls and keeps more abundant records than its forbears of 1863 or even 1978. These changes should make process-based constraints harder to evade—and thus more credible as alternatives to rigid quantitative limits. Moreover, unlike insider lending, interbank liabilities rarely involve managerial self-dealing.

INSIDER LENDING

The key statute here is 12 U.S.C. § 375b. We encourage students to read the original, although for purposes of class discussion the book adequately describes this and other relevant statutes.

We start by establishing the rationale for regulating insider lending. The dangers of abusive self-dealing are patent, and insider lending has contributed to the failure of many small depository institutions. But the potential for insider abuse does not end the matter; we must still ask why public policy does not rely on private mechanisms to control insider lending. Small shareholders have little incentive to police insider lending: the cost of monitoring will exceed a shareholder's pro rata share of the benefit. Large shareholders have little incentive to monitor insider lending insofar as such shareholders themselves benefit from such lending. And insured depositors have no incentive to such lending. Thus the existence of federal deposit insurance appears to furnish a strong rationale for regulation.

We also approach the issue from the other side, asking why—given the potential for abuse—the law should not categorically prohibit insider lending. The students often offer two main answers: First, that such a rule would hinder the recruitment of savvy outside directors, particularly in the case of small banks in small towns. Second, that loans to insiders can be safer than many other potential investments. Banks usually know more about their insiders than about other prospective borrowers, and thus can make better-informed credit decisions with lower investigation costs. Insiders (so long as they remain insiders) have additional incentives to honor their obligations. And an insider loan may be easier to administer than other loans. Why, then, does § 375b(2)(A)(i) require that insider loans be on terms no more favorable than similar loans to outsiders?

Insider Lending Problems *(pages 342-45)*

Problem 1—Neptune Financial Corporation

Neptune Financial Corporation, a financial holding company, owns all the voting shares of Rho Bank, Sigma Bank, and Neptune Capital Corporation. Sigma Bank, a state nonmember bank, has $30 million in tier 1 capital and no tier 2 capital. State law sets the bank's lending limit at 20 percent of capital, with another 15 percent of capital permissible (for a total of 35 percent of capital) if fully secured by sound collateral. Bilge is Neptune Financial Corporation's chief executive officer. Orlop is president of Rho Bank. Strake is president of Sigma Bank. Mizzen is a director of Neptune Capital Corporation. Strake, as president of Sigma Bank, authorizes the following transactions:

(a)   a $1 million mortgage loan to Bilge to finance the purchase of a vacation home;

(b)   a $200,000 unsecured loan to Orlop's son, Jibe, so that Jibe may post cash bail while awaiting trial on drug-trafficking charges;

(c)   a $5 million loan to Mizzen to start an electronic-commerce business, fully secured by a mortgage on Mizzen's downstate farm;

(d)   a $3 million loan to finance the expansion of Gudgeon & Pintle, Ltd., which operates a prosperous chain of clothing stores, and of which Bilge owns 30 percent of the voting shares; and

(e)   a $5 million line of credit to Up with Bilge, a campaign committee financing Bilge's gubernatorial candidacy.

Do Sigma Bank's extensions of credit comply with applicable law?

Under 12 U.S.C. § 375b(4), a state bank's extensions of credit to any insider must comply with the national bank lending limit, regardless of any more permissive state law. As Sigma Bank has $30 million in capital, its extensions of credit to an insider generally cannot exceed $7.5 million (25 percent of the bank's capital), and any extensions of credit exceeding $4.5 million (15 percent of capital) must be fully secured by readily marketable collateral. Moreover, extensions of credit to an insider can exceed $1.5 million (5 percent of capital) only with prior approval by the bank's board of directors. Id. § 375b(3)(A).

§ 375b(8) generally treats an executive officer or director of the bank's parent company—or of any affiliated entity—as an executive officer or director (as the case may be) of the bank. Thus Bilge, as an executive officer of the holding company, faces the same restrictions as if she were an executive officer of the bank. Similarly, Mizzen faces the same restrictions as if she were a director of Sigma Bank—as we have no indication that Sigma Bank's board of directors has excluded her under § 375b(8)(B) from participating in the bank's affairs.

(a) *$1 Million Mortgage Loan to Bilge:* Raises no issues.

(b) *$200,000 Unsecured Loan to Jibe:* One can make a strong case that Sigma Bank's $200,000 loan to Jibe is unsafe and unsound: Jibe faces drug-trafficking charges, which raise questions about his trustworthiness and his ability to repay the loan if convicted; and the loan is, moreover, unsecured. Given these adverse circumstances, one might infer that the bank made the loan as a favor to Orlop. But without evidence that the loan is actually to Orlop, the loan is not technically an insider-lending violation.

(c) *$5 Million Loan to Mizzen:* This loan amounts to 16.7 percent of Sigma Bank's capital and violates § 375b in at least two ways. First, it violates the national bank lending limit. Under 12 U.S.C. § 84(a)(2), the amount exceeding 15 percent of capital must be fully secured by readily marketable collateral. Mizzen's farm, although fully securing the loan, does not meet the marketability criteria. Second, the loan did not receive prior approval by the bank's board of directors.

(d) $3 Million Loan to Gudgeon & Pintle: As Bilge owns 30 percent of the voting shares of Gudgeon & Pintle, that company constitutes a "related interest" of Bilge under § 375b(9)(G)—and § 375b in effect aggregates the $3 million loan to Gudgeon & Pintle with the $1 million mortgage loan to Bilge, bringing to $4 million (13 percent of capital) Sigma Bank's total extensions of credit to Bilge. Accordingly, the $3 million loan violates § 375b(3)(A) because it lacked prior approval by the bank's board of directors.

(e) $5 Million Line of Credit to Up with Bilge: Under § 375b(9)(G)(ii), Up with Bilge constitutes a related interest of Bilge. Granting the campaign committee a line of credit constitutes an extension of credit under § 375b(D)(i)—regardless of whether the committee ever actually draws on the line of credit—and brings Sigma Bank's total extensions of credit to Bilge and her related interests to $9 million (30 percent of capital). Thus granting the line of credit violates § 375b in at least two ways: first, because that action lacked prior approval by the bank's board of directors; second, because the bank's aggregate extensions of credit to Bilge and her related interests exceed the limit on a national bank's loans to one borrower (15 percent of capital, with another 10 percent of capital permissible only if fully secured by qualifying collateral, which was not the case here).

Problem 2—Tau Bank

(a) May Tau Bank and Upsilon Bank informally agree to make large loans to each other's insiders? This nice scheme points to gaps in the relevant statutes. § 375b will not apply because the two banks are not affiliated. § 1972(2) will apply only if the two banks are correspondents. And § 1972(2), even if applicable, does not include quantitative limits like

those in §§ 375a and 375b. But regulators could attack the scheme as an unsafe and unsound practice: e.g., for any failure to apply proper credit analysis and credit standards.

(b) May Tau Bank make a $200,000 loan to Jesse Jones? § 375b generally does not cover loans to bank insiders' parents and other relatives.

(c) May the bank make a $1 million loan to Barny Smith's campaign committee? Here the loan would indirectly further the bank president's ambassadorial ambitions. The insider lending statutes would not apply, but regulators could take enforcement action if the loan were unsafe and unsound under the circumstances.

(d) May the bank adopt the proposed plan in response to Chi Bank's hostile tender offer? The plan would amount to an unusual sort of poison pill: if an officer or director left the bank after a change in control, that person could borrow $10 million from the bank for ten years at the lowest prime rate prevailing at any time during the preceding five years. Such loans would violate § 375b(2)(A)(i) if made at rates below those prevailing at the time for comparable transactions with outsiders—e.g., because market interest rates had risen, or because the bank would not otherwise have made $10 million prime-rate loans to unaffiliated individuals of comparable creditworthiness. Indeed, if the plan would grant insiders a legally binding (albeit contingent) line of credit—on terms not available to outsiders—then adopting the plan might itself constitute a preferential loan.

Chapter 5: Geographic Limitations

We now turn to the geographic limitations on the banking business. This is a field of regulation that is currently under great stress, and that may, in the relatively near future, be deregulated completely. Congress fundamentally changed the ground rules in the Riegle-Neal Interstate Banking and Branching Efficiency Act. For the time being, however, geographic limitations remain an important part of banking regulation.

We start teaching this section by making sure students understand what the restrictions are. As applied to commercial banks there are basically three important restrictions: (1) the McFadden Act; and (2) state law restrictions on bank expansion; and (3) antitrust regulation. A different, but related, set of restrictions applies to thrift institutions; these we discuss in the body of the material rather than confusing students at the outset with an added layer of complexity.

The McFadden Act governs branching by national banks. It states essentially that national banks can branch within their home states on the same terms and conditions as a similarly situated state chartered bank; but that national banks cannot branch out of their home states. There are lots of wrinkles, but that's a good preliminary summary.

RATIONALE FOR GEOGRAPHIC RESTRICTIONS

We sometimes start teaching this material by considering the general merits of government restrictions on geographic bank expansion. We ask our students to identify some of the pros and cons of this form of regulation. Usually they come up with some or all of the following:

Some of the costs of geographic restrictions typically identified by students include the following: (1) geographic restrictions stymie competition in the banking industry; (2) geographic restrictions harm consumer convenience by preventing the development of nationwide branching networks of the type available in Canada, where a depositor can go to a branch of a big Canadian bank virtually anywhere in the country and engage in general banking transactions; (3) geographic restrictions interfere with the efficient transfer of funds throughout the banking system, and thus impair the ability of the system to direct funds to efficient users; (4) geographic restrictions prevent banks from growing large enough to take advantage of economies of scale; and (5) geographic restrictions impair the safety and soundness of the banking system by causing banks to operate in an inefficient and geographically undiversified manner.

The arguments supplied in favor of geographic restrictions typically include the following: (1) geographic restrictions prevent undue concentration in banking markets, thus deterring oligopolistic price setting and enhancing competition; (2) geographic restrictions enhance local control over financial institutions; (3) geographic restrictions result in locally-focused institutions that are more likely to extend credit to the local community, in contrast to geographically extended banking where the organization is likely to send credit elsewhere; (4) geographic restrictions prevent the concentration of too much economic power in a single hands, which is a threat to freedom; (5) geographic restrictions discourage the growth of very large banking institutions that would be considered "too large to fail" by the federal regulators and therefore would require costly federal bail-outs; and (6) geographic restrictions improve the safety and soundness of the banking system because they discourage ruinous competition among banks.

We spend some time over these arguments, most importantly the concern over concentration in banking markets, which is related not only to the hypothesis that concentrated markets are prone to cartelization, but also to the fear that concentration in banking will vest excessive political power in a few small institutions.

It's useful to contrast the U.S. banking industry with our near competitors. We ask students to suggest reasons for this striking contrast between the U.S. banking industry and the banking industries in related countries (probable answers include history and the pervasive presence of geographic legal constraints).

We talk about the pros and cons of concentration in banking markets. The leading opponent of interstate bank expansion is the Conference of State Bank Supervisors. The Conference intensely stresses the principle of localism: the American banking system, it says, is characterized by (1) local ownership of financial institutions; (2) local control largely through barriers to massive national institutions; and (3) local political authority over the chartering and operation of financial institutions. We ask students to consider these arguments: what's so great about local control, and so bad about massive national institutions?

Here we try to tease out of students an argument that if institutions become nationally concentrated, there is a danger of a "government-banking complex" in which the banks exercise too much influence over government policymaking and government in turn exercises too much influence over banks. We assess the strengths of this argument. Would big banks pose any more of a danger than, say, big automobile companies, or computer makers? Why? What is special about banks that makes political power so troubling? And is it really true that big banks would exercise undue political power? We note that the small banks exercise tremendous political power through the Independent Bankers Association of America, the Conference of State Bank Supervisors, and others. Are a few large banks likely to exercise more political power than many small banks, or less?

We also suggest an alternative argument for localism. This is that localism in banking is necessary to help maintain the spirit of small towns and local communities. We see something of this in the efforts made to maintain family farms. But what is the value of localism? Is it a concern for not disrupting peoples' lives, on the theory that if small town America is allowed to die it will be very hurtful for people living there? But aren't people's lives frequently disrupted in a dynamic capitalist system as a result of technological, demographic and economic changes?

Perhaps the value of localism here is cultural: maintaining localism in banking preserves local culture of small towns and rural areas (among others) that is part of a cultural "gene pool" for our country that offers important external benefits. The extinction of small towns in America would arguably diminish the whole country by extinguishing an important form of life not otherwise available in the culture, just as the extinction of any species diminishes the gene pool on the planet. But does this make sense? Is there really a distinctive small-town or rural culture in the United States that would be lost if the principle of localism in banking were abandoned?

In general, the discussion of concentration in banking and localism can be fun for the class, especially if students from small towns or rural areas can be encouraged to speak up for (or against) the idea of localism.

BRANCHING RESTRICTIONS

The McFadden Act and Competitive Equality *(pages 349-57)*

In *Plant City* (pages 349-53), a national bank in Plant City, Florida (a major producer of strawberries, if you are interested), sets up an armored car service. The armored car calls at places of business, picks up cash and checks for deposit, and brings cash to customers in exchange for checks delivered to the armored car teller. It operates pursuant to contracts with customers that specifically state that the bank acts as the customer's agent until the funds are actually deposited at the bank's home premises. The armored car service is expressly authorized by an OCC regulation.

We ask students to define the statutory question before the Court. Surprisingly, many in the class often have difficulty doing so—a mark, perhaps, of the fact that they have had inadequate grounding in statutory interpretation in prior courses. The question before the Court, of course, is whether this armored car service is a "branch" for purposes of the McFadden Act. "Branch" is defined in § 36(f) to "include any branch bank[!], branch office, branch agency, additional office, or any branch place of business . . . at which deposits are received, or checks paid, or money lent."

Now the Court treats as the dispositive question here whether the armored car is receiving deposits. (The Court alludes to the question whether checks are being paid, but it doesn't go off on that ground.) We ask students why it isn't perfectly obvious that the armored car is receiving deposits. The customer fills out a deposit slip and gives the slip and the checks or cash to be deposited to the armored car teller, and the checks and cash are then deposited to the customer's account. From the standpoint of the customer, it appears that this is obviously a deposit. We ask whether anything can possibly be said in favor of the comptroller's ruling.

Surprisingly, a number of students usually rush to the comptroller's defense, observing that the contracts establish that the deposit does not occur until the bank's home office actually receives it. Sometimes a student will point out, quite plausibly, that a "deposit" is not made when a person hands money and a deposit slip to a friend and asks her as a favor to drop these off at a bank—the friend is acting as agent for the customer, and the deposit will not occur until the bank receives the funds. Why is the armored car service different?

There are two main counters to this argument. One is the functional argument, that whatever the form of the transaction, the function is that a deposit is made when the funds are given to the armored car. This strikes us, personally, as more plausible than the argument emphasized by the Court, which again recited the principle of "competitive equality" from the *Walker Bank* case. The Court concluded that national banks would get a competitive edge over state-chartered banks if they were allowed to offer this service that state-chartered banks could not.

We attempt to draw out criticisms of the competitive equality principle as applied in this context. Does it mean that national banks must be competitively equal with state-chartered banks in every respect? This can't be right, since the law clearly established differences between national and state-chartered banks that implicated the competitive balance between them. Most significantly, national banks were required at the time to hold non-interest bearing reserves at the Fed but state nonmember banks were not required to hold reserves, thus giving state-chartered nonmember banks a competitive edge over national banks. Wasn't the abstract ideal of competitive equality impossible to achieve in practice; and if so, didn't the Court reify that idea improperly in the *Plant City* case?

We also ask whether, other than the fact that state banks would be disadvantaged, there was anything wrong as a matter of social policy with the Plant City Bank's armored car service? Note that the Court itself acknowledges that there is nothing wrong with the arrangement as a matter of social policy; on the contrary, it says that "the utility of the armored car service [is] obvious: many states permit state chartered banks to use this eminently sensible mode of operations." But then after second-guessing Florida's policy in this regard the Court says that Florida's policy isn't subject to judicial second-guessing. Wasn't the Court simply favoring one policy—competitive equality—over another—consumer convenience and competition? Which policy is more important?

At issue in *Clarke v. Securities Industry Association* (pages 353-56) was whether offices of national banks established to perform discount brokerage services are "branches" subject to the McFadden Act. The parties challenging the national banks' actions rely on 12 U.S.C. § 81, which provides that the "general business" of each national bank shall be transacted in its home office and in any branches maintained under § 36. This seems strong evidence that if you are going to conduct a banking business you must do so either out of your home office or out of a branch.

We ask students to tell us how the Supreme Court gets around this argument. The Court says that the "general business" of banking doesn't mean *all* the business of banking. Some business that is not part of the "general business" can be conducted from offices that are not branches. Still, the statute must mean something—it implies that at least *some* banking business must be conducted at the home office or in branches, but not at nonbranch offices. Then how do you distinguish what must be conducted in the home office or in branches from what may be conducted elsewhere? We ask students to clarify this: the answer is that the Court doesn't provide much guidance on this point.

Another noteworthy feature of this case is its treatment of the legislative history. The Court has little use for a statement by Rep. McFadden to the effect that a branch includes any place where the bank "transacts any business carried on at the main office." This suggests that all banking business must be carried on either at the home office or a branch. Rejecting this inference, the Court observes that McFadden inserted this statement into the Congressional Record while Congress was in recess, and in any event McFadden can't be taken as an impartial interpreter of the bill that bears his name since he didn't like branch banking.

We end this discussion with a discussion of *Department of Banking & Consumer Finance v. Clarke* (pages 356-57). We ask students to identify the scenario which promises to undo all remaining limitations on intrastate branching. The scenario is this (1) nationally chartered thrift institutions are already permitted to branch statewide (indeed, under an OTS proposal, they may be allowed to branch nationwide); (2) state-chartered thrifts prevail on state legislatures to allow them to branch statewide in order to maintain their competitive parity with national thrifts; (3) now under *Deposit Guaranty* national banks branch statewide in those states that allow statewide branching privileges to their state-chartered thrifts; and (4) finally, state-chartered banks demand and obtain similar branching powers from their state legislatures in order to maintain their own competitive position vis-a-vis national banks. The ultimate result: all remaining branching limitations for depository institutions are eliminated.

Interstate Branching *(pages 357-59)*

The governing statute here is the Riegle-Neal Act. That statute allows states to "opt in" to interstate branching, so that banks from other states can open branches in the state enacting the requisite opt in legislation. A more effective method for interstate branching under the Riegle-Neal statute is the interstate merger provision. The law generally permits the federal banking agencies to approve mergers between insured banks with different home states without regard to whether such transaction are prohibited under the laws of any state. The resulting bank may establish, acquire, and operate additional branches at any location where any bank involved in the transaction could have established, acquired, or operated a branch under applicable federal or state law if the bank had not been a party to the merger transaction: in other words, the successor institution acquires the branching rights previously enjoyed by the merging partners. State age laws are preserved. States can avoid the effect of this statute, but only by opting out by enacting legislation during a defined time period.

We ask students to consider why Congress chose different regulatory treatment for mergers than for interstate branching, given that the end result is pretty much the same— interstate branching networks. The answer, obviously, is that Congress was anxious to preserve the charter value of banks, especially small banks, that wanted to be acquired and didn't want competition through branching. The preservation of state age laws is a tip-off that this was indeed the principal motivation for the strategy chosen by Congress in the two settings.

Trust Offices *(pages 359-60)*

This material illustrates another issue in the geographic control over bank expansion. The comptroller failed in an effort to obtain broader geographic freedom for national bank trust departments than would be available for state bank trust departments. But this defeat occurred in 1977, when the courts were quite hostile to geographic expansion by national banks. Query if the same result would obtain today. Beyond this, the comptroller says that national bank trust departments in a state where it conducts its "core" fiduciary functions, it can market these services to residents of any other state, regardless of the laws those states may have in place restricting trust activities. This could be a major factor in undermining state regulation of bank trust departments, because national banks can simply move their trust businesses to a friendly state and from that haven, offer trust services nationwide.

GEOGRAPHIC EXPANSION BY BANK HOLDING COMPANIES

We now turn to the potential use of the bank holding company form to expand geographically. The first point to stress to students is that a bank holding company is a substitute for branching, although an imperfect one. Among other things, operating a subsidiary bank is different from operating a branch because the subsidiary bank must be maintained as a separate corporate entity. It must have its own board of directors and observe the necessary corporate formalities. More importantly, it must comply independently with capital adequacy standards, community reinvestment rules, and various other limitations on business expansion. And it must comply with the restrictions on transactions between affiliates found in § 23 of the Federal Reserve Act (discussed in the previous chapter).

The McFadden Act: A Reprise *(pages 360-62)*

The book first considers the application of the McFadden Act to geographic expansion by bank holding companies. The *Michigan National* case (pages 360-61) illustrates the problem. Here a major bank holding company applies to the Federal Reserve Board for an order approving the acquisition of a new bank subsidiary, and the Board uses the opportunity to address the legality of its "ATS" program. The ATS program is a system that essentially allows customers of any subsidiary bank to make deposits or withdrawals at any other subsidiary bank, or make payments on loans extended by any subsidiary bank. The question at issue is whether this program constitutes illegal branch banking. The Fed says it is; but is this right?

Interstate Expansion Through Nondepository Institutions *(pages 362-68)*

There is no limitation in federal law on the ability of a bank holding company to conduct business directly or through subsidiary corporations anywhere in the country (or the world) so long as the subsidiaries are not "banks". Obviously a bank holding company that is barred from expanding through subsidiary banks is likely to try to do so through nonbanks. States are likely to attempt to prevent such expansion if powerful in-state interests object to it.

The issue in these cases, when a state has attempted to bar interstate expansion by bank holding companies through nonbanks, is the constitutionality of the state legislation under the Dormant Commerce Clause. Some of your students will probably have taken constitutional law and know what the Dormant Commerce Clause is; others probably will not. A brief introduction to the Dormant Commerce Clause for the uninformed is usually in order.

The legal issues under the Dormant Commerce Clause are illustrated by *Lewis v. BT Investment Managers, Inc.* (page 362-68). A New York bank holding company sought approval for an investment management subsidiary to operate in Florida. The office would "[p]rovide portfolio advice" as well as "general economic information and advice." Investment advisors in Florida get wind of the application and freak out—as the Court says, "the reaction of the Florida financial community to BT's proposed investment subsidiary was decidedly negative." So the local investment advisors goad the state to action. The revised statute prohibits out-of-state bank holding companies from owning or controlling an investment advisory firm within the state.

The Court rejects the Florida statute as inconsistent with the Dormant Commerce Clause. First, the Court found that regardless of whether the statute discriminated against interstate commerce on its face, it failed the *Pike v. Bruce Church* test. We ask a few questions about the analysis.

Was the Court right to reject the argument that the state had a strong local interest in regulating the activities of banks within its borders? Isn't an interest in maintaining local control over banking services the essence of what American banking regulation is all about? Why isn't this sufficient to justify the statute? The court suggests that the argument itself is not "entirely clear of any tinge of local parochialism." But how does this jibe this with its earlier statement that "we readily accept . . . that both as a matter of history and as a matter of present commercial reality, banking and related financial activities are of profound local concern. . . sound financial institutions and honest financial practices are essential to the health of any state's economy and to the well-being of its people."

Interstate Expansion Through Depository Institutions *(pages 368-69)*

Here the law changed profoundly in 1994 as a result of the Riegle-Neal Act, which repealed the Douglas Amendment to the BHCA and, with it, a substantial body of doctrine governing bank holding company expansion into other state via bank subsidiaries. Now a BHC can acquire a subsidiary bank in any other state, notwithstanding inconsistent provisions of state law. Again, however, state age laws are preserved.

Concentration Rules Under the Riegle-Neal Act *(pages 369-71)*

The Riegle-Neal Act concentration limits cannot really be justified under traditional antitrust principles, although they appear to have a motivation not unlike the policies of the antitrust laws. It is worth exploring in class whether these concentration limits are grounded in a sound and rational social policy. For example, can they be justified on the ground that it is extremely dangerous for the nation to allow a depository institution to grow excessively large, given the potential for abuse that might inhere in such massive size? Does this make sense? Some have compared massive interstate banking organizations to "dinosaurs"—but dinosaurs were among the most successful life forms on the history of the planet!

Geographic Expansion Problems

Professor Carnell uses the following problems to get students to grapple with the federal statutes governing geographic expansion by banks and bank holding companies. (Problems appear here in italics, with suggested answers in roman type.)

Assume that the FDIC insures all of the banks in the following problems:

Problem 1—Columbia National Bank

Columbia National Bank, headquartered in Columbia County, wants to start developing business in Bradford County, a nearby county in the same state. State law prohibits state banks from branching across county lines.

(a) Can Columbia National Bank establish a branch in Bradford County? No. A national bank may branch only to the extent "authorized to State banks by the statute law of the State in question." 12 U.S.C. § 36(c).

(b) Assume that state law defines a "branch" as "any office at or from which a bank conducts financial activities." Can Columbia National Bank establish an office in Bradford County to solicit loan business? An office to conduct a securities brokerage business? The state law definition of "branch" does not control for purposes of § 36. Under § 36(j) "branch" includes a place of business "at which deposits are received, or checks paid, or money lent." If a bank does not take deposits, pay checks, or loan money at a particular office, the bank has a strong argument that the office is not a "branch" for purposes of § 36. Indeed, in *Clarke v. Securities Industry Association* (pages 353-56), the Supreme Court held in 1987 that a discount securities brokerage office did not constitute a "branch" for purposes of § 36. The Court left open the possibility that other "core banking functions"—beyond the three listed in § 36(j)—might render an office a "branch." But given the broad trend toward liberalizing geographic restrictions, neither the OCC nor the courts would be likely to find that additional functions render an office an impermissible branch. Accordingly, Columbia National Bank should be able to establish both a loan production office and a securities brokerage office in Bradford County if those offices do not take deposits, pay checks, or loan money.

Problem 2—Kryptalina

The state of Kryptalina has no statute specifically governing branching by state banks. But since 1931 the Kryptalina banking commissioner has interpreted a statute that authorizes state banks to "conduct the business of banking" as allowing state banks to branch statewide. Can a national bank headquartered in Kryptalina branch statewide? No. Under § 36(c), a national bank may branch only to the extent "authorized to State banks by the statute law of the State in question by language specifically granting such authority affirmatively and not merely by implication or recognition." Here the state statute permits branching not expressly but "merely by implication."

Problem 3—Strictivania

The state of Strictivania has a statute permitting state banks to branch only within 50 miles of their home county but permitting state thrift institutions to branch statewide. What are the branching rights of a national bank headquartered in Strictivania? § 36(l) defines "State bank" as including "trust companies, savings banks, or other such corporations or institutions carrying on the banking business under the authority of State laws." Here the issue is whether Strictivania thrifts conduct enough bank-like activities so that they carry on a "banking business" for purposes of § 36(l). If so, then a national bank headquartered in Strictivania can branch statewide.

Problem 4—New Strictshire

Kryptalina Bancorporation, a bank holding company whose home state is Kryptalina, wants to acquire the Bank of New Strictshire, the oldest bank in the state of New Strictshire. New Strictshire has never authorized interstate banking. Kryptalina Bancorporation already controls two banks, although neither is located in New Strictshire. Can Kryptalina Bancorporation acquire the Bank of New Strictshire? Under § 1842(d)(1)(A), the Federal Reserve Board can permit an adequately capitalized, adequately managed bank holding company to acquire an out-of-state bank "without regard to whether such transaction is prohibited under the laws of any State." Thus it is irrelevant that New Strictshire has not authorized interstate banking. A bank holding company is "adequately capitalized" if its capital "meets or exceeds all applicable Federal regulatory capital standards." Id. § 1841(o)(1).

Problem 5—Presto Financial Corporation

Presto Financial Corporation (Presto) controls PrestoBank of Alachusetts and PrestoBank of Floribraska, both national banks. Presto has controlled both banks for the past decade. It now wants to merge PrestoBank of Alachusetts into PrestoBank of Floribraska, so that after the transaction PrestoBank of Floribraska will have branches in both Floribraska and Alachusetts. Neither Floribraska nor Alachusetts have statutes specifically permitting or prohibiting such a merger. May Presto proceed with the merger? § 1831u generally permits a federal banking agency to approve a merger between FDIC-insured banks with different home states "without regard to whether such transaction is prohibited under the law of any State." Both banks must be adequately capitalized for purposes of the prompt corrective action statute and "adequately managed" (i.e., must have satisfactory examination ratings for management). § 1831u(a)(2) permitted a state to opt-out of such interstate mergers through legislation enacted after September 29, 1994, and before June 1, 1997. As neither Floribraska nor Alachusetts enacted such a statute, Presto may proceed with the merger upon receiving proper regulatory approval.

Problem 6—PrestoBank

PrestoBank of Floribraska wants to establish a branch in the state of Texahoma, where it currently has no branches.

(a) If Texahoma has no statute specifically permitting or prohibiting such branching, may PrestoBank establish the branch? No. Under § 36(g)(1)(A)(ii) an out-of-state bank can enter a state by branching only if the state has enacted a law that "expressly permits all out-of-State banks to establish de novo branches in such State." The bank must be adequately capitalized and adequately managed. Id. §§ 36(g)(2)(A), 1831u(b)(4). If Texahoma has no statute specifically permitting out-of-state banks to establish de novo branches in the state, PrestoBank cannot establish a branch there.

(b) PrestoBank of Floribraska does no business in Strictivania. If Texahoma has a statute specifically permitting banks from any state except Strictivania to establish branches in Texahoma, may PrestoBank establish a branch in Texahoma?
Under § 36(g)(1)(A) the host state—in this case Texahoma—cannot pick and choose which states' banks may enter by de novo interstate branching. As the Texahoma statute discriminates against banks from Strictivania, the statute does not qualify under § 36(g)(1)(A) and thus presumably does not permit banks from Floribraska to enter by de novo branching.

INTERNET BANKING

The Internet is already affecting many areas of the banking business, and will certainly continue to influence events even more profoundly in the future. The selection here discusses the problem of the "location" of an Internet bank. While such banks may be operated out of servers that have a physical location, and may offer mailing addresses, they effectively have no location as far as the consumer is concerned, other than in cyberspace. This fact raises perplexing issues for bank regulation, which has for several hundred years been premised on the idea that the regulation of a bank is properly a function of its physical location. When a bank has, effectively, no physical location, who (if anyone) can regulate it? Notice that this is not only a problem for domestic banking; an Internet bank could be run out of any country in the world and could, from that country, provide a range of banking services within the United States.

The book gives the example of the European Union Bank, an Internet bank which was actually chartered in Antigua, and which offered banking services around the world on the World Wide Web. The Idaho department of finance took the lead in sanctioning this bank for poor management, even before it was intervened by the banking authorities in Antigua. Given the result, it is very likely that the Idaho authorities acted properly and deserve high marks for their swift intervention. But if Idaho can regulate an Internet bank doing business out of Antigua, then isn't it the case that, as regards Internet banking, Idaho (or any other state or jurisdiction with substantive bank regulatory powers) rules the world? Isn't there a serious danger that the valuable contributions of the Internet will be seriously undermined if local authorities can intervene in this fashion?

As yet, we have no authoritative banking cases on point. The book includes an excerpt from the leading case in the field, *American Libraries Association v. Pataki* (pages 372-77). At issue in that case is the validity of state regulation of Internet business under the federal Commerce Clause. The decision contains an excellent description of the Internet and its operations, which can easily be adapted to understand the possible shape of banking on the Internet. The result of this decision is a strong protection of Internet commerce under the "dormant" Commerce Clause. If that decision carries over to the banking context, it might impose significant limits on efforts by state banking regulators to control the operations of Internet banks with physical locations in other states. On the other hand, the instructor might bring out the fact that there are potential First Amendment considerations at play in *American Libraries* that may explain part of the decision. Those considerations are largely absent in the context of an Internet bank, and thus the scope of state regulatory power may be greater in the banking context. Further, note that insofar as the decision in *American Libraries* is based on the Commerce Clause, it would not appear to limit the power of the *federal* banking agencies from regulating the activities of an Internet bank.

Question 3. Internet banks pose an obvious threat to the future validity of the dual banking system. It might be worth encouraging students to speculate on the future of the system in light of this technological development.

ANTITRUST CONSIDERATIONS

Introduction *(pages 378-83)*

Geographic expansion inevitably raises antitrust concerns. The book outlines the law applicable to bank antitrust. This is another of those areas where you as a teacher are likely to confront a wide disparity in sophistication among students. Those who have taken antitrust will find this material relatively easy going, whereas those who have not taken antitrust may find it difficult. We have attempted to present the material at a level which should be relatively accessible to all students, yet without being so simplistic as to lose students who have already taken a class in antitrust law. Fortunately, bank antitrust contains enough unique difficulties and problems that even the antitrust experts in the class will probably find new and challenging questions to address.

In general the substantive antitrust standards applicable to banks are similar to the standards applicable to industries generally. The banking statutes contain language that closely tracks §§ 1 and 2 of the Sherman Act and § 7 of the Clayton Act. But these similarities conceal practical differences:

1. The antitrust statutes apply against the background of the McFadden Act, which has had the effect of deterring geographic expansion by banks and which are justified in large measure on antitrust-type grounds: preventing undue concentration of financial resources that might stymie competition in banking markets.

2. These statutes are enforced by different groups. The Bank Merger Act, the Change in Bank Control Act, the Bank Holding Company Act, and the Savings and Loan Holding Company Act each commit enforcement power to a designated federal banking agency. The general antitrust laws, on the other hand, are enforced by the Department of Justice and the Federal Trade Commission.

3. The bank antitrust statutes contain a convenience and needs defense that is not available to ordinary industries. A merger may be able to proceed, notwithstanding the fact that it would otherwise violate substantive antitrust standards, if it can be shown that the anti-competitive effects are outweighed by the probable effect of the merger in meeting the convenience and needs of the community to be served.

4. Most of these bank antitrust statutes require prior regulatory approval. The general antitrust statutes may require pre-merger notification, in the case of the Hart-Scott-Rodino Act, but do not require prior approval.

5. Several of the bank antitrust statutes contain a safe harbor rule that protect bank mergers from antitrust attack if the transaction is not challenged within a very short period of time after it is approved.

As the book observes, we have three separate bodies of law all apparently intended to serve roughly the same public policy objectives and all applicable to bank mergers: (1) the McFadden Act; (2) the bank merger statutes; and (3) the general antitrust statutes. We ask students whether this is any way to run an airline—or a banking industry. Why shouldn't we just have one body of law, the general antitrust statutes?

We then proceed to the substantive analysis. What is the goal of antitrust analysis here, as elsewhere? It is to prevent the creation or enhancement of market power. Market power, roughly defined, is the ability of a single firm or group of firms profitably to maintain price above competitive levels for a significant period. Or if we are concerned about buyers, it is the ability of a single buyer or group of buyers to depress the price paid for a product below its competitive level for a significant period of time. If they can do so they have market power.

In bank merger cases, antitrust analysis asks whether the entity that survives the merger will have market power. How do you determine whether it will have market power? The first step in the analysis is to identify the relevant markets. You can't know if there is market power unless you know what the market is. And of course there are two relevant markets for any firm: a geographic market and a product market.

Market Definition *(pages 383-415)*

How do you identify the relevant geographic product and geographic markets? The Justice Department defines it by doing a thought experiment. A market is an area and product line such that a hypothetical, profit-maximizing firm, not subject to price regulation, that was the only present and future seller of those products in that area would impose a "small but significant and nontransitory" increase in price above prevailing or likely future levels.

To define the market you might start with a very small market—for example, the local neighborhood in the case of geographic markets, or the precise product in the case of product markets (e.g., 90 day certificates of deposit). You then perform the Justice Department's thought experiment. When the starting point is an extremely narrow market, the thought experiment will usually result in the conclusion that a monopolist in the market could not impose a nontransitory price increase. Faced with the price increase, customers would go elsewhere or find substitutes, something that would not be difficult if the market is very narrowly defined.

If the initial market definition does not generate a market with market power, the thought experiment proceeds to broaden the market definition and ask whether a hypothetical monopolist in the broader market would be able to profitably to raise prices. The market is identified as soon as the expanded definition generates a hypothetical monopolist that can profitably raise prices.

While this thought experiment is elegant, it is highly abstract. The practical realities of defining the relevant product and geographic markets are much more messy. In the case of bank antitrust, we will see that the process is extraordinarily confused and conceptually unsatisfying, a consequence of binding Supreme Court precedents that do not reflect current realities in banking markets.

Product markets in banking. The leading case here is *Philadelphia National Bank* (pages 387-99). This case involves the merger of the second and third largest commercial banks in the Philadelphia metropolitan area, consisting of Philadelphia and three contiguous counties in Pennsylvania. PNB is the nation's 21st largest bank with assets of over $1 billion; Girard is slightly smaller with assets of over $750,000,000. The resulting bank would have approximately 36 percent of total assets and total deposits in the four county area. The two largest institutions after the merger would have 59 percent of assets and 58 percent of deposits; and the four firm concentration percentage would be 78 percent of assets and 77 percent of deposits.

Now the opinion gives a snapshot of the banking industry in 1963 and draws heavily from this snapshot in its analysis of antitrust principles as applied to banks. We consider the question following the decision, p. 399, pointing out that many if not most of the key factual premises on which the opinion was ostensibly based are no longer true. We ask what should the precedential value of the opinion be if its underlying factual assumptions are so out of date.

We ask students to identify the court's rule regarding the relevant product market in bank merger cases. What is the product market? It's "the cluster of products (various kinds of credit) and services (such as checking accounts and trust administration) denoted by the term 'commercial banking.'"

This is sometimes called the "cluster" approach, which says that the relevant product market in bank merger cases is a cluster of different products and services commonly provided by commercial banks.

We ask students to consider whether the cluster approach makes sense. Wouldn't it be better to adopt a product-oriented approach? Why not segment the product market into a variety of submarkets, as is done in other industries? When you get a conglomerate merger, the Justice Department doesn't look at the conglomerate's activities *in toto* as a distinct product line. It disaggregates those activities into distinct markets and asks with respect to each market whether the merger would lead to impermissible market power. So why not the same thing with banks?

One answer to this question is that the disaggregation approach itself would be difficult to achieve. It's not clear how broad the submarkets should be under the disaggregation approach. Should consumer lending be disaggregated from commercial lending? Should consumer home mortgage lending be separated from consumer personal credit? Obviously any product market definition must be administratively workable, and if product markets are disaggregated too much the whole enterprise becomes unwieldy.

We ask students, however, whether workable guidelines could be developed which, if not precisely accurate, are nevertheless more accurate than the outdated *Philadelphia Bank* cluster approach. How about: (1) depository services; (2) commercial lending; and (3) consumer lending, including home mortgage and personal unsecured loans?

We ask whether the Court's cluster approach is likely to result in more stringent or less stringent antitrust scrutiny of bank mergers. The answer is somewhat subtle.

There are cases where the cluster approach would result in more *lenient* scrutiny— i.e., where mergers would be approved under the cluster approach that would be rejected under a product-oriented or disaggregated approach. Say that you have a city with lots of banks, but where only a few banks engage in commercial lending. Also there are virtually no nonbank commercial lenders in this town. A merger of the two leading banks, both of which do commercial lending, would create a surviving institution with only 20 percent of the banking market evaluated according to the cluster approach, but with 90 percent of the commercial lending market. The disaggregating approach would prohibit the merger because it would tend to create a monopoly in the commercial lending market, but the cluster approach would permit the merger because it would result in an institution controlling only 20 percent of the banking market.

More frequently, however, the cluster approach would result in more *stringent* scrutiny—i.e., mergers would be disapproved under the cluster approach that would be approved under the disaggregated or product-oriented approach. Whenever there is significant nonbank competition in the various product lines, the cluster approach is likely to be more stringent because the impact of this nonbank competition is not taken into account in the cluster approach. The only market is the commercial banking market, and nonbank competitors are not in the banking market. As nonbank competition has grown—especially with the granting of checking account privileges to thrift institutions in the 1970s and 80s— the cluster approach increasingly fails to take account of commercial realities (or so we believe).

Product Market Definition (pages 399-408)

Consider *Connecticut National Bank* (page 399-403). This case considers the question of whether thrifts should be included in the line of commerce. The trial court here concluded that savings banks should be included in the line of commerce, stating that "the cold hard realities of the situation are that savings and commercial banks are fierce competitors in this state," and that under state law savings banks would soon be permitted to offer one of the traditional indicia of commercial banks, personal checking accounts. But the Supreme Court rejected this argument, saying "despite the strides that savings banks in Connecticut have made toward parity with commercial banks, the latter continue to be able to provide a cluster of services that the former cannot, particular with regard to commercial customers, and this Court has repeatedly held that is the unique cluster of services provided by commercial banks that sets them apart for purposes of § 7." The Court noted that the commercial lending business continued to be dominated by commercial banks, and that savings banks were going to be allowed to offer only consumer checking accounts, not accounts for commercial customers.

So in *Connecticut National Bank* the Court reached the precipice and drew back, continuing to adhere to the *Philadelphia Bank* market definition. As we will see, however, this is not the end of the story, for the banking agencies and the Department of Justice have developed and are applying their own ideas about product market definition despite the apparently binding injunctions of the Supreme Court in the *Philadelphia National Bank* and *Connecticut National Bank* cases.

Geographic Market Definition (pages 408-15)

We turn to the question of geographic market definition. Again our starting place is *Philadelphia National Bank.* We again ask our students to identify the rule of the case as applied to geographic markets. The Court says: it's the area "where the banks have their offices." We can call this the "office" approach. The Court explains the rule as follows: "in banking, as in most service industries, convenience of location is essential to effective competition. Individuals and corporations typically confer the bulk of their patronage on banks in their local community; they find it impractical to conduct their banking business at a distance. The factor of inconvenience localizes banking competition as effectively as high transportation costs in other industries. Therefore . . . the four-county area in which appellees' offices are located would seem to be the relevant geographical market."

We ask whether this makes sense. Isn't it an incredibly rough approximation? We suggest that students consider the following argument: A local area approach doesn't even work very well for consumer accounts, given that you can bank by mail and get cash from an ATM network. It's very easy now to conduct your consumer checking accounts at a distance. But the unreality of it all becomes even greater as we move into things like commercial loans or acceptance of large denomination CD's. Aren't these instruments offered in much broader geographic markets than the local market identified by the Supreme Court in *Philadelphia Bank?*

The Court's answer to this critique is this: "that in banking the relevant geographical market is a function of each separate customer's economic scale means simply that a workable compromise must be found: some fair intermediate delineation which avoids the indefensible extremes of drawing the market either so expansively as to make the effect of the merger upon competition seem insignificant, because only the very largest bank customers are taken into account in defining the market, or so narrowly as to place appellees in different markets, because only the smallest customers are considered." In other words, the office approach is justified as a rule of administrative convenience, admittedly imperfect though it may be.

We ask students to consider the connection between the Court's ruling on product markets and it s ruling on geographic markets. Having concluded that banking is a cluster of services the Court then needed a *single* geographic market to define for the cluster. A disaggregated approach would use different geographic markets for each distinct product line. Thus the Court's commitment to a cluster approach to product markets nearly forced it to adopt a single rough-and-ready test for defining the relevant geographic market.

We ask students to consider whether, even if the geographic market definition in *Philadelphia National Bank* made some sense at the time that case was decided, it makes sense today given the obviously broader geographic areas in which banks do business today. Again the Court reached this issue, and backed away, in the *Connecticut National Bank* case (second excerpt from the case, pages 409-12). Here the trial court had ruled that the relevant geographic market was the state as a whole. This deviated from the office approach in *Philadelphia National Bank* because there were parts of the state in which one or the other of the merging firms did no business. Even though there was apparently a messy checkerboard pattern of branch offices at various places in the state the Supreme Court adhered to the localized approach. It said, essentially: look where each bank has an office, then draw a line around each office delineating the geographic area served by that office, and then take the two maps and put them together and see how much overlap there is.

Market Share Analysis *(pages 415-22)*

We now turn to the substantive test for determining whether a merger between two banking institutions will result in an unacceptable lessening of competition under antitrust standards. Again we are brought back for the substantive test to *Philadelphia Bank*, where the Court says that the substantive test is this: "we think that a merger which produces a firm controlling an undue percentage share of the relevant market, and results in a significant increase in the concentration of firms in that market, is so inherently likely to lessen competition substantially that it must be enjoined in the absence of evidence clearly showing that the merger is not likely to have such anticompetitive effects."

We ask students to apply this test to a numerical example. The goal is to illustrate that the test itself is full of weasel words: an "undue" percentage share of the relevant market, a "significant" increase in the concentration of firms in that market and so on. How do you apply these words in practice?

We then contrast two methodologies for quantifying the reduction in competition resulting from a proposed merger. The old methodology was to calculate concentration ratios: you would look at the percentage of the market controlled by the four top firms before and after the merger, and ask whether the merger creates an undue increase in concentration. Or you could use a five firm ratio.

We show students that this kind of aggregate ratio has some inadequacies as an analytical tool. For example, consider the following three banking markets. Assume for expository purposes that there is no threat of potential competition: the existing firms in the market are the only realistic competitors in the future.

FIRM	MARKET 1	MARKET 2	MARKET 3
1	20%	77%	20%
2	20%	1%	20%
3	20%	1%	20%
4	20%	1%	20%
5	20%	1%	1%
6	—	1%	1%
7, etc.	—	1%	1%

What is the four-firm concentration ratio in each of these markets? It's 80 percent—they all have the same ratio. Yet there are obviously powerful differences here. We ask what they are.

As far as antitrust policy is concerned, Market 2 is clearly the most problematic; one firm alone controls 77 percent of the entire market. This creates a situation not that different from a monopoly—it would not be too inaccurate to say that this market is effectively monopolized by the top firm. It is true that there are a substantial number of small firms waiting in the wings, but the existing market structure indicates that Firm 1 apparently possesses the ability to hold this competition at bay, perhaps by the threat of predatory pricing.

Market 1 is somewhat less problematic, but still presents a serious threat to competition because it is dominated by five and only five firms. The chance of cartelization is relatively great here, but because of the difficulties inherent in any cartel, we are probably not quite as worried about an oligopolistic situation like Market 1 as we are about a monopolistic situation like Market 2. And because there are no smaller firms in the market, there are no actual competitors waiting to take advantage of any cartel pricing (we defer the question of potential competition).

Market 3 presents less of a concern. True, there are only four big firms in the market, and this creates dangers of cartelization that might be even worse than Market 1, because the costs of organizing a four-firm cartel are less than the costs of organizing a five-firm cartel. But Market 3 is characterized by a large number of smaller firms that can be expected to compete if a cartel is formed and to undermine its pricing strategy.

So the gross four-firm concentration ratio of 80 percent covers all sorts of differences that are important for antitrust policy. Further, consider what we learn from increases in concentration ratios as a result of a merger. A merger in the top two firms in Market 1 would increase the concentration ratio by 20 percent to 100 percent. This seems very bad. In Market 2 a merger of the top two firms would increase the concentration ratio by only 1 percent, to 81 percent. This seems much less problematic. But the fact is that *any* increase in the market power of a monopoly might be very threatening to competition. In Market 3 a merger of the top two firms increases the concentration ratio again by only 1 percent, to 81 percent, but again this figure seems deceptive because we have doubled the size of the largest firm in the market. Surely this presents a greater threat to competition than might be inferred from a simple 1 percent increase in the concentration ratio.

We use this demonstration of the inadequacies of concentration ratios as measures of competition to illustrate the advantages of the Justice Department's preferred measure, the Herfindahl-Hirschman Index or HHI. The HHI is simply the sum of the squares the market shares of the individual firms in the market.

If we apply the HHI analysis to the three markets given above we find very different results. What's the index for Market 1? 20^2 x 5, or 2000. Market 2? 77^2 + 23, or 5952. So these two markets have the same four-firm concentration ratios, but the HHI for Market 2 is *three times* greater than the HHI for market 1. What about Market 3? The HHI is 20^2 x 4 + 20, or 1620. The HHI index shows this to be the least problematic market from an antitrust standpoint, which seems to accord well with our intuitions.

The other neat feature of the HHI index is how you calculate increases resulting from mergers. You don't need to do a separate concentration ratio on the market after the merger. All you do is sum the prior market shares and multiply by 2. Why is this? Before the merger the two market shares contribute to the overall HHI index by being squared and added: $a^2 + b^2$. After the merger you have a single firm with a market share of $(a + b)$; it contributes to the HHI index by $(a + b)^2$ or $a^2 + 2ab + b^2$. The difference between the contribution of the two firms separately and the contribution of the two firms merged is $2ab$; this is the amount that the HHI index is increased by the merger.

So if we are looking at a merger of the two top firms in our respective markets, we simply calculate $2ab$. In Market 1 the HHI prior to the merger was 2000; after the merger it is increased by 2x20x20, or 800; the post-merger HHI is 2800. For Market 2 the HHI was 5952. After the merger it is increased by 2x77x1, or 154; the post-merger HHI is 6106. For Market 3, the pre-merger HHI was 1600; post-merger is 1600 plus 2x20x20, or 800, increasing the index to 2400.

Now the Justice Department's general approach to HHI measurements is set forth in the Merger Guidelines. If the post-merger HHI is under 1000 the Department leaves it alone. If the post-merger HHI is between 1000 and 1800, the Justice Department becomes concerned, but will generally allow the merger to go through if the HHI is increased by less than 100 points. If the post-merger HHI is over 1800 the Department is likely to challenge the merger if it results in an increase of more than 50 points. We can see that a merger of the top two firms in any of the markets we have been considering in the examples above would result in a likely challenge by the Department.

After this introduction to methodology we turn to a consideration of how these guidelines are applied in bank merger cases. Our text here, which is chosen more or less arbitrarily from the *Federal Reserve Bulletin*, is the *AmSouth Bancorporation* order (pages 419-21). A bank holding company has 18.1 percent of total statewide deposits and is the largest firm in the state. The bank to be acquired is the 6th largest bank in the state with total deposits representing 1.4 percent of statewide deposits. This doesn't present any real problems for the use of the guidelines on a statewide basis.

The problematic area is the Tuscaloosa market. Here the acquiring firm controls 2.5 percent of deposits in Tuscaloosa but the bank to be acquired is the largest bank in the market with 52.7 percent of the deposits. Moreover, the Tuscaloosa market is highly concentrated already with 97 percent of total deposits controlled by the four largest firms. The HHI for the market is 4046 and would increase as a result of the merger by 265 points to 4311.

We ask students how would this ordinarily be analyzed under the guidelines. It is clearly, unequivocally no good.

Consider the Justice Department's statement that if the post-merger HHI is above 1800—and here the post merger HHI of 4311 is more than *twice* 1800—and the HHI increases by 100 or more—here it increases by 265 points—"only in extraordinary cases will [mitigating] factors establish that the merger is not likely substantially to lessen competition."

Consider also the leading firm proviso of the guidelines, which says that the Department is so concerned about mergers involving a dominant firm in the market—one controlling a market share of 35 percent or more—that it is "likely" to challenge mergers that otherwise might pass muster under the guidelines. Here we have a dominant firm—the acquired bank has 52.7 percent of total assets in the market—and the acquiring bank has 2.5 percent. So even if this merger were OK under the guidelines—which it most definitely is not—the Justice Department would ordinarily challenge it.

Yet that doesn't happen here. We ask students to tell us why not. Usually students start by pointing to note 3 of the order, where the Justice Department is recorded as adopting a special test for bank merger cases: "The Department has informed the Board that a bank merger generally will not be challenged . . . unless the post-merger HHI is at least 1800 and the merger increases the HHI by at least 200 points." So there is a special rule applicable as a matter of custom for bank mergers. Why? Because of the existence of limited-purpose lenders and other nondepository financial entities.

We ask students to consider whether this special rule for bank merger cases is consistent with *Connecticut National Bank*. Recall that the Supreme Court there said that thrifts should not be included in the line of commerce applicable to commercial banks, but here the Department is taking explicit account of thrift competition.

We then ask whether this merger passes muster even under the Department's stated policy for bank mergers. The answer is obviously no: The post-merger is over 1800 and the HHI is increased by more than 200. So why in heaven's name is this merger approved?

Here students usually suggest that the answer is in note 5. Here the Board analyzes the merger as if 50 percent of the thrift deposits are included in the relevant market. So calculated, the merger fits within the Justice Department's guidelines (barely) because the post-merger HHI would be 2833 and the HHI would increase 159.

At this point one or two students usually have their hands in the air, ready to point to the problem with the Board's approach. The problem is that it double counts thrift competition: first, to get the Justice Department's lenient merger standards for bank mergers, and again to get the Board's modification of the Justice Department's rule. We ask whether the agencies really ought to be fudging the analysis, much less double chocolate fudging as the Board has done here. Isn't it time for the agencies to come right out and admit that the *Philadelphia National Bank* and *Connecticut National Bank* cases are no longer workable, rather than engaging in the type of charade we see in this case?

Concluding this material, we ask what is wrong with the remedy proposed by the dissenting members—that AmSouth should divest itself of enough of its Tuscaloosa offices or at least of offices "equivalent to its present position in the market"—presumably this means that it could divest offices currently held by the acquired bank. Isn't this a sensible solution? The students usually explain that the acquisition of the Tuscaloosa market appears to have been the whole reason for the merger in the first place, so if AmSouth is required to divest that market it might not engage in the merger at all. One answer is that the dissenting members don't call for total divestiture, only divestiture of AmSouth's market share; AmSouth could still gain a dominant position in the market by virtue of the deposits of the acquired firm. Another answer is that if AmSouth is not willing to divest, then let it not engage in the transaction in the first place. Given the availability of divestiture as a less draconian remedy to outright rejection of the merger, isn't the Board going overboard in approving mergers of this sort?

Entry Analysis and Potential Competition *(pages 422-25)*

The unit on bank antitrust ends with a brief excursion into the potential competition doctrine. The basic idea here is that it's not enough just to examine how competition in a market will be reduced as a result of a merger. This doesn't take into account the restraining force that *potential* competitors exercise on anti-competitive behavior. If you have a merger that increases the potential for cartelization, that may not be so problematic if there are lots of other firms waiting in the wings and ready to enter at a moment's notice if they see profit margins increasing as a result of cartelization. The existence of such potential competition both breaks down cartels if they exist and deters the formation of cartels in the first place because the existing market participants know that any cartel activity will be destroyed by new entry.

We ask students whether the potential competition doctrine increases or decreases the stringency of antitrust scrutiny. Potential competition has a curious double-edged quality. On the one hand it seems to justify all sorts of mergers among firms *already* in the market that would not otherwise be possible because it suggests that concentration ratios—even sophisticated ones like HHI—overstate the danger to competition posed by an intramarket merger. We see this consideration reflected in the 1992 Merger Guidelines on "Committed Entry" (page 423-24). On the other hand, the doctrine affords a basis for challenging mergers between a firm *in* the market and an *outside* firm even though by definition such mergers would not result in an increase in concentration within the market and so would otherwise be OK under the antitrust laws. So the upshot is that potential competition makes intramarket mergers easier and extramarket mergers (somewhat) more difficult.

Beyond identifying the issues, we don't do that much with potential competition other than to ask why it might be more important in banking markets than in other markets. There are two answers, both suggested at note 1. We find it worth going over these answers, since often students don't fully grasp the reasons for special importance of potential competition in bank merger cases.

First, the special importance of potential competition in banking merger cases stems from the existence of the geographic restraints on bank expansion discussed already in this chapter. These mean that often there are only a limited number of bank institutions waiting in the wings, which is an essential precondition to potential competition. In other industries where geographic constraints are not present, the number of potential competitors is likely to be large, so the loss of any one potential competitor as a result of a merger with a major firm in the market is not likely to raise significant antitrust concerns.

Second, the importance of potential competition in banking stems from the artificially narrow nature of geographic market definitions in banking. Because the Supreme Court has defined the geographic market for banking to be essentially local, there are many competitors that would be defined as *potential* competitors in banking markets where similarly situated institutions would be considered *actual* competitors in other industries. The artificial narrowness of geographic markets in banking understates the loss of competitiveness from a merger between firms in two narrow geographic markets. The only way to pick this loss up is to deal with it through the potential competition doctrine.

We conclude this section by noting that the rapid liberalization of geographic constraints in banking markets over the past ten years has reduced considerably the importance of the potential competition doctrine even in this industry, since there are now a large number of potential competitors for most banking markets. The loss of potential competition resulting from a bank merger is thus unlikely to raise antitrust concerns today, although in unusual cases it may still do so.

Chapter 6: Affiliations Between Banks and Other Companies

INTRODUCTION

The chapter begins with an example designed to introduce students to the relevant terminology: "holding company," "holding company affiliate," "subsidiary," and the all-inclusive "affiliate." These are all statutory terms except for "holding company affiliate," which we use to distinguish from other kinds of affiliates (e.g., subsidiaries) a company affiliated through a common parent.

BANK HOLDING COMPANY ACT BASICS

A "bank holding company" is a company having control of a bank. So we review the key concepts: "company," control," and "bank." "Company is the most straightforward of the three—broadly defined to encompass most business entities. Statutory "control" can exist without actual control, as the Mulberry Bank example on page 431 makes clear. "Bank" has a narrower meaning than one might expect, and excludes numerous entities with bank charters and even FDIC insurance (e.g., credit card banks, industrial banks, and trust companies).

The story of the nonbank bank loophole (pages 432-33) provides an opportunity to make important points in class about the process of regulation and the role of lawyers in that process. The loophole once constituted one of the main gaps in the entire structure of federal banking regulation. Congress inadvertently created the loophole when accommodating a senator's desire to let a diversified firm retain control of a single trust company. By its terms the loophole permitted *any* company to engage in *all* financial and nonfinancial activities—and to own banks nationwide—as long as the company's subsidiary banks adhered to some modest limits on their activities. Market participants did not immediately exploit the loophole. But when sophisticated lawyers scrutinized the statutory text itself (as distinguished from the conventional expectations surrounding that text), they recognized its sweeping implications and counseled their clients on how to take advantage of that text. We will encounter this process of demystifying the statutory text several times along the way—notably in how regulators interpreted the McFadden Act to give national banks in many states greatly expanded branching rights (pages 356-57); reinterpreted an obscure 1916 statute to let national banks sell insurance nationwide (pages 540-50); and reinterpreted the Glass-Steagall Act to permit the very sorts of banking-securities affiliations that the Act had sought to preclude (page 582). These examples show how smart, creative lawyers—unintimidated by conventional expectations—can strip away the haze around a statute and open the way to outcomes that would have astonished the authors of the statute.

We emphasize to students that financial holding companies are, by definition, also bank holding companies: i.e., a financial holding company is a bank holding companies that meets certain criteria. See 12 U.S.C. § 1841(p). Thus unless otherwise specified, any statute applicable to a bank holding company applies to a financial holding company.

FINANCIAL HOLDING COMPANIES

A bank holding company that qualifies as a "financial holding company" (under the criteria discussed on pages 445-46) can affiliate with companies engaged in any activity that is "financial," "incidental" to financial activities, or "complementary" to financial activities. Congress has classified a long list of activities as "financial" (pages 446-48). The Federal Reserve Board can find additional activities to be financial under standards that embody a strong bent toward inclusion (pages 448-49). And the standards under which the Fed can find activities to be complementary set such minimal thresholds as to make it difficult to question any such finding (pages 449 and 454).

What Is Merchant Banking *(pages 449-52)*

Of the "financial" activities listed in 12 U.S.C. § 1843(k)(4)-(5), many students find merchant banking the most difficult to grasp. Under Secretary Gensler's congressional testimony elucidates what merchant banking is and how it works (pages 449-52).

Questions and Comments *(pages 453-55)*

1. Will allowing banks to affiliate with a wide range of other companies benefit consumers? Whether and how consumers win or lose from financial modernization provides grist for lively class discussion. Many students may find that the contrasting views of Secretary Rubin and Ralph Nader both have their appeal. Rubin stresses the potential for efficiency gains; Nader stresses how ordinary people may see little improvement in the price, quality, or availability of basic financial services. Note how, quite apart from differences in philosophy and tone, Rubin and Nader make very different kinds of points. Rubin points to *potential* gains and argues that competitive pressures should help achieve them. Nader compares the shortcomings of the deregulated *present* (e.g., charging ordinary people high fees and relegating them to impersonal toll-free numbers) with a tidy, regulated *past* in which banks—barred from paying market rates on deposits and shielded from nonbank competition—extensively cross-subsidized services.

The effects of financial deregulation arguably manifest what the economist Joseph Schumpeter called the "creative destruction" in capitalism. Wal-Mart may serve to exemplify creative destruction—and, more broadly, the tradeoffs of modernization (a point for which we are indebted to Lawrence H. Summers, now president of Harvard). Wal-Mart has brought small-town America a wide selection of goods at low prices (which is what most consumers say they want). But in so doing it has also helped undermine the locally owned retailers that were long the mainstays of Main Street. Thus we may simultaneously gain and lose: gaining greater selection and lower prices even as we lose the Main Street we once knew.

One may view populist critics like Nader as harping on the disadvantages of modernization and deregulation even as they take for granted gains in price competition and customer convenience. Ordinary people must now pay higher fees and endure more impersonal service than they did four decades ago. But those with money to invest can much more readily earn a market rate of return on that money. And customers can conduct many financial transactions without having to appear in person, during notoriously limited "bankers' hours," in the lobby of their own bank. Nader might reply that for many people, particularly those with low incomes or low balances, the trade-offs have still been for the worse. Free-marketers might retort that market forces would, in any event, have ended the cozy world of Regulation Q and frustrated any effort to institutionalize cross-subsidies for lower- and middle-income consumers. Free-marketers might add that market forces, if allowed to work, should ultimately constrain excessive fees (e.g., for ATM use).

3. What lawful business activity could not qualify as "complementary"? Questions 2 through 4 underscore points made on pages 448-49: that the applicable standards make it easy to find activities "financial," "incidental," or "complementary." Here in class discussion we go on to ask students how they would anticipate regulators actually going about making such decisions—given the pro-inclusion tilt of the statutory standards for finding additional activities "financial" or "incidental" and the low statutory thresholds for finding activities "complementary." Regulators have enormous discretion and the real constraints on that discretion are likely to be less statutory than political (e.g., "If we allow this, will anyone powerful get really angry at us?").

5. If you were designing from scratch a statute allowing financial holding companies to engage in "financial," "incidental," and "complementary" activities," where would you draw the lines? Again, the question calls on students to grapple with the forward-leaning, inclusive tilt of the statutory criteria.

Financial Holding Company Problems *(pages 455-56)*

Problem 1—Oldman Sax

The Oldman Sax Group, an elite investment banking firm that includes an SEC-registered broker-dealer, is also the nation's largest owner of bowling alleys. Oldman acquired the bowling alleys years ago, rightly anticipating that bowling would become more popular as the Baby Boom generation aged. Oldman intends to sell the bowling alleys eventually, at whatever time will maximize the return on its investment. May Oldman acquire a bank and become a financial holding company? Why?

This problem, loosely drawn from Goldman Sachs' ownership of bowling alleys, poses the challenge of fitting the hypothetical Oldman Sax within the activity restrictions of the BHC Act. Oldman has three potential avenues available: (1) the two-year divestiture period available to any company that becomes a bank holding company; (2) the special grandfather rights available under 12 U.S.C. § 1843(n) to companies that become financial holding companies without having been bank holding companies; and (3) the merchant banking powers of financial holding companies.

First, Oldman could simply acquire a bank and become a bank holding company, as Travelers did by acquiring Citicorp (pages 442-43). Oldman would then have two years (or such additional time as the Fed might allow) to divest itself of the bowling alleys. But this is the least satisfactory solution. Oldman could acquire no additional bowling alleys and would have to divest itself of its existing bowling alleys. Moreover, prospective buyers' knowledge of the divestiture deadline could prevent Oldman from getting top dollar for those properties.

Second, Oldman could continue under § 1843(n) the kinds of bowling alley activities it engaged in as of September 30, 1999, if Oldman becomes a financial holding company without having been a bank holding company. Under § 1843(n), Oldman must: (a) derive at least 85 percent of its annual consolidated gross revenues (excluding revenues from subsidiary depository institutions) from "financial" or "incidental" activities; (b) not expand the grandfathered nonfinancial activities by merger; (c) not cross-market products or services of a grandfathered company (e.g., bowling) or a company held under the merchant banking or insurance company investment provisions of § 1843(k)(4)(H)-(I); and (d) not permit a grandfathered company to engage in a "covered transaction" (page 473) with an affiliated depository institution. Although page 460 describes grandfather rights under § 1843(n) as lasting for ten years, the statute imposes no time limit on such rights.

Third, Oldman's ownership of shares in bowling alleys would qualify as merchant banking if Oldman: (1) acquired the shares as part of a bona fide underwriting, merchant banking, or investment banking activity; (2) did not hold the shares through a depository institution or subsidiary of such an institution; (3) held the shares for a period to enable their sale on a reasonable basis; (4) did not routinely manage the bowling alleys except as necessary to obtain a reasonable return on its investment. Id. § 1843(k)(4)(H).

Problem 2—Near Bancshares

Near Bancshares, a bank holding company, controls two banks: FatBank and LeanBank. Near Bancshares has owned FatBank since 1970. It acquired LeanBank ten months ago. FatBank has $5 billion in total assets, $3.2 billion in risk-weighted assets, $500 million in tier 1 capital, and $100 million in tier 2 capital. When most recently examined, FatBank received satisfactory ratings for management and community reinvestment. LeanBank has $1 billion in total assets, $760 million in risk-weighted assets, $40 million in tier 1 capital, and $60 million in tier 2 capital. When most recently examined, LeanBank received a satisfactory rating for management and a "needs to improve" rating for community reinvestment. May Near Bancshares become a financial holding company?

For a bank holding company to qualify as a financial holding company, (1) all of its subsidiary insured depository institutions must be well capitalized and well managed; (2) each of those institutions, when most recently examined, must have received a satisfactory CRA rating; and (3) the holding company must have filed with the Federal Reserve Board an election to become a financial holding company.

FatBank is well-capitalized (10 percent leverage ratio; 18.8 percent total risk-based capital ratio), well-managed, and has a satisfactory CRA rating. Lean Bank, although well-managed, is only adequately capitalized (4 percent leverage ratio) and has a "needs to improve" CRA rating.

Near Bancshares could qualify as a financial holding company in two basic ways. First, it could take steps to increase the capital and improve the CRA performance of LeanBank. Assuming that LeanBank continues to have $1 billion in total assets, it needs at least $10 million in additional tier 1 capital, which Near could infuse by purchasing from the bank that amount of the bank's common shares or cumulative perpetual preferred shares. If Near lacked sufficient resources of its own to make that investment, it could have FatBank pay Near a dividend out of FatBank's surplus capital. Moreover, as Near acquired LeanBank within the past year, § 2903(c)(2) would permit LeanBank to deal with its CRA problem by submitting to its regulator an acceptable plan for improving its CRA performance.

Second, Near could probably qualify as a financial holding company by merging LeanBank into FatBank. FatBank would be well-capitalized even after the merger (9 percent leverage ratio; 17.7 percent total risk-based capital ratio). Moreover, one could reasonably expect that FatBank—four times the size of LeanBank—would retain its satisfactory CRA rating after the merger. (FatBank could preempt possible criticism based on LeanBank's CRA deficiencies by offering its own plan for correcting any post-merger remnants of those deficiencies.)

Problem 3—VelociCorp

VelociCorp, a financial holding company, wants to acquire Lizzi Motors, which specializes in manufacturing and leasing armored cars. What are the best arguments in support of allowing the acquisition?

VelociCorp could argue that manufacturing and leasing armored cars literally involves "[p]roviding [a] device . . . for transferring money or other financial assets," which the Fed can define as "financial" under 12 U.S.C. § 1843(k)(5)(B)(ii).

More conventionally, VelociCorp could argue that the Fed should find the activity "financial" or "incidental" under § 1843(k)(3) or "complementary" under § 1843(k)(1)(B). More specifically, VelociCorp could argue that the activity is "incidental" or "complementary" to the following activities:

- Transferring, exchanging, or safeguarding money or securities under § 1843(k)(4)(A).

- Leasing—approved under § 1843(c)(8) before the Gramm-Leach-Bliley Act and thus "financial" under § 1843(k)(4)(F).

- Providing courier services for checks, documents, and written instruments (excluding currency and bearer-type negotiable instruments) exchanged among financial institutions—also approved under § 1843(c)(8) before Gramm-Leach-Bliley.

Problem 4—Black Sheep Bancshares

Black Sheep Bancshares, a bank holding company, owns BaaBank and BaaCapital. BaaCapital has for years engaged, pursuant to section 4(c)(8) of the Bank Holding Company Act, in underwriting and dealing in a full range of securities, including government, municipal, and corporate securities. The Federal Reserve Board has forbidden BaaCapital from deriving more than 25 percent of its revenues from activities involving corporate securities and other securities that a national bank cannot underwrite and deal in directly. Bank Sheep Bancshares now wishes to be free from this restriction—a restriction that does not apply to financial holding companies. BaaBank has $10 billion in assets and $9.55 billion in liabilities. How can it get relief?

Black Sheep Bancshares cannot qualify as a financial holding company without raising its capital ratio. It could reduce its assets, or could increase its capital by retaining earnings or selling securities. More conveniently for Black Sheep Bancshares, the Fed could use its authority under § 1843(c)(8) to ease the 25-percent-of-revenue restriction.

Problem 5—Hedgehog Group

The Hedgehog Group manages the Hedgehog Fund, a hedge fund that invests in debt and equity securities of U.S. and foreign companies. The Hedgehog Group has $500,000 in total assets and $50,000 in total liabilities. The Hedgehog Fund has $2.0 billion in total assets, $1.95 billion in total liabilities, and less than 100 investors. The fund accepts investments only from sophisticated investors with very high net worth. May the Hedgehog Group acquire a bank?

The Hedgehog Group itself is almost certainly well capitalized: it has $500,000 in total assets and only $50,000 in total liabilities, which suggests a capital-to-assets ratio of some 90 percent ($450,000 in capital ÷ $500,000 in total assets). The issue here is whether the Hedgehog Fund's assets count as part of the Hedgehog Group's total assets for purposes of the Fed's holding company capital standards. In The Bessemer Group, 82 Fed. Reserve Bull. 569 (1996), the Federal Reserve Board required a bank holding company seeking to sponsor and manage hedge funds (specifically, leveraged limited partnerships) to consolidate the hedge funds' assets and liabilities with the holding company's assets and liabilities for regulatory capital purposes. The board stressed the risk that the holding company would rescue a faltering hedge fund to protect its own reputation. But § 1844(c)(3) now prohibits the Fed from imposing any capital requirement on a registered investment adviser that is a functionally regulated, nondepository subsidiary of a bank holding company.

Problem 6—Governmental Impasse

6. The Department of the Treasury and the Federal Reserve Board reach an impasse over what activities to permit in subsidiaries of banks under 12 U.S.C. § 24a. The Federal Reserve Board has used its authority under section 24a(b)(1)(B) to veto the Treasury's proposal to determine that certain activities are financial or incidental to financial activities under section 24a(b)(1)(A)(ii) and therefore permissible for subsidiaries of banks. In response, the Treasury has used its authority under 12 U.S.C. § 1843(k)(2) to veto the Federal Reserve Board's proposal to determine that those same activities are financial or incidental to financial activities and therefore permissible for financial holding companies. Assuming that the Treasury-Fed deadlock continued, would there be any way for a financial holding company to conduct the activities in question?

The Fed could still allow the activity as "complementary."

THRIFT HOLDING COMPANIES

On way to teach this material is to use it as a vehicle for exploring the policies that underlie holding company regulation. The following table summarizes some of the key differences in financial holding company, bank holding company, and unitary thrift holding company regulation. We list four objective differences and then add our own broad-brush point about the implicit premise of each of these types of holding company regulation:

KEY DIFFERENCES IN HOLDING COMPANY REGULATION

CRITERION	FINANCIAL HC	BANK HC	UNITARY THRIFT HC
Regulator	Federal Reserve	Federal Reserve	OTS
Permissible Activities	Financial, incidental, and complementary	Closely related to banking	If all subsidiary thrifts meet QTL test: *any* activity if HC has grandfather rights; same as *FHC* if HC lacks grandfather rights. If any subsidiary thrift fails QTL test, same as *BHC*
Requisite Qualifications	All subsidiary depository institutions must be well-capitalized and well-managed, and must have satisfactory CRA record	None	All subsidiary thrift institutions must meet QTL test
Consolidated HC Capital Requirements	Yes, but not for functionally regulated components	Yes	No
Overarching Implicit Premise	Need some HC regulation, but it can be much looser than traditional bank regulation	HC needs much bank-like regulation	No need to regulate HC; regulation should focus instead on depository institution and its transactions with affiliates

One can ask students, "How does the regulation of thrift holding companies differ from the regulation of financial holding companies?" From there one can explore the rationale for the differences and the extent to which the differences matter from the standpoint of good public policy.

One can also discuss the rationale for—and wisdom of—the Gramm-Leach-Bliley Act's decision to place most nonfinancial activities off-limits to future unitary thrift holding companies.

AFFILIATION WITH NONFINANCIAL COMPANIES: THE DEBATE OVER SEPARATING BANKING AND COMMERCE

Whether to permit nonfinancial companies to affiliate with banks has generated lively debate over the past quarter-century. This section deals with that debate in three ways.

First, pages 460-64 set forth arguments for and against such affiliations. The professor can ask students which side has the better of the exchange—and invite students to enter the fray with arguments of their own.

Second, pages 464-66 discuss the extent to which the Gramm-Leach-Bliley Act—although nominally maintaining a separation between banking and nonfinancial activities—allows significant nonfinancial affiliations by classifying merchant banking and insurance company investments as "financial." This stretching of "financial," together with regulators' authority to allow additional nonfinancial activities as "incidental" or "complementary" (pages 448-49 and 454-55), raises questions about the extent to which the Act actually maintains a meaningful separation between banking and nonfinancial activities.

Third, pages 467-71 present Peter Wallison's provocative paper arguing that—quite apart from any such stretching of "financial"—the Gramm-Leach-Bliley eliminated any policy basis for separating banking from nonfinancial activities by permitting banks to affiliate with *financial* companies. Wallison sees no tenable distinction between financial and nonfinancial activities. He welcomes the breakdown of the banking-commerce separation because he believes that breakdown will ultimately force policymakers to abandon the notion of banks as special and to let the federal safety net for banks wither away. The questions on pages 471-72 (particularly Questions 2-5) provide springboards for class discussion of Wallison's ideas. Question 6 provides an opportunity to revisit the Corrigan-Aspinwall debate over the specialness of banking (pages 81-92) in light of what students have learned since the beginning of the course.

RESTRICTIONS ON BANKS' TRANSACTIONS WITH AFFILIATES: SECTIONS 23A AND 23B

There are at least two reasons for studying sections 23A and 23B (12 U.S.C. §§ 371c & 371c-1). First, those sections are fundamental to maintaining some economic separation between a federally insured bank and its affiliates. They should become all the more important as banks affiliate with a broader range of nonbanking companies and as those nonbank affiliates tend to become larger and more important parts of bank holding companies. Indeed, one could see those sections—together with the requirement that financial holding companies' subsidiary banks be well-capitalized and well-managed—as the "constitution" of financial modernization.

Second, sections 23A and 23B also offer the challenge of grappling with a short but difficult modern banking statute dealing with matters remote from most students' experience. One of us tells his students, "You may read section 23A, feel you've started to understand it, and then—when you return to it—find it has vanished from your mind. But if you stick with it, you'll master it and sharpen your ability to master other statutes."

1. What explains the exceptions from section 23A for (1) loans secured by U.S. government securities or by segregated, earmarked accounts at the lending bank; (2) giving immediate credit for items (e.g., checks) submitted for collection in the ordinary course of business; (3) purchasing assets with a readily identifiable market price at that price; and (4) investing in a bank service corporation? These transactions present fairly low risk. The first is exceedingly safe, the second quite safe. (Note that a check, if dishonored, loses the benefit of the exception for items submitted for collection in the ordinary course of business.) In the case of the third type of transaction, purchasing at a readily identifiable market price provides strong evidence of regularity. Bank service corporations conduct activities that banks could conduct directly in the bank; the fact that the service corporation is a separate legal entity does not make the bank's investment in it any more risky.

2. What do you think of the arguments made by Fischel, Rosenfield, and Stillman? Are transactions between a bank and its affiliates really like taking money from one pocket and putting it into another? Fischel, Rosenfield, and Stillman rightly argue that "The firm as a whole [i.e., the bank and all of its affiliates as a consolidated entity] cannot reduce the cost of borrowing by charging an uneconomical transfer price." But in the context of protecting the federal deposit insurance funds, "the firm as a whole" is *not* the issue. Thus if a bank lends to an affiliate at a below-market rate, the affiliate's gain is the bank's loss—and such losses could conceivably cause the bank to fail. Moreover, economic theory suggests that management will seek to maximize the profits of the consolidated entity—even at the price of exposing the bank to additional risk. Without the federal safety net, the bank's parent holding company might be indifferent to whether the bank or the affiliate bore a particular cost. But insofar as the safety net imparts a subsidy to insured banks, the holding company has incentives to shift costs to those banks and thus further exploit the subsidy. Thus sections 23A and 23B properly seek to limit the potential for shifting costs to banks from their uninsured affiliates.

Affiliate Transaction Problems *(pages 480-82)*

Problem 1—Apex Financial

> Apex Financial, Inc., owns both Apex Bank and Apex Insurance Agency. The insurance agency wants to buy a new office building for $450,000 and has applied to the bank for a $350,000 first-mortgage loan to help finance the purchase. The bank has total assets of $50 million, total liabilities of $47 million, and no outstanding covered transactions with the insurance agency or any other affiliate. May the bank make the loan?

No. The bank and the insurance agency are "affiliates" under section 23A(b)(1)(A). As the bank has $3 million in capital, the $350,000 loan would violate section 23A's 10 percent of capital limit on covered transactions with any one affiliate. The transaction would also fail to meet the collateral requirements of section 23A(c)(1)(d), under which real estate used as collateral must be worth at least 130 percent of the covered transaction, and 130 percent of $350,000 = $455,000.

Problem 2—DoubleWide

Members of the Traylor family own both DoubleWide Industries, Inc., and DoubleWide Bank. DoubleWide Industries manufactures and sells mobile homes. The Traylors intend for the bank, which just received its charter, to specialize in financing the sale of mobile homes—especially mobile homes manufactured by DoubleWide Industries. The bank's business plan envisions that half of the bank's assets will consist of loans purchased from DoubleWide Industries. May the bank proceed with the business plan?

No. Although the bank and DoubleWide Industries are owned by members of a family (rather than by a company), such common ownership still makes DoubleWide Industries an "affiliate" of the bank under section 23A(b)(1)(C)(i) ("any company that is controlled . . . by or for the benefit of shareholders who . . . control . . . the . . . bank"). Alternatively, the Federal Reserve Board could classify DoubleWide Industries as an "affiliate" by determining under section 23A(b)(1)(E) that the bank's relationship with that company may affect the bank's covered transactions with that company to the detriment of the bank.

Section 23A(b)(7) generally defines the purchase of assets from an affiliate as a "covered transaction." Accordingly, the 10-percent-of-capital limit would apply to the bank's covered transactions with that company—and prevent the bank from carrying out its business plan in its current form.

Problem 3—DoubleWide Redux

Same as Problem 2 except that DoubleWide Bank will originate the loans itself (rather than purchasing the loans from DoubleWide Industries). May the bank proceed with that approach?

Here, instead of buying loans originated by DoubleWide, the bank will make loans directly to buyers of DoubleWide mobile homes. The bank can therefore argue that if it makes its own independent credit judgments, the arrangement should pass muster under sections 23A and 23B. But the Federal Reserve Board would probably assert under the attribution rule in section 23A(a)(2) that the extensions of credit indirectly finance the sales department of DoubleWide Industries and thus constitute covered transactions. That argument would be even stronger if, in making loans to DoubleWide buyers, the bank in any way relies on or defers to DoubleWide. Regulators would, in any event, scrutinize the concentration of credit risk in mobile home loans.

Problem 4—Artemis Corporation

Artemis Corporation has two subsidiaries: Artemis Bank and Artemis Mortgage Company. The bank has $1 billion in total assets and $900 million in total liabilities. The mortgage company has never before had dealings with the bank, but is now temporarily short of cash and wants to borrow as much as possible from the bank for six months. It offers the bank $10 million in top-quality mortgages as collateral for the loan. What is the most that the bank can lend to the mortgage company on that collateral? Why?

The bank cannot lend more than $7.7 million because, under section 23A's collateral rules, the mortgages used as collateral must be worth at least 130 percent of the amount of the loan. 12 U.S.C. § 371c(c)(1)(d). On the facts presented, the collateral rules are more restrictive than the 10 percent limit ($10 million). $10 million = 130 percent of $7.7 million.

Problem 5—Spartan Financial

Spartan Financial Corporation owns Alpha Bank and three nonbank corporations: Beta Corp., Gamma Corp., and Delta Corp. The bank has outstanding the following transactions:
- $35 million loan to Beta;
- $10 million in standby letters of credit on behalf of Gamma;
- $25 million investment in bonds issued by Delta; and
- $15 million loan to Delta fully secured by U.S. Treasury securities.

In addition, the bank has outstanding a $10 million loan to Arcadian Mills, Inc., an unaffiliated corporation, secured by $15 million in shares of Spartan Financial. The bank has $6 billion in total assets and $5.6 billion in total liabilities. Is the bank in compliance with section 23A?

The bank has $400 million in capital, making the 10 percent limit $40 million and the 20 percent limit $80 million. Under section 23A(d)(4)(A), a loan fully secured by U.S. government obligations—such as the $15 million loan to Delta—does not count as an extension of credit for purposes of the 10 and 20 percent limits. On the other hand, under section 23A(d)(7)(D), the loan to Arcadian Mills constitutes a covered transaction because the collateral consists of securities issued by Spartan Financial, an affiliate of the bank. The bank's covered transactions with all affiliates total $80 million, of which no more than $35 million is with any one affiliate. Assuming compliance with section 23A(c)'s collateral requirement, the transactions comply with section 23A.

Problem 6—Chekhov Bancorporation

Chekhov Bancorporation controls three banks. It owns 90 percent of the voting shares of Olga Bank, 80 percent of the voting shares of Masha Bank, and 70 percent of the voting shares of Irina Bank. Each of the three banks has $2 billion in total assets and $1.9 billion in total liabilities.

This problem highlights various aspects of section 23A's "sister-bank exemption," using names from Anton Chekhov's 1901 play, *The Three Sisters*.

(a) May Olga Bank make a $120 million loan to Masha Bank? Yes, as long as the loan is safe and sound. Because the same company owns at least 80 percent of the voting shares of both Olga Bank and Masha Bank, section 23A(d)(1)—the so-called "sister-bank exemption"—exempts covered transactions from the 10 and 20 percent limits and from the collateral requirement. Section 23A(a)(4) still requires that the transaction be safe and sound.

(b) May Masha Bank issue a standby letter of credit guaranteeing $200 million in loans that Olga Bank is selling? Same answer as for Problem 6(a): Yes, under the sister-bank exemption—as long as the transaction is safe and sound.

(c) May Olga Bank make a $12 million loan to Irina Bank? No. Chekhov Bancorporation owns 90 percent of Olga Bank but only 70 percent of Irina Bank, making the sister-bank exemption inapplicable to covered transactions between the two banks. Accordingly, section 23A's 10 percent and 20 percent limits apply. The loan would violate the 10 percent limit.

(d) May Irina Bank accept $18.5 million of Olga Bank bonds as collateral for a $14 million loan to Dr. Chebutykin, who has no ties to Olga Bank or Irina Bank? No. Under section 23A(b)(7)(D), accepting securities issued by an affiliate as collateral for a loan to anyone constitutes a covered transaction. Cf. loan to Arcadian Mills in Problem 5.

(e) May Irina Bank purchase Masha Bank's past-due $5,000 loan to Colonel Vershinin? May Olga Bank? As the loan is more than 30 days past due, it constitutes a "low-quality asset" under section 23A(b)(10)(C). Section 23A(a)(3) prohibits a bank from purchasing a low-quality asset from an affiliate. This prohibition applies even under the sister-bank exemption. 12 U.S.C. § 371c(d)(1). Accordingly neither Olga Bank nor Irina Bank can purchase the loan from Masha Bank.

(f) May Olga Bank make a $15 million loan to Chekhov Bancorporation? No. The loan would exceed the 10 percent limit. The sister-bank exemption applies only among FDIC-insured depository institutions.

Problem 7—Chekhov Redux

Same basic facts as in problem 6, except that Olga Bank has $2 billion in total assets and $1.95 billion in total liabilities. May Olga Bank make a $6 million loan to Masha Bank?

Olga Bank is now significantly undercapitalized (leverage ratio < 3 percent). Under the prompt corrective action statute, the appropriate federal banking agency must prohibit a significantly undercapitalized depository institution from using the sister-bank exemption unless the agency determines that the prohibition would not further the purpose of the prompt corrective action statute (i.e., would not help avoid or minimize loss to the deposit insurance fund). 12 U.S.C. § 1831o(f)(2)(B)(i), (3)(B).

Problem 8—Bengal Bancshares

Bengal Bankshares owns: Tiger Bank; Tiger Securities Corporation, a registered broker-dealer; Tiger Capital Corporation, which engages in merchant banking; and Tiger Leasing Corporation, which leases equipment. Tiger Bank has $10 billion in total assets, $9 billion in total liabilities, and no outstanding covered transactions.

(a) Tiger Leasing applies to borrow $100 million from the bank and offers the bank a security interest in leases having a market value of $130 million. May the bank make the loan at 2 percentage points below the bank's prime rate? The loan would comply with section 23A's collateral requirement and 10 and 20 percent limits. But the below-prime interest rate would almost certainly violate section 23B(a)(1), under which a bank may engage in a covered transaction (and various other transactions) with an affiliate only on arm's-length terms: specifically, "on terms and under circumstances . . . that are substantially the same, or at least as favorable to the bank . . ., as those prevailing at the time for comparable transactions with or involving other unaffiliated companies."

(b) Bengal Bankshares, having decided to consolidate its corporate family's leasing activities in Tiger Leasing, instructs Tiger Bank to sell its existing leases to Tiger Leasing at book value. May the bank proceed with the sale? Section 23B(a)(1) applies to a bank's sale of assets to an affiliate, even though such a sale is not a "covered transaction" as defined in section 23A(b)(7). Sale at book value would satisfy section 23B(a)(1)(A) only if such a price were "substantially the same, or at least as favorable to the bank . . ., as those prevailing at the time for comparable transactions with or involving other unaffiliated companies."

(c) Bengal Bankshares and Tiger Bank enter into a contract under which the bank will furnish data-processing services to the holding company and its nonbank subsidiaries for $2,000 per month. May the bank proceed under the contract? Section 23B(2)(C) makes the arm's-length standard of section 23B(a)(1) applicable to "the furnishing of services to an affiliate under contract . . . or otherwise." To assess whether the contract would meet that standard, one should ascertain market prices for data-processing services and the bank's own data-processing cost-structure.

(d) Tiger Securities is underwriting the initial public offering of Airhead.com's stock. May Tiger Bank purchase one-tenth of the offering for itself or its trust customers? The bank generally cannot purchase equity securities for its own account. 12 U.S.C. §§ 24(Seventh), 1831a(c)(2). Section 23B(b)(1)(B) generally prohibits the bank from knowingly acquiring any security while any affiliate is serving as a principal underwriter of that security. Under section 23B(b)(2), a majority of the bank's outside directors can approve the acquisition of such securities, but only if they (1) do so "before such securities are initially offered for sale to the public" and (2) determine "that the purchase is a sound investment for the bank irrespective of the fact that an affiliate of the bank is a principal underwriter of the securities." Note that the second requirement, added by the Gramm-Leach-Bliley Act, is phrased in a way that does not literally cover acquisitions as a fiduciary ("a sound investment for the bank").

Problem 9—Atlas Financial Group

Atlas Financial Group owns Atlas Bank, Atlas Insurance Company, and Atlas Securities Corporation. May affiliates of the bank use in their advertising the slogans or statements on page 482?

In each case, the issue is whether the statement or slogan comports with section 23B(c) of the Federal Reserve Act, which forbids a bank to "publish any advertisement . . . stating or suggesting that the bank shall in any way be responsible for the obligations of its affiliates."

ACTIVITY RESTRICTIONS ON BANKS WITHIN A HOLDING COMPANY

Merchants National holds that the BHC Act does *not* apply to banks controlled by bank holding companies. Thus such a bank may, to the extent permitted under its charter and other applicable law (such as 12 U.S.C. § 1831a), engage in activities impermissible for its parent holding company.

The Second Circuit's opinion is striking for its clarity and candor. It uses plain, direct language to shed light on abstruse issues, including thorny textual arguments over the reach of the BHC Act's activity restrictions. It acknowledges the strengths and weaknesses of both sides' arguments (page 487-88) before concluding that *Chevron* deference requires the court to uphold the Federal Reserve Board's interpretation of those restrictions.

Questions and Comments (page 489)

1. Why did the Fed disclaim regulatory authority over activities conducted in a bank (as distinguished from a subsidiary of a bank)? Is this renunciation consistent with regulators' general propensity to protect and expand their bureaucratic turf? This is a genuine case of regulatory turf-renunciation. Events had backed the Fed into a corner. Many bankers believed that they needed new powers, particularly the power to sell insurance, in order to remain competitive with nonbank financial institutions. Yet the BHC Act generally barred bank holding companies from selling insurance—and Congress was then more inclined to widen that prohibition than to repeal it. Accordingly, bankers seeking expanded insurance powers looked to state bank charters, especially in states (like Indiana) that already authorized their state banks to sell insurance.

Thus the *Merchants National* case confronted the Fed with a cruel dilemma. The Fed could side with the banks—and give concrete expression to its support for bank entry into insurance sales—at the cost of relinquishing a long-held jurisdictional claim. Or it could advance the jurisdictional claim and thereby further the insurance agents' efforts to halt bank entry and roll back even established bank insurance activities. Had the Fed sided with the insurance agents, banks, bank trade associations, and state bank regulators might well have turned against the Fed in ways that could ultimately have gravely weakened the Fed's regulatory authority under any financial modernization legislation.

2. Why did the Fed assert authority to regulate the activities of a subsidiary of a bank controlled by a bank holding company even as it disclaimed authority to regulate the activities of the bank itself? Banks had not invested heavily in subsidiaries as a means of exercising new powers. Bankers felt less strongly about the powers of subsidiaries than about the powers of banks themselves. And in many cases (e.g., selling insurance) banks had authority to do directly what they could do through a subsidiary, so that if the subsidiary route became unavailable banks could still conduct the activity in the bank itself. Hence the Fed could maintain its jurisdictional claims over subsidiaries without incurring the sort of political and policy costs it might have faced had it sided with the insurance agents in *Merchants National*.

Whether the BHC Act's Activity Restrictions Apply to Subsidiaries of Banks *(pages 490-95)*

Citicorp Delaware (pages 490-94) resolved the issue left open in *Merchants National*: it held that the BHC Act's activity restrictions did *not* apply to subsidiaries of a bank holding company's banks.

Question and Comment 1 on pages 494-95 explains why the Delaware statute went to such lengths to authorize the activity in question—insurance underwriting—not only in a subsidiary of the bank but in a separately regulated division of the bank. The statute had sought to bring the activity within the Federal Reserve Board's Regulation Y, which specifically permitted a subsidiary of a bank to engage in activities permissible for the bank itself. But the Fed held that the statute required so great a separation between the bank and its insurance division that the bank itself would not actually be underwriting insurance.

The Second Circuit overturned the Fed's order, holding it inconsistent with *Merchants National*. Underscoring the strength of *Chevron* deference, the court went on to declare that it would probably have upheld the Fed both in *Merchants* and here if in *Merchants* the Fed had construed the BHC Act's activity restrictions as applicable to all entities directly or indirectly controlled by a bank holding company (page 494). But the court reasoned that the construction of the Act upheld in *Merchants* now bound the Fed as well as the court, and precluded the Fed from applying those restrictions to subsidiaries of banks.

Questions and Comments (pages 494-95)

5. How can one reconcile the Fed's concern about statutes like Delaware's promoting "potentially destructive competition among the states with adverse consequences for . . . safety and soundness . . . and the federal deposit insurance funds" with the Fed's support for regulatory competition during the debate over consolidating the federal banking agencies? These positions are difficult to reconcile. The Fed's criticism of the Delaware statute was consistent with the Fed's longstanding opposition to regulatory "competition in laxity"—a view most notably articulated by Fed Chairman Arthur Burns. But in resisting regulatory consolidation the Fed chose to stress the benefits of regulatory competition (pages 74-75) and suggest that adequate safeguards already existed to contain the adverse effects of such competition (cf. the safeguards referred to in Question and Comment 3 on page 489).

6. Would the reasoning of Citibank Delaware apply to subsidiaries of national banks? It should. One could make dual-banking arguments for giving state banks additional leeway. But the relevant provisions of the BHC Act drew no distinction between national and state banks.

Subsidiaries and the Spread of Safety-Net Subsidy *(pages 495-505)*

Given that the BHC Act's activity restrictions do not apply to subsidiaries of banks, what activities *should* public policy permit such subsidiaries to conduct? This question occasioned great controversy during congressional consideration of the Gramm-Leach-Bliley Act. The debate between the Fed and the Treasury, excerpted here, provides an opportunity to examine the subsidiary model itself and—more broadly—the dynamics of affiliation between banks and other companies and the efficacy of safeguards like section 23A in maintaining an economic separation between banks and affiliates.

Key issues here include the following: (1) Does the federal safety net give banks a meaningful net subsidy? (2) If so, can that subsidy be contained by prudential safeguards like section 23A? (3) Is either the holding company or the subsidiary model better for that purpose? Grappling with such issues will strengthen students' understanding of the dynamics of affiliation generally.

Subsidiaries Under Existing Law *(pages 505-09)*

In prescribing regulations to implement the subsidiary provisions of the Gramm-Leach-Bliley Act, the FDIC set some limits on the lenient treatment of state nonmember banks (discussed on page 507). The FDIC rejected the argument that to engage as principal in newly authorized financial activities, subsidiaries of state nonmember banks need comply only with 12 U.S.C. § 1831a(d)(1)—rather than with the more stringent restrictions and requirements of § 1831w(a). 66 Fed. Reg. 1018, 1022-23 (2001). Accordingly, such banks must be well-capitalized after complying with the capital-deduction requirement. The FDIC also required state nonmember banks with such subsidiaries to be well-managed. 12 C.F.R. § 362.18.

Questions and Comments (pages 508-09)

1. What institutional interests do the Federal Reserve Board and the Treasury have in the debate over allowing subsidiaries of banks to conduct nonbanking activities? The Fed regulates all bank holding companies—and thus stands to lose power if banks can form affiliations through subsidiaries (over which it would generally have authority only if it were the primary federal regulator of the parent bank). The Treasury's Office of the Comptroller of the Currency regulates national banks. The OCC stands to gain importance insofar as national banks can form affiliations through subsidiaries (and not just through the BHC Act). Broad scope for such affiliations may also reduce the likelihood of national banks converting to state charters—and leaving the OCC less able to support itself from user fees.

6. Does the public interest justify prohibiting subsidiaries of banks from holding merchant banking investments? Arguments in favor of the prohibition: (1) creditors of a troubled portfolio company might pierce the corporate veil and hold not only the subsidiary but its parent bank liable for the portfolio company's obligations; and (2) the federal safety net may permit the bank to fund its investment in the subsidiary more cheaply than the bank holding company might fund its investment in a holding company affiliate (pages 496-99). Arguments against the prohibition: (1) piercing the corporate veil to hold a bank liable for the obligations of a portfolio company is unlikely in any event, and is no more likely under the subsidiary model than under the holding company model; (2) banks could not spread a subsidy any more readily to subsidiaries than to holding company affiliates—and having subsidiaries hold merchant banking investments would actually be subsidy-reducing, as the bank's equity in those investments would increase the assets available to the bank's depositors and the FDIC (pages 503-05).

7. *Why apply weaker restrictions and requirements to subsidiaries of state banks than to subsidiaries of national banks?* The Fed had an interest in placating customary allies like state bank supervisors. Hence it argued for giving state nonmember banks favored treatment to improve the prospects for enacting the Gramm-Leach-Bliley Act with its Fed-Treasury agreement on subsidiaries (an arguably ironic stance given the Fed's previously stated preference for having no legislation rather than legislation allowing expanded powers through subsidiaries; see page 496). The Treasury had its own reasons for applying weaker rules to state nonmember banks. It calculated that such treatment would ultimately help undercut the stricter treatment of national and state member banks. Experience with state nonmember banks could help rebut the Fed's arguments about the perils of subsidy-spreading—and facilitate future legislation cleaning up the anomalies in the name of regulatory burden relief.

Chapter 7: Insurance and Securities Powers of Banking Institutions

This chapter is new in the Third Edition. It deals with the insurance and securities powers of depository institutions and their affiliates, as fundamentally modified by the Gramm-Leach-Bliley Act of 1999. Because the chapter is entirely new, we have only limited experience teaching from it. Accordingly, the following pages in this Teacher's Manual are based more on predictions of what students will find interesting than on the results of actual experience in the classroom. The authors, of course, encourage instructors who adopt the book to experiment in teaching this as well as other chapters, and to let any of us know of your successes (or failures).

INSURANCE POWERS OF BANKING INSTITUTIONS

The first part of the chapter deals with insurance. This has been perhaps the most hotly contested area in the entire politics of banking regulation over the past decade, as banks found themselves confronted by an equally powerful, committed rival in the form of the insurance industry, which wanted to resist bank encroachment into its business while at the same time poaching on the business of banking. The book discusses the principal reason why this conflict occurred: banks and insurance firms, despite their differences, are in many respects involved in functionally similar businesses. It is a good idea to ask students to identify the similarities and differences between the banking and insurance functions, and to test the limits of what those features might be. Structurally, banks and insurance firms are both financial intermediaries, although an important difference is that insurance firms do not have high levels of demand debt in their balance sheets. Nevertheless, both banks and insurance firms rely on the law of large numbers in order to operate according to a principle of fractional reserves. In the case of banks, the assumption is that only a small fraction of depositors will want to withdraw funds on any given day. For insurance firms, the assumption is that the risks insured against will not come to pass for more than a relatively small fraction of policyholders at any given time. Both these assumptions could be wrong, of course. In the case of a run, depositors line up to withdraw funds; and in the case of an unforeseen catastrophe (e.g., a thousand-year storm), policyholders may make claims against their insurance companies *en masse*. Neither banks nor insurance companies have the reserves on hand to pay out these kinds of mass claims.

Banks and insurance companies share in common the fact that they are relied on by their customers as a safe bulwark against risk. People get insurance in order to protect themselves against bad things from happening. People sometimes go to banks in order to obtain an investment that is absolutely secure, and people accept checks because they believe that the payments system will be secure against the risk of failure of banks in the chain of payments. These are fundamental assumptions that undergird much of our economic system. If people could not have a high degree of certainty that their claims against banks or insurance companies would be honored, the economic system would be quite different than it is now. For both these reasons—that banks and insurance companies are vulnerable to mass claims, and that banks and insurance companies are bulwarks against risk in the economic system—it is considered important to protect claimants against the threat of loss, at least to a substantial extent. Accordingly, regulators act to protect claimants against the possibility that they will not be repaid.

There are also important synergies of operation between banks and insurance firms, both because the customer base can be consolidated, and because both firms, as intermediaries, make investments in other firms that require expertise and monitoring. Thus there may be economies of scope and scale in the combination of banking and insurance. It's probable also that many people would like the convenience of doing all their financial business with a single financial services "supermarket" whose reputation they trust and on whose solvency they rely.

It's worth spending quite a bit of class time on these issues, since they are fundamental, and basic to the combinations of banking and insurance that we are witnessing as the Third Edition goes to press. If the class goes well, there will be several students who know the industries and will volunteer their personal perspective on the issues.

Having brought out the similarities between banking and insurance, it's worth exploring the differences in regulatory treatment. Actually, banks and insurance firms are, in some respects, regulated similarly. Both are comprehensively regulated, and are subject to much stricter scrutiny by the government than other types of firms. Both operate under minimum capital requirements. Both have insurance schemes in place administered by government intended to protect consumer claimants. But in other respects, having to do as much with history as with function, there are huge regulatory differences. Most importantly, insurance is nearly entirely regulated at the state level (a consequence of the McCarran-Ferguson Act), whereas banks are regulated at both the state and federal level and, arguably, are principal regulated by the federal government. Also, even though the regulatory schemes for the two industries look alike in some respects, there are big differences in detail. The minimum capital system for insurance is different than the minimum capital rules for banks; indeed, the accounting conventions in use for the two firms are not in all respects congruent. Insurance is indeed available for claimants in both industries, but it is administered differently: in banking, it's a system of federal deposit insurance and is uniform across the country; in insurance, states insure policyholders located in their borders.

Thus, despite the obvious potential advantages of consolidation, putting these industries together faces daunting political, legal, and technical problems. These problems, however, are now being addressed as a result of the enactment of the Gramm-Leach-Bliley Act in the closing days of 1999. That statute creates an exquisitely balanced regime that preserves the interests of both industries, and both sets of regulatory authorities, while permitting fairly broad consolidations between banks and insurance firms. It could be worth exploring, briefly, the nature of some of these subtle political compromises in the form of the various pre-emption rules of the statute discussed on pages 515-516.

Insurance Powers Conducted by a Depository Institution Directly *(pages 516-51)*

The chapter starts with a discussion of the power of banks to conduct insurance activities directly. This situation should be distinguished from one in which insurance is offered through an affiliate, subsidiary, or parent institution of the bank. The issues here are complex and interesting. However, as the book notes, since the GLB Act allows a clear avenue for conducting insurance activities through one of these other forms, there is less pressure today on a bank to offer insurance services directly.

The Line Between Banking and Insurance (pages 517-30)

The *NationsBank v. VALIC* case (pages 517-19) involved a challenge to the power of national banks to act as agents in the sale of annuities. It's worth bringing out for students precisely what's at stake here. First, you might discuss the nature of an annuity. One of the founders of the concept of an annuity described it as such: "till death do us part." Actually, an annuity is simply the payout of money over time. But if the time period of the payout is specified as the life of a person, the party offering the annuity is in effect offering a form of insurance. The holder of the annuity is in effect insuring against the risk of living too long rather than too briefly. Annuities therefore serve an opposite function to life insurance contracts, but they depend for their value, as does life insurance, on the expected mortality of a person.

After clarifying what an annuity is, you might ask students to clarify what the national bank was doing in this case. The purpose of the question is to distinguish the function of acting as agent from that of underwriting. The bank here was not underwriting annuities, in that it was not offering contracts that it promised to perform itself. Rather the bank was offering for sale annuity products underwritten by others. The bank's interest was in obtaining sales commissions for the sales. Thus, the bank did not take on the mortality risk that is inherent in the annuity contract.

The court here, in a reprise of matters covered in Chapter 3, concluded that the comptroller was within his discretion in concluding that banks could broker annuities under 12 U.S.C. § 24(7). You might ask students to note the highly deferential attitude displayed by the court towards the comptroller's decision, an attitude that contrasts markedly with the tone previously expressed by courts towards comptroller decisions in earlier decades. The more interesting part of this case concerns the impact of 12 U.S.C. § 92, which allows banks to act as agent for the sale of insurance products in towns of 5,000 or less. The insurance parties argued that the statute, by negative implication, precluded national banks from acting as agent to sell insurance in larger towns. However, the Supreme Court never reached that issue, concluding instead that the comptroller properly concluded that annuities are not insurance.

The questions and comments after *VALIC* (pages 519-20) raise significant doubts about the correctness of the Court's holding as a matter of economic reasoning. Although some annuities are not tied to mortality, most are. And annuities are a product traditionally offered by insurance companies, not banks. You might use these problems as a means for probing the determinants of the Court's ruling. Was the Court motivated by the *Chevron* principle of deference to agency interpretations? But should that principle have applied here, where the banking agencies were interpreting an unfamiliar term and doing so against the backdrop of strong disagreement by an industry that was both powerfully affected by the decision and that had little, if any, influence within the comptroller's office? Other than deference, are there justifications for the decision? Perhaps the Court was influenced by the underlying policy. Since brokering annuities poses no investment risk for banks—they do not assume mortality risk when they act as agents—it is hard to see the harm to the public from allowing banks to do so, and rather easy to see some possible benefits (consumers would have another source for insurance products). Was the decision based on policy grounds? Should it have been?

The decision in *Blackfeet National Bank* (pages 520-28) involved the question of whether a national bank could issue a "retirement CD." In teaching this case, it might be fruitful to invite students to explain, precisely, the nature of the activity being challenged (discussed on page 521). You can invite students to explain why this instrument might be a desirable investment, and indicate who the likely buyers would be (obviously, people who want to invest funds for retirement).

Here the result is different than in *NationsBank v. VALIC*: the national bank was not permitted to conduct the activity in question. This presents an obvious topic for class discussion, namely, why the difference? One answer is the formality of the decision by the comptroller. In the former case, the comptroller had granted formal permission to engage in the questioned activity; in *Blackfeet*, the comptroller had simply not objected. But in both cases, the comptroller had permitted the activity in question after administrative consideration, and it's not at all clear that the fact the latter case was a "no action" letter makes a difference under *Chevron*.

What you look for is a student who can identify the distinction between brokering and underwriting. In the present case, unlike the *NationsBank* case, the bank was assuming the actuarial risk. This is the distinction that the court highlights. From a functional perspective, the court notes that protection against the risk of insolvency is the key, and this risk is posed when a bank underwrites rather than acts as agent in the sale of a product. But you might question this reasoning on two grounds. First, banking regulation is at least as concerned about insolvency risk as is insurance regulation, so it's not clear that insolvency risk should be the touchstone for distinguishing between banking products and insurance products. Second, the court offers no reason why insolvency risk should be a reason for distinguishing the products in any event. Isn't the essence of insurance, rather, the fact that a party takes on the risk of a future event? Can the decision in this case be reconciled with *NationsBank*, where the court held that annuities were not insurance, even though the payout often depending on the mortality of the annuity holder as determined by actuarial tables?

Having discussed the definitional question, you might consider drawing out of students the doctrinal issue under the McCarran-Ferguson Act. Even if the national bank could offer this product under the National Bank Act, the McCarran-Ferguson Act might allow the state regulators to forbid the activity. You can ask what the court means by "reverse pre-emption" here.

The court holds that issuing the retirement CD is the "business of insurance" for purposes of the McCarran-Ferguson Act. How can this be so if a national bank is authorized to issue the instrument as part of or incidental to the "business of banking" under § 24(7)? Logically, the same activity could be both the business of banking *and* the business of insurance; the statutes don't say they are mutually exclusive. And *a fortiori* something could be incidental to the business of banking and part of the business of insurance at the same time. But can the same logic be used for § 92, which was the key statute at issue in *NationsBank*. That statute used the term "insurance", and the Supreme Court held that the annuities in issue were not insurance products, right? But perhaps "insurance" means something different in the context of § 92 as in the context of the McCarran-Ferguson Act. The relevant test for defining "insurance" under the McCarran-Ferguson Act is the three-part *Pireno* test described on pages 526-27, which is not necessarily the same as the test for defining "insurance" in § 92. In any event, these doctrinal issues can be the basis for a provocative class discussion.

The final issue in the case, which students might also be encouraged to identify, is whether, if issuing a retirement CD qualifies as the business of insurance under the McCarran-Ferguson Act, the National Bank Act "specifically relates" to the business of insurance so as to overcome the pre-emption of federal law that would otherwise apply. The court rejected the bank's argument, on the ground that the provisions relied on by the comptroller—most importantly, § 24(7)—were general and did not relate specifically to insurance.

Question 5 (page 529): you might ask this question. After all, what *is* wrong with national banks offering a product such as the Retirement CD? If it's not a good product, customers won't buy it, right? Do you really think the risk of bank insolvency was greater than the risk of insurance company insolvency? Wasn't the Retirement CD in fact safer than a similar insurance product, because it was insured by the federal government up to $100,000?

The Gramm-Leach-Bliley definition of insurance (pages 529-30) is excerpted as a possible statutory response to the question of how to define "insurance" for purposes of drawing regulatory boundaries. Note that for the most part, the drafters simply avoided attempting a functional definition, relying instead on whether a product was regulated as insurance under the relevant state insurance law. This provision is in effect now as a means for regulating insurance underwriting powers of depository institutions, a topic that is introduced by the concluding sections of the *Blackfeet* case. Notice that the new definition appears to confirm the result in *Blackfeet*, since annuity contracts subject to § 72 of the Internal Revenue Code are treated as "insurance."

Insurance Underwriting Powers Of Depository Institutions (pages 530-39)

The general rule is that national banks can't underwrite insurance—a rule generally applied to state chartered banks by § 1831a(b). A key question here is one already asked: what would be so terrible—other than the harm to the insurance industry—if banks could underwrite insurance directly?

The Gramm-Leach-Bliley Act provides an exception for grandfathered insurance activities. One such activity might be standby letters of credit. These have long been permitted by the comptroller, under a line of authority extending back many years. The issue with respect to standby letters of credit is to distinguish them from guarantees. It has long been black letter law that banks are not permitted to act as guarantors, but they can act as issuers of standby letters of credit. The interesting question is, why? This is addressed in the *Republic National Bank* case (pages 531-36).

Republic National Bank is fun to teach. You might introduce the case by observing that if national banks can't generally act as insurance agents—where they do not assume any significant risk—then surely they cannot perform an insurance underwriting function, where they actually take on customer risk. This is indeed the general rule, expressed in the black-letter maxim that national banks cannot act as guarantors. Yet in this case we see that national banks can provide a service—the standby letter of credit—that is functionally equivalent to a guarantee for most purposes.

We teach the case by contrasting the standby letter of credit with the standard commercial letter of credit. In the straight letter of credit, the bank expects the beneficiary to present the draft and accompanying documentation. The straight letter of credit is in most functional senses a loan. We ask students to suggest reasons why it might have commercial advantages over a loan (after all, if it was strictly equivalent to a loan, banks would probably content themselves with making loans). One advantage offered by the straight letter of credit, from the bank's perspective, is that the customer is strictly limited in the use of the bank's funds. This way the bank can reduce its credit risk by ensuring that the customer uses the loan proceeds for purposes approved in advance by the bank. Probably more importantly, the straight letter of credit facilitates the transaction between the account party and the beneficiary. The beneficiary wants assurance that it will be paid for the goods supplied, and the letter of credit provides such assurance. The account party, on the other hand, may not want to pay for the goods prior to delivery and inspection, since if the goods are not conforming the buyer may want to reject and not pay. The letter of credit serves both needs. It assures the beneficiary that if the requisite documentation is obtained—which means, usually, that the buyer must accept the goods upon delivery—then payment will be forthcoming. At the same time it provides the buyer with assurance that if the goods are not conforming the buyer can reject the delivery and the seller will not be able to draw on the letter of credit.

The straight letter of credit has been around for hundreds of years and is completely unproblematic. Having discussed its features, we then ask students to describe why the standby letter of credit is different. The answer, of course, is that in a standby letter of credit arrangement the bank hopes and expects *not* to have to pay on the letter. The beneficiary under a standby letter of credit draws on the letter only if the account party defaults on the underlying obligation. And if the account party has defaulted on the underlying obligation, it is unlikely that the bank on which the letter is drawn will be able to obtain the money back from the account party.

This principle is illustrated by the *Republic National Bank* case, involving a standby letter of credit for the benefit of the trustee of a perpetual care fund for a cemetery. The ostensible account party is B&H Amusement Rides, which is the obligor on a $50,000 note to the fund. The purpose of the letter of credit is to facilitate the sale of the cemetery; the potential buyer is leery (rightly so, in retrospect) about the B&H note, and wants assurance that the perpetual care fund will be able to recover on the debt (otherwise there might not be enough money in the fund to pay for the upkeep of the cemetery, thus reducing the cemetery's value to the potential buyers). We ask students what is in it for B&H Amusement Rides to obtain the letter of credit; the answer is probably nothing—the real party in interest is probably the seller of the cemetery which probably induced B&H to obtain the letter of credit and paid the bank's fee.

Now B&H defaults on the note, and the beneficiary presents a draft and supporting documentation to the issuing bank conforming with the terms of the letter of credit. The issuing bank, not surprisingly, doesn't want to pay on the letter, and claims that the letter is *ultra vires*. We ask at this point why, putting aside the equities of the situation (the bank trying to wriggle out of a bad deal), the bank isn't right. What possible difference is there between this arrangement and an outright guarantee of B&H's debt to the fund trustee?

The court offers a distinction: in the standby letter of credit the bank is not obliged to determine the rights of its account party vis-à-vis the beneficiary. Its only obligation is to pay on the letter if conforming documentation is provided. In the guarantee, on the other hand, the guarantor has to pay off only if the beneficiary of the guarantee has *in fact* breached the underlying obligation, and thus the guarantor must examine the respective rights of the underlying parties.

This is the standard distinction between standby letters of credit and guarantees, but query if it makes much sense. Why isn't it the case that a bank is better off as a guarantor than as the issuer of a standby letter of credit? As a guarantor the bank can assert the rights of the account party against the beneficiary. In a standby letter of credit the bank is denied the right to assert these defenses. So if the concern is about bank safety and soundness, arguably the guarantee is better than the standby letter of credit. The court does make the point that the standby letter of credit avoids protracted litigation, but again wouldn't a national bank prefer having defenses, even if they have to be asserted in litigation, to having no defenses at all? Moreover, the standby letter of credit is not an absolute guarantee against litigation; the account party may try to enjoin the bank from paying out on the letter, although such suits are difficult to win under the U.C.C.

Insurance Agency Activities by Depository Institutions *(pages 539-51)*

We return to the statute, 12 U.S.C. § 92, that permits national banks to act as agents for the sale of insurance products in small towns. You might ask students to speculate about why Congress enacted this statute. It would be fun to highlight the irony that such a simple-sounding provision has caused so much trouble, including the apparently inadvertent repeal of the statute during the codification of the revised statutes, and the repeal of the repeal by a Supreme Court that called a halt to literalism in interpretation in the *National Bank of Oregon* case.

Another fascinating issue is the comptroller's effort to interpret the statute as not prohibiting insurance agency sales in larger towns. That the comptroller would have the nerve to endorse such an interpretation may be one of the reasons that the courts were, for several years, very hard on the comptroller's exercise of discretion in interpreting the banking statutes.

But notice the cases cited on pages 541-42, some of which upheld the comptroller's continuing efforts to allow banks to sell more limited, "special-purpose" insurance products in towns larger than 5,000 souls.

The biggest issue, however, is the one treated by the D.C. Circuit in *IIAA v. Ludwig* (pages 543-44). Although it is very doubtful that Congress believed, when it enacted § 92, that it was authorizing national banks to establish insurance offices in small towns and from those locations to market insurance on a nationwide basis, the statute did not in terms prohibit such activity. The legislative record was blank on the topic, however—perhaps because the idea of nationwide marketing from small towns would not have even occurred to a member of Congress in 1916, when § 92 was enacted. Nevertheless, the D.C. Circuit endorsed the idea. You might explore with students whether the decision was based on law, or policy. Note also various other end-runs around the statute permitted by the comptroller in recent years (page 545).

Barnett Bank of Marion County v. Nelson (pages 546-50) involved a Florida statute that prohibited anyone affiliated with a financial institution from acting as an insurance agent in the state, except that an unaffiliated small town bank could sell insurance in a small town. Barnett Bank, as part of a bank holding company, did not qualify for the exemption.

The Supreme Court held first that § 92 pre-empted the Florida statute. You might probe as to whether this analysis is completely convincing. Was there anything illogical in the position that § 92 removed *federal* obstacles to national bank insurance sales in small towns, but had no effect on *state* obstacles? Note, further, that the Florida statute did not on its face discriminate against national banks; it applied to all banks, state or federal—although, realistically, most national banks are parts of holding companies so that the small town exemption under state law would apply principally to state chartered banks.

The Court then addressed the impact of the McCarran-Ferguson Act, a special statute setting forth the scope of federal regulation of insurance. You might remind students of the treatment of a related issue in the *Blackfeet* case (if they—or you—can remember back that far!). The McCarran-Ferguson Act provides that a federal statute is not be read as pre-empting state laws enacted "for the purpose of regulating the business of insurance" unless the federal statute "specifically relate to the business of insurance." 15 U.S.C. § 1012(b). The Court held that § 92 "specifically relates" to the business of insurance, and therefore ruled that the National Bank Act pre-empted the Florida statute, notwithstanding the anti-pre-emption rule of the McCarran-Ferguson Act.

Questions and Comments *(pages 550-51)*

2. It can be fruitful to ask students how far the *Barnett* pre-emption rule goes.

3. *Duryee* is a nice example of the issues that arise in the wake of *Barnett*.

4. A cute issue is whether the state regulation in question relates to the business of insurance. If it doesn't, the McCarran-Ferguson Act's reverse preemption is not triggered in the

first place. The question illustrates that it may sometimes be hard to categorize a state regulation in this manner.

Insurance Powers of Affiliates and Subsidiaries *(pages 551-54)*

We move now from the insurance activities (acting as agent or underwriting various insurance and insurance-related products) of banks directly, to the perhaps more salient issue of the insurance powers of affiliates and subsidiaries of banking firms. Here the Gramm-Leach-Bliley Act has revolutionized the ground rules. As to insurance underwriting, the Act permits financial holding companies or their subsidiaries to engage in a full range of insurance powers, including the power to underwrite. For the definition of financial holding company, see page 445. Notice that this authorization doesn't apply to the depository institution itself. Important here, also, is the principle of functional regulation; if the holding company affiliate is underwriting insurance, it will be regulated by the relevant state insurance commissioner.

Importantly, the power to underwrite insurance was denied to subsidiaries of depository institutions. This is part of the upshot of the dispute between the Federal Reserve and the Treasury about the proper vehicle for expanded bank powers. As discussed on pages 495-95, the Fed wanted expanded powers to be restricted to affiliates of a holding company (which the Fed would regulate). The Treasury wanted similar powers for subsidiaries of banks (which the OCC, part of the Treasury, would regulate in the case of national banks). Congress split the baby, giving expanded authority to subsidiaries of banks but reserving a few important powers to affiliates of a financial holding company; insurance underwriting is the most important of these.

Insurance agency activities are freely permitted both to subsidiaries of banks and to holding company affiliates. Financial holding companies and their subsidiaries qualify. So do "financial subsidiaries" as defined in the GLB law. The statute also has a special provision for "financial agency subsidiaries" which do not act as principal in providing financial products; these need not jump through all the hoops necessary to become a "financial subsidiary."

SECURITIES POWERS OF BANKING INSTITUTIONS

In some respects, analysis of the securities powers of banking institutions parallels the discussion of the insurance powers. There are important differences, however, so we treat them differently in the book. One important difference has to do with history. Prior to the GLB act, bank involvement in securities activities was regulated by a different statutory scheme than bank involvement in insurance. For insurance, the relevant statutes were 12 U.S.C. §§ 24(7) and 92 and the McCarran-Ferguson Act. For securities, the relevant statute was the Glass-Steagall Act, which has largely, although not wholly, been repealed by the GLB act.

Theses statutory differences led to differences in business practice. While until the GLB law, the line between banking and insurance remained relatively steady, the situation was different in the case of securities. It was long supposed, after the Great Depression, that the Glass-Steagall Act enacted in 1933 had created a virtually impregnable wall between investment banking (i.e., the securities business) and commercial banking. When the wall came under stress in the early 1970s, the Supreme Court shored it up with an important decision, *Investment Co.*

Inst. v. Camp, excerpted on page 566. Yet as market conditions changed, and memories of the Great Depression began to fade, banking and securities lawyers found that the Glass-Steagall Act hardly created the wall of separation that had once been supposed. In fact, the language of the Glass-Steagall Act, as opposed to the folklore surrounding it, allowed a remarkably large amount of interaction between banks and securities firms. By the time the GLB act came along, the larger banks were acting as full-service investment banks through so-called "section 20" subsidiaries (a reference to section 20 of the Glass-Steagall Act). The GLB Act's repeal of most remaining restrictions on affiliations between banks and securities firms thus represented more the administration of a *quietus* rather than a revolutionary development in the law. Nevertheless, the topic of securities powers of banking institutions remains important and, in some respects, controversial.

We begin the discussion of this issue with a reprise of a functional analysis. Just as there are very significant similarities between banking and insurance, there are large areas of overlap between investment and commercial banking. These are largely obvious, although it is fun to have students think them through. But there is one very significant difference between banks and securities firms. Banks engage in intermediated finance, whereas securities firms are principally in the business of providing direct finance. The book discusses this fundamental distinction on pages 554-55. It is worth explaining in detail to students, as it is one of the most important features of the system for capital formation in the United States and around the world.

You might remind students at this point of the basic cross-cutting principle of the GLB Act, namely that of functional regulation. Regardless of where a particular activity is undertaken, it will be regulated according to function by the same regulator that, prior to the GLB Act, was responsible for that function. In the case of the securities activities of banks, this principle has the important consequence of subjecting banks, for the first time, to the jurisdiction of the SEC as regards their activities as brokers and dealers in securities. Now, if a banking firm acts as a broker or dealer, it must obtain a broker-dealer license from the SEC and comply with the SEC's broker-dealer regulations. However, as described on page 556, certain traditional bank activities were grandfathered.

In introducing this topic, we find it useful to fix definitions in students' minds. It's worth spending some time, therefore, on the definitions of brokerage, dealing, and underwriting, as set forth informally on page 557. Some students need to feel comfortable with these definitions in order not to be scared by the material that follows.

Securities Activities Conducted by a Depository Institution Directly *(pages 557-82)*

The book treats the material in two steps, starting with securities activities conducted by a depository institution directly. Part of the language in § 24(7) was enacted as § 16 of the Glass-Steagall Act, and was not repealed by the GLB act. This language constrains the kinds of securities activities that national and state member banks can engage in directly. The related provision of the Glass-Steagall Act, § 21, draws the same line but does so from the perspective of securities firms. This was also left intact by the GLB Act. We recommend that you spend class time carefully going over the wording of these two provisions, which are excerpted on pages 557-58.

What Is a "Security"? (pages 559-65)

The next topic is the definition of a "security" for purposes of these laws. *Bankers Trust I* (pages 559-63) addresses the issue in the context of bank sales of commercial paper (CP). It's worth spending some time to acquaint your students with the characteristics of CPAGE Essentially, it's short term corporate IOUs. Usually, CP is issued by highly rated corporations, but any firm can issue it if it finds a buyer. CP is not typically sold to individuals, but rather is marketed over-the-counter to institutional investors, including banks. The U.S. has had an active CP market since the Nineteenth Century; in fact, this was one of the principal means by which bank deposits raised in one part of the country could be used to supply credit to borrowers located elsewhere. CP has many characteristics of a commercial loan; it is typically short-term, unsecured, corporate debt. In Bankers Trust I, the Fed attempted to equate CP to loans, and thus to declare that they were not securities subject to the Glass-Steagall Act. Here the Supreme Court refuses to defer to the administrative interpretation, and speaks about the intent of Congress to separate as far as possible commercial from investment banking.

You might take students through the statutory language, as an exercise. The book also supplies the relevant definitions of "security" from the 33 and 34 Acts, which are useful for comparison. You can also use this case to ask why the Supreme Court did not defer to the Fed's interpretation of the applicable statute. Was the Fed so far off base, or was the Court concerned about the policy implications of allowing the Fed to exclude CP from the Glass-Steagall Act's prohibitions? Relevant here is the court's emphasis on the purposes of the act being to erect a wall of separation between investment and commercial banking.

The next topic is that of underwriting or dealing in securities. Section 24(7), as described in the book, generally allows national banks to act as brokers of securities (although this was in question for many years during the heyday of the "wall" metaphor). But acting as underwriter or dealer are more restricted. The statute is complex, but as interpreted by the comptroller, it divides the universe of securities into three parts, distinguished according to the activities (brokering, dealing, or underwriting) permitted to national banks. (You should also recall the discussion on pages 153-56 of bank investments in securities, which is relevant but not repeated here.) A most important provision is that which allows banks to underwrite and deal without limitation in U.S. government debt; this has allowed major banks to be primary dealers in U.S. treasury securities, a large and economically important market.

Investment Company Institute v. Camp (pages 566-73) deals with the issue of underwriting and dealing in securities. It also represents the high-water mark of the folklore that the Glass-Steagall Act had creating an impregnable wall between investment and commercial banking. The language in the case about the "subtle hazards" of bank/securities affiliation was exceedingly influential for many years. Although Supreme Court has never repudiated that language, it is doubtful that a court today would view the subtle hazards in quite the same way.

In teaching this case, we like to have students describe the nature of the program in question. It really turns out to be an open-end investment company managed by the bank. It's interesting to have students identify the "security" that is in issue. The Supreme Court's opinion never clear does so. The security in question, however, is rather clearly the units of participation in the fund. Then you can ask students if they understand what the bank did that was wrong under the Glass-Steagall Act. Again, the Court was not very specific, but it seems clear that the problem was that the bank itself was acting as underwriter of these securities. The bank was therefore underwriting securities, in violation of both §§ 16 and 21 of the Glass Steagall Act.

The *Camp* case is still important, although much less so than formerly as a result of the enactment of the GLB Act. It's worth spending some class time on the case bringing out the various "subtle hazards" identified by the court. You can clarify the discussion by drawing a chart on the board showing a model of the bank and its securities affiliate. You can then ask students if they agree with the Court's "subtle hazards" analysis, referring if necessary to the challenging article by Fischel, Rosenfeld and Stillman at note 4, page 574.

In *Camp*, there was little question that the bank was underwriting the securities. But what does it mean to "underwrite"? This question was raised in *Securities Industry Assn' v. Board of Governors* (pages 575-78). This is a decision by the D.C. Circuit on remand from the Supreme Court's opinion, excerpted previously in the book, which held that CP is a "security" for purposes of the Glass-Steagall Act. Here Judge Bork concludes that because the bank was only engaged in privately placing CP to sophisticated clients, it was not "underwriting" and therefore was not in violation of the Act. The court also holds that the private placement of CP was not in contradiction of the purposes of the statute as identified in *Camp*. Thus, what appeared to be a high wall between investment and commercial banking was not so high after all.

Securities Brokerage (pages 579-82)

Securities brokerage is the issue in Securities Industry Association v. Comptroller of the Currency (pages 579-81). Here a national bank acquired a discount broker, with the comptroller's approval. The SIA claimed that the comptroller exceeded his authority because the acquisition violated §§ 16 and 21 of the Glass-Steagall Act. What is interesting about this case is not the outcome—the court found nothing wrong with a national bank acquiring a securities brokerage—but the fact that the SIA seriously believed it had a chance to win a case in the face of the clear language of the Glass-Steagall Act which seemed to permit the activity. You might challenge your students to come up with a plausible argument to support the SIA's position, given the statutory language.

Note that the operation of a securities brokerage today, after the enactment of the GLB Act, must comply with the SEC's broker-dealer rules and regulations.

Securities Powers of Affiliates and Subsidiaries of Depository Institutions *(pages 582-88)*

Here, as in the case of insurance powers, the law has been revolutionized by the enactment of the Gramm-Leach-Bliley Act. The Act jettisoned the prior regulatory scheme, which had been structured around § 20 of the Glass-Steagall Act. The GLB law repealed § 20 and substituted a new, permissive regulatory scheme.

Much of this scheme has already been described in Chapter 6. If an holding company qualifies under GLB as a "financial holding company," it can conduct, either directly or through a financial subsidiary, a full range of activities that are either "financial in nature," or "incidental to [an activity that is financial in nature]." This includes all traditional investment banking activities. Thus, there is no impediment to a qualifying financial holding company acting as a full-service investment bank. There is also a set of rules providing limited permission for financial holding companies and their nonbank affiliates to engage in "merchant banking" and, as to insurance company affiliates, to "portfolio investment" activities. These are basically investments in equity positions that may even give the investor control of the business in question.

It's worth discussing the pros and cons of the universal banking concept in this regard (page 586). German-style universal banks, which can conduct a full range of banking, investment banking, and insurance activities, are often held up as a model that the U.S. banking system should emulate. Scholars are divided on whether these universal banks operate more efficiently than U.S. style institutions, which have traditionally stayed only in the banking business. With developments over the past twenty years, and especially with the enactment of the Gramm-Leach-Bliley Act, it is now possible for American banks to move strongly in the direction of the German model. You might mention this to your students, and raise the question whether this international convergence, in which (contrary to the pattern observed elsewhere) the U.S. is moving in the direction of the rest of the world, is a good or a bad thing.

Finally, the book discusses the securities powers of subsidiaries of depository institutions. In general, qualifying financial subsidiaries may engage in the same securities activities permitted to financial holding companies. There's an interesting rule, described on page 587, for decision-making by federal agencies as to the permissible activities for financial subsidiaries; in theory, the Treasury could give such subsidiaries broader powers than are available to financial holding companies, but the Fed's veto power over any such decision renders that possibility largely theoretical. As in the case of insurance powers, the powers of financial subsidiaries are more limited in some respects that the powers of affiliates of financial holding companies—most importantly, the ability to act as principal in merchant banking activities.

Chapter 8: Investment Companies and the Regulation of the Mutual Fund Industry

INTRODUCTION

Chapter 8 deals with the regulation of the mutual fund industry. One tricky thing that makes it difficult to teach this subject matter is that students have vastly different perspectives on the material. Some students understand (and believe) that markets are efficient, that diversification is important, and that index funds are the best strategic choice for long-term investors. Other students have no idea what mutual funds are. Still others understand mutual funds but believe that old-fashioned stock-picking is the best way to go.

We find that a good way to prompt a spirited classroom discussion is to ask students to define what a mutual fund is and to provide their own opinions about the role that mutual funds should play in investing. Students often are unaware of the distinction between index funds—which are designed simply to track the performance of broad market indices such as the Standard and Poors 500—and traditional mutual funds, which are managed by investment advisors who attempt to hand-pick individual stocks that will outperform the market.

We tell students that stock picking is for people who (contrary to virtually all known research in the field of corporate finance) think that they can beat the market by themselves. On the other hand, traditional mutual funds are for people who think that even if they can't beat the market themselves, mutual fund managers (or at least some mutual fund managers) can. Finally, index funds are for people who either (a) don't believe that anybody except insiders consistently can beat the market; or (b) don't think that they can pick a mutual fund manager who is likely to be able to beat the market. We find that this analysis pushes students to focus on the fact that the most important distinguishing characteristic of a traditional mutual fund is its manager. From a legal perspective, this means that disclosures related to who the manager is may be of great relevance to investors.

We find that most students are unaware of the distinction between (1) closed end investment companies (called closed end funds), which issue a fixed number of shares that trade on a secondary market like the New York Stock Exchange; and (2) open end investment companies (called open-end funds), which (a) sell shares to the public and then permit investors to redeem (sell) the shares previously purchased; and (b) to continually purchase additional shares at a price called the "net asset value" (NAV), which is the marked value of the *pro rata* portion of the portfolio represented by each share.

In the introductory material in the casebook we "tip our hand" a little bit as to our own opinions about the value of mutual funds when we say "[a]s U.S. investors have become more sophisticated, they have come to appreciate the benefits of diversification." Mutual funds permit small investors to enjoy the benefits of diversification. It is probably important to get the students to understand how mutual funds and banks compete and also to understand why mutual funds have experienced such explosive growth in recent years.

THE INVESTMENT COMPANY ACT OF 1940

The Investment Company Act (popularly known as the 1940 Act or simply the '40 Act) requires investment companies to register with the SEC. The registration statements filed with the SEC must contain information about the investment objectives and strategies of the fund. Once the investment company is up and running, the fund may not change its investment objectives without obtaining approval from a majority of fund investors (query whether majority approval is sufficient).

The material in this section discusses the important relationship between the fund sponsor and the fund adviser. Fund sponsors organize funds. Generally sponsors do this because they know that if the fund is organized successfully (i.e. if it attracts a sufficient number of investors to get off the ground), they will become the adviser to the fund. As the fund's adviser, the sponsor is entitled to compensation for its work in making the investment decisions for the fund. This compensation typically comes in the form of management fees (an annual fee which is typically a percentage of the assets that the fund has under management). Some funds also charge a "front-end load" which is an intial sales charge, calculated as a percentage of each investor's initial investment.

The case book (page 594) contains what we hope is a useful organization chart of a mutual fund. We emphasize to our students that the pedagogic point of this organizational chart is to stress the analogies between a mutual fund and an ordinary corporation. For example, like shareholders everywhere, people who invest in mutual funds have the right to vote for the board of directors of the fund, as well as to vote on fundamental policy changes proposed for the fund. In addition, the '40 Act gives investors an additional right: the right to vote on changes to the investment advisor's contract. Similarly, like boards of directors of corporations generally, the board of a mutual fund: (a) owes fiduciary duties to the investors in the company (i.e. to investors of the mutual fund), and (b) has the authority to manage the business affairs of a fund. However, like corporate boards generally, as a practical matter, mutual fund boards appoint the investment adviser, and the investment adviser actually runs the fund on a day-to-day basis. Moreover, like a garden variety corporation, the adviser (management) has a lot to say about who goes on the fund's board, and board members typically do not rock the boat too much.

What is an Investment Company? *(pages 591-609)*

SEC v. Fifth Avenue Coach Lines (pages 594-600) and the case that follows it illustrate two points. The first is that the legal definition of a "mutual fund" is broad enough to encompass certain businesses that we do not commonly think of as mutual funds (or do not want us to think of them as mutual funds). The second point is that the Securities and Exchange Commission (SEC), which regulates the mutual fund industry and interprets and enforces the Investment Company Act of 1940, has considerable latitude to interpret the legal definition of what constitutes a mutual fund.

First we establish the facts. The defendants in this case include the infamous Roy Cohn. (Cohn was an assistant U.S. attorney on the prosecution team that succeeded in having Ethel and Julius Rosenberg sentenced to death for selling nuclear secrets to the Soviet Union. Cohn was an aide to the red-baiting Senator Joseph McCarthy, and lead counsel to the House Un-American Activities Committee during the Army-McCarthy hearings. Cohn, incidentally, is portrayed in the Pulitzer Prize-winning play "Angels in America," which depicts gay life in New York City. The role of Roy Cohn was played by the actor James Woods in the biographical film "Citizen Cohn." Mr. Cohn's file in the Federal Bureau of Investigation's "Freedom of Information Act Reading Room is 3,854 pages long.)

Fifth Avenue Coach Lines owned Surface Transit. Fifth and Surface operated municipal transit systems in New York City. In March 1962 the City of New York condemned all of Fifth's New York City bus lines, which constituted the vast majority of Fifth's assets. Finally, after much litigation, Fifth received an initial compensation award in 1966. Rather than return the condemnation award to the shareholders, Fifth's management decided to use the money to buy other companies. The issue in the case is whether Fifth Avenue became an investment company after it received this condemnation award.

In 1965, before receiving any money from the City of New York, Fifth Avenue told shareholders in its annual report that it would make "proper and advantageous investments for the benefit of the Company" as soon as it received its condemnation award." The SEC used this statement to argue that Fifth Avenue became an investment company the instant it received its cash award in October 1966. The SEC based this conclusion on § 3(a)(1) of the Investment Company Act, which says that "a company is an investment company if it... holds itself out as being engaged primarily in... or proposes to engage primarily in" the business of investing, reinvesting or trading in securities. The U.S. Court of Appeals for the Second Circuit rejects this argument because, in its view, Fifth Avenues "predictions" about what it planned to do in the future were "too general" to justify the legal conclusion that the company was "holding out" or "proposing" to engage in the business of investing. Moreover, the court rejected the SEC's argument that Fifth Avenue was an investment company as soon as it got the money and deposited it in cds and other interest-bearing money market instruments. The SEC took the position that these activities constituted investing, and that Fifth Avenue was thus an investment company under the provisions of § 3(a)(1), which say that an investment company is a company that "is engaged primarily in the business of investing, reinvesting or trading in securities." The court holds that "merely putting one's money in the bank" is not investing within the meaning of § 3(a)(1) even if one does earn interest. As a matter of statutory interpretation, the court reasons that "surely a company which has come into possession of a substantial amount of cash is entitled to a reasonable time to decide what to do with it without violating the Investment Company Act."

Eventually Fifth Avenue started buying stock. Interestingly, even then the court does not immediately conclude that Fifth Avenue became an investment company simply by buying stock. Rather, the court says that it was not an investment company during this period of transition. Instead, Fifth Avenue only became an investment company once investing became its primary business. The court reasoned that when a company sells its assets it does not become an investment company: it simply becomes a company with a lot of cash and "no real business." Later, when the company spends the cash, it "becomes engaged in a business of some sort." The court found that the business that Fifth Avenue entered was the business of investing in securities. For this reason, the court finds that Fifth Avenue was an investment company.

Fifth Avenue's defense was that it was not buying stock for the purpose of investing, but rather for the purpose of obtaining control of other companies for the purpose of actively managing them. Importantly, the court finds that the Investment Company Act does not create an exception for companies that are engaged in the business of acquiring stock in order to acquire control over other companies.

Section 3(a)(3) of the Investment Company Act provides another definition of the term "investment company." Under § 3(a)(3), a company is an investment company if the value of its investment securities exceeds 40 percent of its total assets. This test involves a simple division problem in which the firm's total assets constitute the denominator, and the firm's investment securities constitute the numerator. Arguments arise over these values. The statute provides some guidance, by requiring that "government securities and cash items" be excluded from total assets when the calculation is made. This provision, of course, helps the SEC in this case because it reduces the total assets of the company, thereby reducing the value of the investment securities necessary to comprise 40 percent of total assets. In *SEC v. Fifth Avenue*, Fifth Avenue and the SEC also quibbled over whether certain IOUs due the company were investment securities. The statute (Investment Company Act § 2(a)(3) defines investment security to include all securities except government securities and securities issued by majority owned subsidiaries of the owner. The definition specifically includes "evidence of indebtedness" among its list of things that constitutes a security.

However the Second Circuit carves out some exceptions from this definition in its *Fifth Avenue* opinion. The SEC was incredibly aggressive in its attempt to expand the jurisdictional boundaries of what constitutes a security under the Investment Company Act. For example, at one point Fifth Avenue owed $175,000 to a certain Krock. Fifth Avenue claimed that it paid this debt twice and that Krock thus owed Fifth Avenue $175,000. The SEC wanted to include this amount as an investment security in its calculation. The court rejected this contention noting that "the court does not see how a claim for the return of a payment erroneously made can conceivably be called an investment." Similarly the SEC claimed that some 90-day CDs were investment securities. The court found that these items were cash, and should not be counted at all.

In discussing this case we try to get the students to see how these arguments by the SEC are a form of turf grabbing. By including debts and CDs in its definition of investment security, the SEC was trying to expand significantly the number of businesses that must be considered investment companies subject to its regulations.

We also think it is important to discuss why the SEC was going after Fifth Avenue. There is a danger that companies could become investment companies through the back door by slowly shifting their assets from operating assets to investments. Note that there was no vote by Fifth Avenue shareholders on the company's decision not to return the money received when the company's assets were taken by the City of New York. Of course, had Fifth Avenue been an investment company, the shareholders would have been entitled to vote on this "fundamental policy change."

SEC v. ICOS Corp. (pages 600-04) is a nice example of how technological change and changes in market conditions can put stress on regulation, as well as how a bureaucracy such as the SEC might respond. ICOS was a biotech company engaged in drug research. It raised a substantial amount of money through public and private offerings of equity. ICOS wanted to invest the funds it did not need immediately.

We ask students how ICOS could have avoided being classified as an investment company. One way would be to raise funds only as needed. It doesn't take long for students to see that this would be cumbersome and inefficient because of the economies of scale involved in raising money. Alternatively, ICOS could have invested its extra cash in government securities because such securities are excluded from the definition of investment securities in § 3(a)(3). ICOS did not want to do this because the returns on such securities is very low. Finally, § 3(b)(2) permits the SEC to exclude issuers from being categorized as investment companies if they are "engaged primarily in a business other than investing, reinvesting, owning, holding, or trading in securities."

Before *ICOS* the SEC applied the so-called *Tonopah* analysis (discussed on page 602) and looked primarily at the nature of a company's assets and the sources of a company's income to determine whether the company was entitled to an exemption under 3(b)(2). Under this analysis, ICOS could not avoid the conclusion that it was an investment company: the majority of its assets were in securities, and 77 percent of its income came from securities activities.

We try and make sure that our students understand why this will be true for the virtually all high-tech firms, biotech firms, and other firms focused on research and development. The SEC concedes that the *Tonopah* analysis is unsuited to such firms (which, didn't exist in 1947 when *Tonopah* was decided). In place of the *Tonopah* analysis, the SEC says that for a firm involved in research and development it will look at: (a) whether the firm's research and development expenditures are greater than its gross investment income); (b) the nature of its expenses—i.e., whether "a substantial portion" of the firm's expenses are for research and development activities, and whether its expenses for investments (which include research, selection, supervision and custody of investments) are de minimis compared to its gross expenses for all purposes; and (c) whether the company invests in securities in a manner consistent with the goal of preserving its assets until they are needed for R&D.

We note that the SEC revised its position because Congress was on the verge of passing legislation to protect the high tech industry from SEC regulation. We ask whether the regulations promulgated by the SEC could provide a loophole for firms like Fifth Avenue (preceding case).

Notes and Comments (pages 604-09)

2. We discuss the definition of "security" in the Investment Company Act as compared with how other securities laws define the term.

6. The first sentence contains a typo; it should read "An interesting defense offered in SEC v. Fifth Avenue Coach Lines was that Fifth Avenue was not an investment company because the company planned to use its new-found cash to purchase control of other companies in order to become a conglomerate."

8. This note, largely self-explanatory, contains very important information on the (pass-through) taxation of mutual funds. We point out that if Fifth Avenue had won its case against the SEC and persuaded the court that it was not an investment company, any dividends received from companies in which Fifth Avenue had invested would be subject to triple taxation because the portfolio company earning the dividends would have to pay taxes on the earnings, then Fifth Avenue would have to pay corporate income tax on the earnings, and then any shareholder receiving the dividend would have to pay income tax on that distribution. By contrast, if Fifth Avenue qualified as a regulated investment company under Subchapter M of the Internal Revenue Code, it would avoid taxation on these dividend distributions.

We generally spend a bit of time discussing the various arguments (summarized in notes 8 and 9) for why investment companies don't take a more active role in corporate governance. We find considerable merit to the arguments advanced by both Professor Mark Roe (note 8) and Professor Jill Fisch (note 9) and Professors Ron Gilson and Reinier Kraakman (also note 9).

The Structure of the Investment Company Act *(pages 609-10)*

This material is largely self-explanatory. We ask students what sort of disclosure is most useful to investors. Investment performance by the fund is often mentioned. But here we point out that if a fund frequently changes advisers, past performance may be meaningless. We suggest that the competence of the adviser is very important. This leads to our discussion of the Investment Advisers Act of 1940 (pages 610-11).

THE DUTIES OF MUTUAL FUND ADVISERS

Rosenfeld v. E.R. Black (pages 611-16) is a well-known opinion by Judge Henry J. Friendly. The starting point for understanding this case is an awareness that (a) investment advisers earn big fees for managing mutual funds; and (b) investment advisers sometimes transfer their job as investment adviser to other firms. At its core the opinion deals with the thorny issue of whether an investment adviser can *sell* or otherwise *profit from* its decision to get out of the investment advisory business and transfer the work to another adviser. In this case, the investment banking firm of Lazard Freres was getting out of the business of serving as investment adviser. The reason that Lazard wanted to get out of this business was because the fund was shrinking in size. Mutual funds that don't perform well often shrink in size. In this case, the fund was shrinking in size because, unlike most open-end funds, Lazard did not offer new shares to investors on a continuous basis. It seems that, unlike investment banks that routinely deal with small, non-institutional, retail investors, Lazard did not have an extensive retail sales force that could sell mutual funds to small investors. Thus, redemptions by investors who bought in the fund's initial offering were not matched by corresponding sales to new investors. This shrinkage apparently occurred faster than Lazard had anticipated when it organized the fund.

Lazard thought that the fund would be successful if, and only if, it could continually offer its shares for sale. Since Lazard would have to make fundamental changes to its sales force in order to do this, it decided to transfer its advisory business to another firm. This possibility seemed particularly attractive when it learned that Moody's Investor Service, a subsidiary of Dun & Bradstreet, was considering entering the mutual funds business.

In other words, Lazard wanted out of this business because it no longer fit its business strategy, and Moody's wanted into the business because of the fees involved. The issue is whether Lazard could profit from the transfer. Lazard shareholders were to vote on the proposed transaction. The proxy statement provided to fund investors for the purpose of obtaining their votes disclosed that Moody's was going to do the following things for Lazard's benefit: (1) make certain executives available for the purpose of certain undefined "consulting," (2) to use its best efforts to get certain Lazard personnel to go to work for Moody's, (3) to make certain Lazard research reports available, (4) to provide advice with respect to European economic and monetary conditions; and (5) to serve as a director of the Moody's fund. The disclosure document said that, in exchange for these benefits, Dun and Bradstreet, the owners of Moody's, had agreed to give Lazard "75,000 shares of its common stock, par value $1 per share." The disclosure document somehow neglected to mention that the shares were selling at around $37 per share at the time of the transaction, considerably in excess of the $1 par value referred to in the proxy statement.

The transaction between Lazard and Dun & Bradstreet/Moody's was overwhelmingly approved by the investors. The plaintiffs were fund investors who argued that the 75,000 shares of stock given to Lazard were not given in exchange for the consulting services and other services described in the preceding paragraph. Rather, the plaintiffs alleged that Moody's gave the shares to Lazard to compensate Lazard for arranging to have Moody's named as investment adviser to the fund. This, the plaintiffs alleged conflicted with the well-known principle that directors and other fiduciaries may not personally profit from, much less sell, their corporate offices. As Judge Friendly points out, "a fiduciary endeavoring to influence the selection of a successor must do so with an eye single to the best interests of the beneficiaries." Judge Friendly says that the issue of whether Moody's motivation for giving the 75,000 shares of stock to Lazard was (a) illegally to compensate Lazard for transferring its advisory business to Moody's; or (b) legal compensation for consulting and other services was factual, and had to go to a jury.

In addition, Judge Friendly is sympathetic to the plaintiffs contention that the disclosure of the stock compensation as being at the price of "par value $1 per share" was not only devoid of meaning for shareholders but tended to mislead them (even though the market value of the shares could easily have been determined by looking in the financial pages of a newspaper or calling a stock broker. Judge Friendly rejecting the lower courts' doubts about the materiality of the information, decides that summary judgment was not properly granted to the plaintiffs because a jury of other fact-finders easily could have determined that the statement was an omission of a material fact necessary to make a statement actually made not false or misleading.

We spend some time exploring the implications of this case. Clearly it is important that investment advisors protect investors from incompetent or dishonest fund managers when they are transferring fund assets. This seems like a critical aspect of advisers' fiduciary duties.

Questions and Comments (page 616)

1. We emphasize the fact that even if Lazard had fully disclosed its compensation, it still would have had a problem under Judge Friendly's analysis, because a jury might nonetheless determine that the firm was being improperly compensated for selling its

advisory business, rather than for providing consulting services. This would still be an issue of fact for a jury to decide.

2. Why didn't Lazard just liquidate the fund and return the proceeds to investors if it wanted to get out of the advisory business? One answer is taxes. Investors would be responsible for paying capital gains taxes on gains from the sale, and they might not want to do this. Also, the fund might think that some of its investments were undervalued.

REGULATION OF MUTUAL FUND INVESTMENTS

The rules regarding investments by money market mutual funds are particularly relevant to students of banking because money market mutual funds (MMMFs) provide the most competition for the checking accounts traditionally offered by banks. MMMFs must invest in high quality securities that present minimal credit risks to investors. The 1940 Act requires that funds that call themselves "money market" funds, meet certain standards regarding quality and liquidity. MMMFs generally try to make sure that their net asset value remains at $1 per share. Since 1977 when Merrill Lynch introduced its cash management account, a standard feature of MMMFs is that investors can withdraw their funds by writing a check. MMMFs tend to grow during times of rapidly rising interest rates. As a historical matter, we point out to our students that the Federal Reserve used to have a regulation called Reg Q which restricted the interest that commercial banks could pay to depositors. This regulation created pressure for the development of an alternative savings vehicle for investors when market interest rates rose above the amount that banks were permitted to pay depositors under Reg Q. MMMFs were the answer to this regulation.

We use this as an opportunity to review the principal differences between mutual funds and banks: (1) MMMFs pass more risk back to investors. For example, banks shield depositors from the credit risk associated with their deposits. Mutual funds pass along any changes in value in the underlying investments directly to the depositors. These changes in value can come either in the form of a deterioration in credit risk or a reduction in interest rates. Of course MMMFs avoid the problem of credit risk by making very high quality, short-term investments.

People put their money into both checking accounts and into money market mutual funds in order to deal with the fact that their demand for cash is uncertain. People simply do not know how much cash they will need and when they will need it. Money market mutual funds solve this problem by investing in highly liquid money market instruments characterized by low credit risk and low interest rate risk. Gary Gorton & George Pennacchi, *Money Market Mutual Funds and Finance Companies: Are They the Banks of the Future?*, in Michael Klausner & Lawrence White, *Structural Change in Banking* 180 (1993). By matching the term structure of their assets with the term structure of their liabilities, money market mutual funds can make credible promises to their investors that their money will be there for them when they need it. The problem with this strategy is that it is wasteful. We know, in fact, that not all depositors will need access to their funds simultaneously on short notice. Statistical inference allows banks to predict with great accuracy what depositors' demands for liquidity will be for money market mutual funds. This allows banks to invest depositors' money that will not be needed for depositors' short-term liquidity needs in illiquid assets that offer higher rates of return. By contrast, because they erroneously assume that all depositors will want their funds simultaneously, mutual funds are quite limited in how then can invest their clients' money. And, this makes mutual funds imperfect substitutes for banks, and in turn, suggests that a market niche for banks is likely to remain.

Those mutual funds that invest money in high-yielding investments cannot promise investors that all of their principal will be returned. This makes non-money market mutual funds poor substitutes for checking accounts because investors who need liquidity must be able to know with certainty how much money they will have available at any particular time. Money market mutual funds solve this problem by fixing the price of their share, usually at a value of $1.00. *See* 17 C.F.R. § 270.2a-7 (designed to reduce the volatility of money market mutual funds by restricting the types of securities that money market mutual funds can hold). Once this price is fixed, mutual funds strive mightily to make sure that their net asset value does not fall below $1.00 per share (and thus"break the buck"). The Investment Company Act of 1940, which regulates mutual funds, permits money market mutual funds to choose whether to fix their share values at a particular level (such as $1.00) or else to mark to market—i.e., adjust the price of their shares each day to reflect changes in the market values of the underlying assets. Gorton & Pennacchi, supra, at 181. When money market mutual funds fix their share prices, they cope with changes in the underlying value of fund assets by adjusting the number of shares owned by each money market mutual fund investor, rather than by adjusting the value of each share. It is the ability of money market mutual funds to fix their share prices at $1.00 that allows them to compete with bank checking accounts.

Relative to other mutual funds whose share price is permitted to fluctuate, a MMF's (money market mutual fund's) fixed share price makes redemption of its shares more convenient and allows the account to resemble a bank demand deposit account. This convenience comes from two sources. First, since a shareholder will usually realize no capital gain or loss when selling shares, the need for tax-related record keeping is reduced. Second, as long as a MMF can maintain a fixed price, a shareholder will be certain of her account's minimum balance, since rates of return will always be non-negative. Id.

The point here is that both banks and money market mutual funds compete for depositors' short-term funds. Banks have one big advantage over money market mutual funds, which is that they invest depositors' money in longer-term, higher yielding assets. This allows banks to compete successfully with money market mutual funds for customers.

However, it does not appear that money market mutual funds compete with banks on the basis of price. The interest rates offered customers on money market mutual fund accounts and on checking accounts appear to be quite similar. Richard Pozen, *Comment on Gorton and Pennacchi*, in Klausner & White, supra, at 223-224. However, it seems clear that commercial banks out-compete mutual funds on the vector of customer convenience.

If we look at convenience of withdrawing cash, bank deposits have a significant advantage over MMFs. Banks allow cash withdrawals, not only at a multitude of branches but also through a broad array of ATMs. By contrast, most MMFs do not permit cash withdrawals even at investor centers. Investors typically receive a check from the MMF that must be cashed at a bank. While a few MMFs have allowed ATM access, the fees for ATM access to MMFs typically have been higher than those for ATM access to bank deposits. Id. at 224.

Moreover, many MMFs have only limited checking privileges, allowing checks to be drawn only for limited amounts such as $250 or $500 per check. Banks, of course, generally allow customers to write checks for any amount, no matter how small, and usually do not charge customer fees for checks or account fees to customers who maintain the minimum balances described above.[1]

On a more theoretical note, we observe that an important difference between checking accounts and other investments such as money market mutual funds is the characteristic of "interdependence." Bank depositors are interdependent in a way that no other sorts of investors are. When people invest money in money market mutual funds, they do not care about the savings and consumption patterns of other investors. Because money market mutual funds invest depositors' funds in assets that match the maturity and liquidity structure of their investors, such investors need not concern themselves with when or whether other investors are seeking access to their investments.

The same is not true for bank depositors. Because of the mis-match in the term structure of banks' assets and liabilities, the behavior of other depositors really does matter because it affects the ability of the bank to meet their creditors' claims as they come due in the ordinary course of business. If, for some reason, all or even many of the depositors in a particular bank want to obtain their funds at the same time, there will be a run on the bank

---

[1] *Id.* at 225. One reason why money market mutual funds discourage check-writing more than banks do is that MMFs do not have direct access to the Fed payment system. However, it appears that "the costs of direct access to that system would probably not be worth the benefits for most MMFs." This is largely due to the fact that MMFs are pass-through vehicles that lack the ability to accumulate equity of their own, since earnings in the form of distributions and capital appreciation are immediately passed along to the Funds' customers. However the Fed requires MMMFs to maintain substantial amounts of equity to guarantee that the clearing function will not be impaired.

and the bank will be forced into insolvency. This is true even if the bank is solvent in a balance-sheet sense, i.e., in the sense that the present value of the bank's assets is greater than the present value of its liabilities. But, these assets are illiquid and opaque, meaning that they cannot be sold or even evaluated easily by outside investors. For this reason, if a bank's assets have to be sold hurriedly, in a sort of "fire-sale" fashion, in order to meet the liquidity needs of outside investors, these assets could not be sold at anything close to their fair market value. This is why runs on banks are such fearful events.

MUTUAL FUND DISCLOSURE

We review the material on risk disclosure and prompt the students to discuss whether they think that this information is of value to investors. Clearly the comparisons with indices is important. But how sophisticated do investors have to be to understand things like beta co-efficients? Above all, we want our students to understand that it is not possible to compare the performance of two mutual funds (or two investments of any kind), merely by looking at the *rate of return* promised by the investment. This is because investors also need to know the *risk*. In choosing between two investments with similar rates of return, the fact that one investment has lower risk will make that investment better. At any given rate of return, investors should choose the investment that has the lowest risk. Disclosure is tricky, because investors tend to focus too much on the returns associated with investments without factoring in the risks associated with those investments.

In *Hines v. ESC Strategic Funds, Inc.* (pages 624-29), the defendant fund offered two classes of shares for sale. Class A shares had a very high (4.5 percent) front-end load, and relatively low (1.8 percent) annual operating expenses. Class D shares had a relatively low (1.5 percent) front-end load, but high annual operating expenses (2.3 percent). Presumably, short-term investors would like the Class D shares, while longer-term investors would prefer the Class A shares. The plaintiff in this case had bought the Class A shares.

What was the plaintiff complaining about? She argued that she was a long-term investor who was attracted to the fund on the basis of its representations that it was a "suitable investment for investors seeking long-term capital appreciation." The fund also had disclosed to her that it expected the average holding period of its investments to be 2-5 years, and that the fund was not appropriate for investors with short-term time horizons, or others "seeking to capitalize on short term market fluctuations." The Fund suffered huge losses when Asian and Russian currencies and capital markets experienced significant downturns during the late 1990s.

In early 1999, the fund sent a letter to investors stating that it had decided to liquidate its investments and discontinue operations. Investors were given the option of transferring their investments to another fund within the defendant's family of funds (without any additional front-end sales charge) or to receive a check for the amount of their initial investment. The fund said that it was closing because "it had not attracted sufficient interest among prospective investors and is considered unlikely to do so in the future." Also, the fund was too small. Its size, according to the fund's managers, did not permit it to operate "at a competitive or reasonable expense ratio."

The plaintiff alleges that the fund's prospectus and other public disclosures were materially misleading because they failed to disclose that the fund would "decide to sellout prematurely because they do not like current market conditions or do not believe that they themselves are making enough money from the fund." In particular, the plaintiff claimed that the fund "omitted to tell investors that defendants themselves might liquidate the fund if market conditions or the amount of fees they were earning were not to their liking." The plaintiff stressed that she wanted to be a long-term investor, and had been told by the fund's promoters that this was a long-term investment, but had been forced into a short-term investment by these same promoters when they decided to terminate the fund.

The defendants response to this interesting and rather creative argument by the plaintiffs was to say that the prospectus was not misleading because the prospectus contained such boilerplate cautionary language as: "there can be no assurance that the Fund will achieve its investment objective" and the fund "may liquidate securities without regard to how long they have been held, if such action is considered appropriate" The court discusses several cases in which cautionary language did shield defendants from liability, but says that such language will not provide an effective shield under the facts of this case because they did not caution against the sorts of risks that the plaintiff is complaining about. Specifically, the cautionary language addresses the risk that certain of the fund's investments might tank. It did not caution about the risk that the fund itself would be terminated.

After drawing out the point that there was no disclosure of the risk that the fund itself might be terminated, we ask whether this really matters. Of course, this lack of disclosure is important in this particular case. But if, in the future, funds simply can (as they often do) avoid liability by saying that there is a risk that the fund might be terminated, does this aspect of the case matter very much. Hopefully, this can lead to a discussion of whether investors reading disclosure documents and whether, if they do, this sort of disclosure would mean very much to the average investor.

We also make sure that the students understand that statute under which the plaintiffs are suing. They are suing for generic securities law violations under § 12(2) of the Securities Act of 1933 alleging misrepresentations in the public offering of the mutual fund and § 10b of the Securities Exchange Act of 1934, alleging misrepresentations in connection with the sale of the mutual fund (mutual fund shares are, of course securities).

It appears that an important fact in this case was that the mutual fund knew, but failed to disclose to investors when it circulated the Fund's prospectus, that a minium investment amount was needed to insure the viability of the Fund. This is important because it rebuts the defense that the plaintiff failed to allege that the Fund had the required state of mind to satisfy the scienter requirement of Rule 10b-5.

The scienter requirement under § 12(2) is much weaker. The statute says that anybody who offers or sells a security by means of a prospectus that contains "an untrue statement of a material fact or omits to state a material fact necessary in order to make the statements, in the light of the circumstances under which they were made, not misleading," is liable to purchasers for the amount paid for the securities with interest unless he can "sustain the burden of proof that he did not know, and in the exercise of reasonable care could not have known, of such untruth or omission." This means that to refute the plaintiff's 12(2) claims, the defendants would have had to show either (a) they did not omit to state material facts about the possibility that the fund was closed because the cautionary language in the prospectus provided sufficient warning; (b) they could have determined (after exercising reasonable care) that they would close down if the fund did not attract a sufficient number of investors.

Questions and Comments *(pages 629-30)*

1. This question asks whether the plaintiff really suffered any damages. Here we stress two points. First, the plaintiff suffered damages because of the transaction costs (i.e. the large front-end load that she paid). These damages would have been mitigated, to some extent, because the plaintiff was permitted to roll her investment into another mutual fund without incurring charges. Second, the plaintiff arguably suffered damages to the extent that she lost the opportunity to "ride out" the decline in the market and profit when the fund's investments rebounded. There are two problems with this argument: (a) to make this argument the plaintiff has to concede that the defendants had a good investment strategy with the potential to rebound, which seems inconsistent with the facts; and (b) the plaintiff would not suffer much from any damages if she could simply transfer her money to another fund with the same investment strategy. Presumably this second fund also would have declined in value, enabling the plaintiff to buy in cheaply. We note also that this damages question relates to the plaintiff's 10b-5 claim, not to her § 12(2) claim, because (as discussed above) § 12(2) provides for statutory damages.

Van Kampen Investment Advisory Corp. (pages 630-31): This enforcement vignette provides an interesting window on the way that mutual funds operate. In order to understand this enforcement action, students have to have a little background into the practical world of mutual funds and initial public offering practices in the United States. First, students must understand that (by far) the single-most important factor in determining whether a mutual fund will be successful in attracting investors is its past performance. Funds that show "beat the market" by a considerable margin, or otherwise show strong performance for a quarterly or a year, will enjoy a net investment inflow. Funds that underperform the market will suffer an outflow. Second, we remind the students that fund managers want to show strong performance because their *fees* are based on the size of the fund: they earn a percentage of fund assets. Third, students should know that before starting the expensive process of registering with the SEC and marketing to the public mutual funds often have an "incubator period" during which the funds' promoters will make investments and the fund manager will try to build a "track record." For example, the Van Kampen Growth Fund that was the subject of this SEC enforcement action started out with net assets of only $200,000-380,000 during its incubation period which took place during 1996. During that 1996 period the fund experienced a stellar return of 61.99 percent. Of course, when the fund was marketed to the public during that period, the advisor could trumpet this strong return and lay claim to being the number 1 fund in its category. Even though the fund's disclosure documents cautioned, as all disclosure documents caution, that past performance is no guarantee of future success, investors almost invariably look to past performance when deciding where to invest, so this stellar past performance allowed the fund to grow to $109 million shortly after it was made available to the public after the incubation period.

With the background provided thus far, we ask the students what the fund was accused of doing. But to know this, the students need a bit more background information: they need to know how ipos (initial public offerings) work and they need to know how shares in "hot ipos" are allocated. The critical facts are these: (1) the price at which shares in initial public offerings are offered to the public typically is substantially below the closing price in the first trading days subsequent to the IPO. This phenomenon is known in the world of finance as "ipo underpricing". Typically underpricing is between 20 and 30 percent. This means that anybody lucky enough to be able to buy shares in an initial public offering is almost guaranteed a significant return. This return can be realized by "flipping" the IPO, i.e. by buying it and then selling it shortly thereafter when the price has increased. The investment bankers that manage IPOs discourage flipping, but it happens quite a bit, particularly by retain investors; (2) demand for IPOs frequently outstrips supply: in other words, people who want to buy shares in IPOs frequently are disappointed as all the shares are sold before many buyers can purchase; (3) shares in IPOs in the U.S. do not have to be, and are not distributed "fairly": shares are not, for example distributed on a first-come, first served basis. Rather, shares are distributed according to the preferences of the underwriters. This means that people with "connections" and, above-all, preferred customers such as institutional investors, get preferential treatment.

The Van Kampen Investment Advisory Corporation served as investment advisor to a large number of Van Kampen funds, including the Van Kampen Growth Fund. The Investment Advisory Corporation was accused of using its considerable clout with investment banks to obtain allocations of stock in a large number of so-called "hot IPOs" (i.e. IPOs for which demand greatly outstripped supply at the initial offering price and were likely to experience particularly large price increases after the initial allocation of stock in the IPO).

The Van Kampen Investment Advisory Corporation and its chief investment officer, Alan Sachtleben, were accused by the SEC of making sure that the Van Kampen Growth Fund received a disproportionate share of the stock allocated to the Van Kampen family of funds during its incubation period. These allocations, of course, had a substantial impact on the performance of the growth fund since the fund was so small at that point.

The 61.99 percent return that was advertised by the Van Kampen Growth Fund was misleading, according to the SEC because it did not disclose that IPOs had a large impact on the fund's 1996 return. This, in turn created two disclosure problems associated with the fund's performance. The first problem related to the fund's growth. Once the fund grew from $300,000 to $109 million, IPOs necessarily would be a much smaller percentage of the fund's overall size. For this reason the fund's failure to disclose that such a high percentage of its return was from IPOs was misleading.

The second problem was a bit more subtle. It seemed pretty clear that after the Van Kampen Growth Fund got off the ground, the Van Kampen investment advisors were going to stop giving that particular fund preferential treatment when IPOs were being allocated among the whole range of Van Kampen funds. This, in turn, would reduce the performance of the growth fund.

We find it useful to point out that the use of incubator funds itself is problematic. After all, it hardly seem right that a mutual fund family can start a bunch of mutual funds, and then go to market with only those funds that have done well. After all, if a Van Kampen or a Fidelity start enough incubator funds, some are bound to out-perform the market. Similar disclosure problems exist when funds advertise their performance. If a company has a lot of different funds, the law of averages dictates that some will do better than others, and that some are likely to out-perform the market. Of course, the advisors simply can choose to advertise those funds to the expense of the funds that experience inferior performance. This practice may well mislead investors. If so, it is an on-going problem that the SEC has yet to confront.

SPECIAL PROBLEMS IN CLOSED END MUTUAL FUNDS

In Re Nuveen Fund Litigation (pages 632-38), the final case in this chapter deals with closed-end investment companies. Closed-end funds, unlike open-end funds, do not have to deal with the problem of asset shrinkage because investors cannot redeem their shares by turning them back to the fund and receiving the shares' pro-rata net asset value. Instead, investors who want to liquidate their holdings must sell their shares in the secondary market. Frequently, the price offered by the market is less than the net asset value of the shares. Why this is so is something of a mystery in the world of corporate finance.

Like other fund managers, managers of closed-end mutual funds have incentives to make their funds as large as possible because their fees are based on the size of the funds they manage. One way that closed-end funds can increase in size is by selling additional shares to the public by making additional public offerings of their shares. However, the fact that closed-end funds trade at below NAV makes it impossible for such funds to make public offerings because § 23(b) of the Investment Company Act makes it impossible for funds to sell its common stock at a price below current net asset value except in connection with an offering to the holders for one or more classes of its capital stock.

In other words, in order to grow, closed-end funds often have to sell their shares at below net asset value to existing shareholders. And this creates problems.

This is precisely what happened in *Nuveen Fund Litigation*. Plaintiffs claimed that his rights offering (offering of rights to purchase additional shares) was made only for the purpose of generating fees for the Funds' investment adviser and its controlling parent corporation.

From the perspective of existing investors rights offerings are problematic because they pose a collective action problem for such investors. Shareholders might well be better off as a group if nobody took advantage of the rights offering. However, if any one investor fails to invest while others choose to invest, that investor will suffer dilution from the sale of additional shares at below NAV, as well as from the underwriting fees. For example, suppose that the NAV of a particular fund is $1 per share because the fund has 100 shares outstanding and its assets are worth $100. If the fund makes a rights offering that permits shareholders to buy one additional share for every share owned at a discounted price of 90 cents, and one-half of the shareholders take advantage of this opportunity, the fund will have (assuming no underwriting costs) total assets of $145. With 150 shares outstanding the new NAV will be about 97 cents: each investor who fails to invest will suffer dilution of 3 cents per share (those who do invest will gain if they invest and if others do not: if only half of the investors exercise their rights, the NAV will drop to 97 cents per share. Every share purchased for 90 cents will increase to 97 cents, which will more than offset the loss of 3 cents on the shares already held) Thus, shareholders can eliminate the problem of dilution by buying more shares. If everybody buys at the discounted price the new net asset value will be 95 cents per share: this means that each investor will suffer a 5 cent gain on the new shares purchased, and a 5 cent loss on the old shares (which decline in value from $1 to 95 cents). It is this sort of analysis that drives the plaintiff's contention that the proposed rights offering gave investors the difficult choice of deciding whether : (1) to invest more money in the funds in order to minimize the dilutive effects of the rights offering; (2) refrain from investing more money and suffer dilution from the addition of new shares and the deduction of underwriting fees; or (3) sell their shares in an intentionally depressed market and suffer losses.

The plaintiffs allege that the directors of the mutual fund and the mutual fund's advisor breached their fiduciary duties and that the fund made materially misleading statements in the offering prospectus. The reason that the plaintiffs were successful in fending off the defendants' motion to dismiss was that they were able to discover analysis by the defendants that directly contradicted statements in the prospectus that benefits from improved performance would outweigh the dilutive consequences for shareholders, including non-participating shareholders.

Clearly investors could be harmed by the dilutive effects of these rights offerings. The plaintiffs claimed that the only reason that the advisor proposed the transactions was to generate fees for itself. While the court refused to go so far as to say that a rights offering for less than NAV is a per se violation of the fund managers' fiduciary duties, the defendants will have a problem if they can't come up with any story about how the rights offering might benefit shareholders. What sort of defenses might creative closed-end investment fund managers come up with? They might argue: (1) that increasing the size of the fund will enable them to cut costs, thereby decreasing the funds expense ratio; (2) that increasing the size of the fund will give them more clout with underwriters, thereby allowing them access to "hot IPOs" and other hard-to-get securities; (3) they might argue that the fund needs to grow because it has more investment opportunities than it can pursue at its current size.

This discussion should lead into a discussion of why anybody would invest in a closed-end investment fund in light of the fact that such funds frequently trade at a discount to NAV. There are several answers to this: (1) not all closed-end funds trade at a discount (and those that do, don't trade at a discount all the time; (2) closed end funds have a theoretical advantage over open-end funds: because they do not have to stand ready continually to make redemptions, they can keep a higher percentage of their assets invested in high-yielding assets; (3) closed-end funds provide a very efficient means for investing in illiquid securities and securities that might be hard for investors otherwise to obtain, such as securities issued by developing countries.

We also note that the shares of a closed-end investment company generally fall below NAV shortly after the initial public offering. This means that the underwriters get these securities and sell them, and then the ultimate investors suffer the price decline. See SEC, Proposed Amendments to Registration Form for Closed-End Management Investment Companies, 53 Fed. Reg. 32,993 (1989). Specifically, the SEC's Office of Economic Analysis found that 24 weeks after their initial public offering, closed end funds trade at an average discount of 10 percent. SEC Commissioner turned law professor Joe Grundfest posited that many such shares are purchased by investors who, in his words, simply were "not smart enough" to realize that they were soon going to decline in value. After these investments declined in value they would be purchased by other, smarter investors, who were "smart enough" to realize that closed-end investment funds never trade at a discount. These investors will wait until after an IPO of a closed-end fund, and then buy the shares at a discount. See id. (separate statement of Commissioner Grundfest).

Chapter 9: Examination and Enforcement

BANK SUPERVISION: THE MONITORING SYSTEM

Background *(pages 639-44)*

The chapter begins by noting bank regulators' sweeping powers and formidable reputation—and the failures of bank and thrift regulation during the 1980s and early 1990s. It describes various explanations for those failures. And it encourages students to consider the costs as well as the benefits of regulatory stringency.

The Supervisory System *(pages 644-56)*

We summarize the supervisory system, including the examination process (pages 644-46).

Excerpts from the FDIC's *Manual of Examination Policies* (pages 646-56) explain the federal banking agencies' CAMELS rating system, and set forth the criteria under which examiners assess the six individual CAMELS "components"—Capital adequacy, Asset quality, Management, Earnings, Liquidity, and Sensitivity to market risk—and then assign a "composite" (i.e., overall) CAMELS rating.

Questions and Comments (pages 656-61)

3. Can you think of any potential pitfalls in relying on state supervisors to protect the insurance funds from state-chartered, federally insured institutions? What about potential pitfalls in relying on federal banking agencies other than the FDIC itself? The OCC, Federal Reserve, OTS, and state supervisors may, in varying degrees, have incentives that conflict with the interests of the deposit insurance funds (see page 76). Even the FDIC may have such incentives insofar as it seeks to encourage depository institutions to become or remain state nonmember banks.

9. Should examination reports be made public? What arguments can you develop for and against public disclosure? Arguments for and against such disclosure include the following:

Arguments for: Disclosure will promote greater regulatory accountability and consistency, encourage agencies to learn from their mistakes, and—by facilitating outside scrutiny—promote improvements in examination and supervision. Even if disclosure ends up making the limits of examinations painfully apparent (e.g., if the examination emperor wears only a birthday suit), we will still be still better off realistically recognizing those limits.

Arguments against: Disclosure will discourage open, candid communication by bankers and examiners; make the examination process needlessly adversarial; risk jeopardizing public confidence in banks and the banking system; expose examiners—who jobs are already difficult enough—to pitiless and typically unwarranted hindsight condemnation whenever a bank fails; and divert examiners' energies from assessing and correcting banks' problems to justifying their actions against possible future criticism.

14. Difficulty of challenging examinations: It might be worth addressing the question of whether a depository institution has any redress for an unfair or erroneous examination. For the most part, the answer is no, although if a formal enforcement order is based on an examination, the accuracy of the examination may be brought into question in the enforcement proceedings. But as *Sunshine State Bank* illustrates, courts are loth to substitute their judgment for that of bank examiners. The fact of the matter is that there is little a depository institution can do to challenge an examination once the report is finalized. This means that the institution's practical ability to influence an examination report occurs during the examination itself. We examine the pros and cons of this essentially unreviewable system of examination reports.

ENFORCEMENT

Chapter 9-B begins with two cross-cutting issues: "institution-affiliated parties" and the potential for informal regulatory arm-twisting to conflict with the rule of law. The chapter then takes students through the range of enforcement procedures, starting with the mild and informal and ending with the severe and formal.

Institution-Affiliated Parties *(pages 662-64)*

Questions and Comments *(pages 663-64)*

2. Can the law firm be held liable for the associate's misconduct? We ask students what the rule should be. Holding the firm liable should promote better monitoring of the service-provider; it certainly would give access to a deeper pocket. On the other hand, many firms are loosely structured, so holding the firm liable would amount to imposing strict vicarious liability on persons who bear no fault for the loss.

Administrative Arm-Twisting and the Rule of Law *(pages 664-68)*

Professor Noah's provocative article—questioning the limits of administrative arm-twisting and proposing greater legislative and judicial vigilance—provides ample grist for discussion. Question 1 on page 668 suggests a likely rebuttal argument: that the phenomena Noah criticizes, far from being unintended consequences, are implicit in the supervisory process and in judicial deference to administrative agencies.

Particular Types of Enforcement Action

Questions and Comments (pages 673-75)

3. A cease-and-desist order requiring restitution can have the same effect as a civil judgment requiring restitution. Do civil defendants enjoy any safeguards absent from a cease-and-desist proceeding? In a civil action, the district court tries the case de novo, without any deferring to the agency's factual findings. Civil defendants have the right to trial by jury.

Questions and Comments (pages 684-85)

In *FDIC v. Meyer* (pages 682-84), the Supreme Court considered the rights of an officer of an insolvent depository institution who had been fired by the FDIC in its capacity as receiver. The issue here is whether the FDIC can be liable for money damages for deprivation of an individual's right to property without due process of law. The lower courts held that the FDIC was not immune from civil litigation, in light of the "sue and be sued" clause in its charter, and held further that the plaintiff could bring a constitutional tort action against the agency as well as its officials under a *Bivens* theory. It was clear that the plaintiff had a *Bivens* action against the officer, but this was not an attractive opportunity for several reason. Individual government officials are not likely to have substantial assets with which to satisfy a judgment, and juries are probably much less likely to award substantial damages against individuals as against agencies. Beyond this, individual defendants in *Bivens* actions have the benefit of a qualified immunity defense which might not be available to the agency itself. The Supreme Court, however, puts the quietus on this theory by holding that the *Bivens* remedy lay only against the individual and not against the agency. You can profitably discuss with your class the practical effect of this ruling—namely, that persons fired from their positions after insolvency have little practical hope of obtaining damages for unlawful termination. Is this a fair or equitable result?

Criminal Penalties (pages 719-21)

We ask students to consider whether the beefed-up system of criminal enforcement is justified. An instinctive reaction to the question is that clearly stronger penalties are warranted in order to prosecute and punish those who commit crimes and place the public's money at risk in their management of depository institutions.

However, there are countervailing considerations. At some point the threat of criminal prosecution might become so pervasive that good people would not want to serve in banks; the result could be counterproductive. Moreover, if the goal is deterrence, hasn't that already been largely achieved by the intense heat placed on bank managers for past misdeeds? Do we need a draconian penalty structure in the future?

These are difficult questions to answer, even in principle, but they can lead to stimulating class discussion about the proper objectives and optimal structure of a system of criminal penalties for violations of federal banking law.

Enforcement Problems *(pages 721-22)*

Problem 1—Nightshade Bank

The town of Nightshade, located on the Bering Sea, faces hard times—with its timber mill shuttered, its fishing industry declining, and its bank about to fail. So Ivan Rimsky becomes a local hero when he arrives in town, buys the Nightshade Bank (a state nonmember bank), and restores it to financial health. In just three years, the bank's leverage ratio rises from 3 percent to 10 percent even as the bank's total assets rise from $25 million to $100 million.

(a) What can the FDIC do about Ivan making large loans without checking credit history or requiring financial information? Making large loans without checking the borrower's credit history or requiring appropriate financial information is an unsafe and unsound practice. Accordingly, the agency could seek a cease-and-desist order requiring the bank and Ivan to follow proper credit-underwriting procedures. But if the agency views Ivan as having a generally good record, it would probably content itself with informal criticism or a written agreement—particularly if Ivan makes clear that he now understands the need for proper credit underwriting procedures and will follow them going forward.

(b) What can the FDIC do when Ivan scoffs at normal credit analysis and reaffirms his offhand approach? The more stubbornly Ivan defends his overly casual lending practices—and the more ignorance and insouciance he displays about sound lending practices—the more reason he gives the agency to take formal enforcement action. Note that a cease-and-desist order can limit Ivan's involvement in lending decisions and even require the bank to hire a competent loan officer acceptable to the agency. 12 U.S.C. § 1818(b)(6)(E), (7).

(c) What can the FDIC do when Ivan has the bank buy a $200,000 high-seas speedboat, which he alone uses? As the purchase benefits no one but Ivan (and is not, so far as we know, part of Ivan's agreed-on compensation), it violates Ivan's fiduciary duty of loyalty to the bank.

If spending $200,000 (2 percent of the bank's capital) on something of no use to the bank is an unsafe and unsound practice, the agency can issue a cease-and-desist order requiring the bank to sell the boat. See id. § 1818(b)(6)(C). If having the use of the boat unjustly enriched Ivan, then the order may also require him to make restitution to the bank for that use and to indemnify the bank for any loss it incurs in selling the boat.

The agency can also impose civil money penalties on Ivan. First-tier penalties are unavailable unless Ivan has violated a statute, regulation, final order, or the like. But the agency can impose second-tier penalties for committing a breach of fiduciary duty if the breach either personally benefitted Ivan or caused the bank more than minimal loss. To impose third-tier penalties, the agency would need to show that Ivan: knowingly breached a fiduciary duty or engaged in an unsafe and unsound practice; and knowingly or recklessly either derived a substantial personal benefit or caused the bank a substantial loss. See id. § 1818(i)(2).

If the agency sought to remove Ivan at this stage, it could show breach of fiduciary duty and unsafe and unsound practice (misconduct) and benefit to Ivan and probable loss to the bank (effect). But the agency would have difficulty showing that Ivan acted with personal dishonesty or willful and continuing disregard for the bank's safety and soundness (culpability). See id. § 1818(e).

(d) What can the FDIC do when it uncovers information suggesting that Ivan has ties to organized crime and that five years ago he disappeared by speedboat after looting a bank in the Bahamas? Ivan and the speedboat now look much more sinister. The agency needs to perform an immediate Ivanectomy—i.e., getting Ivan physically out of the bank and preventing him from exercising any control over the bank—until the agency can ascertain whether or not he looted the Bahamian bank. The agency could achieve that result by issuing a temporary cease-and-desist order against the bank or a temporary suspension order against Ivan. Such an order can be issued ex parte, with no prior hearing, and take effect immediately upon service.

To issue a temporary cease-and-desist order, the agency (1) must have served a notice of charges seeking a regular cease-and-desist order, and (2) must determine that the misconduct specified in that notice is likely—before completion of the regular cease-and-desist proceeding—to render the institution insolvent, significantly dissipate its assets or earnings, weaken its condition, or otherwise prejudice the interests of its depositors. Id. § 1818(c). Here the agency could assert that, for various reasons (notably including the possibility that Ivan looted the Bahamian bank), Nightshade Bank's continued employment of Ivan as CEO constitutes an unsafe and unsound practice imminently likely to cause the requisite harm to the bank (e.g., with Ivan "dissipating" the bank's assets by fleeing with them).

Similarly, to issue a suspension order, the agency (1) must have served a notice of its intention to remove or prohibit Ivan, and (2) must determine that the suspension is necessary to protect the bank or its depositors. See id. § 1818(e)(3). If Ivan did loot the Bahamian bank, the agency can remove or prohibit him: Ivan committed a breach his fiduciary duty (misconduct) that benefitted him and caused loss to the bank (effect) and involved personal dishonesty (culpability). See id. § 1818(e).

In addition to its options under § 1818, the FDIC could also effect an Ivanectomy by appointing itself conservator for the bank under § 1821(c)(5)(H) and (10), taking control of the bank, and placing Ivan on leave pending investigation of the Bahamian looting allegations.

(e) Given Ivan's resignation from the bank, can the FDIC take any further action against him? Under § 1818(i)(3) enforcement proceedings may continue despite Ivan's resignation. Obtaining an order removing Ivan or prohibiting him from participating in Nightshade Bank would make particular sense as it would preclude Ivan from future participation in the affairs of any FDIC-insured depository institution. See id. § 1818(e)(7).

(f) What can the U.S. attorney do when Ivan is discovered acting as a credit union director 20 years after disappearing from Nightshade? If the FDIC did issue an order removing or prohibiting Ivan, he would commit a felony by acting as a director of a federally insured credit union without the prior written consent of both the FDIC and the NCUA. See id. § 1818(j).

Problem 2—Bank of Uz

After many years of enviable prosperity, the Bank of Uz and its owner and CEO, Mr. Jobe, face trouble. The bank's second-largest branch collapses during an earthquake, killing three employees and five customers. Terrorists raid the bank picnic, carrying off key lending officers to an unknown fate. Jobe contracts a disfiguring disease and prefers to work in a back office, away from public view. Two of Jobe's former friends, Bill and Eli, are spreading rumors about the impending demise of Jobe and his bank. What action, if any, can the appropriate federal banking agency take under section 1818?

Misfortune does not warrant enforcement action. The problem (loosely drawn from the Book of Job) does not indicate that Jobe or the bank have any responsibility for what has gone wrong.

Problem 3—Bill and Eli as Aleph National Bank Officers

Same as Problem 2, except that Bill and Eli are officers of Aleph National Bank. What action, if any, can the OCC take under section 1818?

This raises the question whether the OCC could take enforcement action against Bill and Eli to avert potential harm to the Bank of Uz, a competing bank. Would an officer of one bank commit an unsafe and unsound practice by knowingly spreading false rumors intended to cause a run on the other bank?

Problem 4—Torpid National Bank

For the past two decades, Luke Warme has served as CEO of Torpid National Bank. The bank has total assets of $100 million and total liabilities of $90 million. Over the past five years, the bank's return on assets has averaged 0.15 percent (compared to a national average of 1.2 percent), placing the bank near the bottom of its peer group. The OCC believes that a talented, energetic CEO could make the bank highly profitable. What action, if any, can the OCC take under section 1818?

If the bank had an unsatisfactory examination rating for earnings, the bank could under § 1818(b)(8) deem the bank to be engaged in an unsafe and unsound practice. The agency could also reclassify the bank from well-capitalized to adequately capitalized under § 1831o(g)(1).

Problem 5—Torpid National Bank as Significantly Undercapitalized

Same as problem 4, except that Torpid National Bank has total assets of $100 million and total liabilities of $97.5 million. What action, if any, can the OCC take under applicable law?

As the bank is now significantly undercapitalized, the agency may: summarily dismiss Luke Warme or other senior managers, without having to show fault; require the bank to hire a competent CEO; and make the new CEO subject to the agency's approval. See id. § 1831o(f)(2)(F).

Chapter 10: Bank Failure

We turn now to a topic in banking law that, until fairly recently, was quite undeveloped: the law of depository institution failure. The reason for the law being undeveloped, of course, was that depository institutions did not fail, at least not in any quantity. For the same reason, the law of bank failure is now developing at an enormous rate, and undoubtedly will continue to do so for some time as the failures of the 1980s and early 1990s wind their way through the judicial system.

We find that student interest in this topic is enhanced if we ask initially about whether any of the students have had an experience with bank failure. These days in a class of any size at least some students have been depositors in a bank or thrift that failed, and usually they are very willing to supply the details. Often their accounts can be used to illustrate some of the legal or policy issues in bank failure law.

We begin this section by observing that bank failure should be conceived of as a specialized form of a bankruptcy regime. We say specialized because banks and thrift institutions are not subject to the bankruptcy law when they fail. There is a statutory exemption in the bankruptcy code for depository institutions (although bank holding companies *are* subject to the bankruptcy code, which has created complicated problems that we will not discuss here).

Although bank failure is specialized, the basic problems for the regime are similar to the problems for any bankruptcy regime. You have an institution whose liabilities exceed its assets. It can't pay off its debts as they arise. The goals of a failure regime in such a situation are three: (1) the institution must be closed and a fiduciary appointed to handle its affairs; (2) the fiduciary must marshal the assets of the failed institution; and (3) the value of the assets must be paid to the creditors of the failed institution (including the FDIC) in order of priority. The chapter is structured according to this organization.

APPOINTMENT OF A FIDUCIARY

First, the institution must be placed under the hands of a third party to administer its reorganization. It can't be left wholly in the hands of existing managers, because the managers have a conflict of interest—they are likely to own stock in the company, and they have reputational capital tied up in the institution, and for these and other reasons they don't usually want the institution to be closed. Moreover, if the institution has failed, this is at least *prima facie* evidence that the existing managers are not the best people to be running the firm. So the bank failure system must provide for the *appointment of a fiduciary*—that is, an impartial third party charged with responsibility for winding up the affairs of the institution.

The traditional rule has been that a depository institution is closed and a fiduciary appointed by the primary banking regulator. National banks would be closed by the comptroller, and state-chartered banks closed by the state banking departments. Similar rules applied to thrift institutions—federally chartered thrifts were closed by the Federal Home Loan Bank Board (now the Office of Thrift Supervision), and state chartered thrifts were closed by the state regulators.

We ask students to identify potential problems with this system. The main problem, of course, is the moral hazard problem for state regulators. The decision whether to close an institution is inevitably political, and at the state level the political dynamic appears to be geared towards allowing institutions to remain open well past the point where they should be closed. The reason is that when an institution is threatened with closure, the parties who are going to lobby the state banking department are generally opposed to closure: these include the management of the institution, who are likely to be politically influential at the state and local level; borrowers from the institution, who again are likely to be influential in local politics and who fear—often with good reason—that their lot will be worse if the institution is closed and their loans are taken over by some other party; and shareholders in the institution (who will include existing management but usually include others as well) whose investments will be wiped out if the institution is closed.

Against this powerful coalition of forces against closure, there is little political influence on the other side. The principal party to be harmed if the institution is kept open past the point of insolvency and continues to lose money is the FDIC. The state regulators realize that if they allow an institution to remain open, it may return to profitability, in which case the local political interests will be satisfied; and if the institution keeps losing money it is the federal government which will eventually pick up the tab. The result, predictably, is that at least some state regulators are likely to delay too long in closing state-chartered institutions. Arguably this is exactly what happened with institutions in Texas and other states that remained open after they had become insolvent, and which continued to lose huge amounts of money before they were eventually closed.

This is not to say that the federal regulators are perfect in their handling of closure policy. Far from it: the FHLBB pursued a deliberate policy of not closing institutions during the early 1980s, largely because the assets of the FSLIC were insufficient to pay out depositors if all insolvent institutions were closed. Arguably the FHLBB gambled that the savings industry would return to profitability over time, much as the managers of individual institutions were gambling on a turnaround for their own institutions. Moreover, powerful politicians at the federal level attempted to influence the FHLBB to exercise "forbearance"—which means nothing other than not closing an institution after it has become insolvent. These efforts generated some of the notable political scandals of the era.

These moral hazard concerns are increasingly being addressed by federal law. First, the problem of moral hazard at the state level is mitigated by explicit closure powers for federal regulators. The OTS can close state-chartered insured thrifts, the Federal Reserve can close state-chartered member banks, and the FDIC can close state-chartered insured nonmember banks. The FDICIA added to the FDIC's closure powers, providing that the FDIC can close any insured institution even if the comptroller or the Fed have not acted. This represents a major federalization of control over closure powers, and appears to respond to the moral hazard problem just described.

FDICIA's prompt corrective action provisions also respond to the problem of undue influence and lobbying at the federal level by limiting and channeling federal regulators' discretion in dealing with capital-deficient depository institutions. This is discussed later in the chapter.

Franklin Savings (pages 728-33) concerns the decision to appoint a fiduciary for an institution. The question was whether the director of the OTS had acted improperly in appointing a conservator for Franklin Savings Association, a state-chartered stock savings and loan.

We start our consideration of this case by treating it as an exemplar for what happened to the savings and loan industry. What you have here is a traditional savings and loan which had been doing business since 1889 in Ottawa, Kansas. It takes deposits and makes first mortgage real estate loans. This is, of course, the Jimmy Stewart bank in *It's a Wonderful Life*.

All this changed in 1981—just the time when the savings and loan industry began to change radically. What you saw with Franklin, as with most of the S&L's that failed during the 1980s, is the "supernova" effect: enormous, dramatic, sudden growth. In Franklin's case, the bank grew from $200 million in deposits in 1981 to over $11 billion in deposits in 1989, its centennial year (and, alas, the year before its demise). Franklin acquired these deposits by bidding in the brokered deposit market. By 1989 over 70% of its deposits were brokered.

Perhaps just as interesting as what it did with its deposits is what it did with its assets. Franklin went into all sorts of complex financial instruments —junk bonds, derivative securities, puts and calls and other sophisticated (some might say hypersophisticated) instruments. Did the managers of Franklin know what they are doing? Probably not. Even the most sophisticated Wall Street money traders hardly knew what to make of these instruments.

Franklin also illustrates another feature of many of these failures—very high compensation and perks for the thrift's incumbent management. One famous (although possibly apocryphal) story has it that two officers of a thrift institution took a two-week trip to France and dined at many of the best restaurants in the world on their expense accounts, on the theory that they had received an application to finance a good quality restaurant and needed to "research" the loan application by testing out other fine restaurants. Whether or not this is true, it's clear that many thrift executives treated themselves very well indeed during the 1980s. In Franklin's case, the institution reported a $9 million loss in 1989, but paid its top 8 executive officers $3.5 million in salaries and bonuses. There may have been unreported perks in addition. These are no Jimmy Stewarts managing this institution.

In 1990 the OTS got fed up and appointed the RTC as conservator. The management challenged the appointment in court, and the case went off on whether the appointment was proper under the applicable statute.

The case is important because it defined the scope of the power of OTS—and implicitly other federal banking agencies—to close depository institutions. We see that the OTS has the discretion under the statute to appoint a receiver *ex parte* if in his (or her) opinion a ground for appointment of a receiver exists. The problematic point is this: what is the scope of judicial review of this decision? All the statute tells us is that "the court shall upon the merits dismiss such action or direct the Director to remove such conservator."

We ask students what in heaven's name this means. The scope of review is really not defined, other than the statement that review must be "on the merits," itself a highly vague phrase. It's odd, too, because modern administrative law statutes usually expressly define the scope of review.

The key battleground is the nature of the administrative record on which the review on the merits is to be conducted. When you have a challenge to the decision of a banking agency to close a depository institution, the agency will supply documentation of its decision and the grounds on which the decision was based. If that documentation is the *exclusive* basis on which the court can base its evaluation of the reasonableness of the agency's action, then the agency has an enormous, practically insurmountable, advantage in the litigation. The agency can easily manipulate the underlying documentation in order to make its decision seem like the epitome of reasonableness.

If, on the other hand, the phrase "on the merits" requires a de novo trial, then the agency loses a lot of control and the party contesting the closure has a much greater chance of winning. That's essentially what the district court did in the present case: as the appeals court noted, the trial court "heard live testimony from twenty-five witnesses; accepted deposition testimony from eighteen witnesses; received over 650 trial exhibits; engaged in credibility determinations regarding competing experts; and basically made its own findings, compared those to the findings of the Director, and decided the conservator was wrongly appointed."

The Tenth Circuit would have none of this, and basically said that the administrative record was to be in the discretion of the OTS, subject to the power of the court to call for supplementation if it were shown that the Director actually relied on documents not provided in the administrative record.

We ask our students to comment on the meaning of this decision for the ability of bank managers to challenge closure decisions. It seems pretty clear that after this decision, a bank manager will have a tough time convincing a court that the decision to close the institution was legally invalid.

We ask whether public policy is well served by giving this degree of discretion to banking agencies to close institutions. What about the danger of arbitrariness or abuse? What about the danger of mistake? What about the deterrent effect this kind of nearly unbridled closure authority may have on the ability of financial institutions to raise capital? For the most part students feel that the agencies' closure powers are justified by the extent of the existing crisis in the banking industry, and that the agencies can be relied on not to abuse their powers, especially given the fact that the resources of the agencies are so taxed at the moment that they are unlikely to go after an institution unless closure is richly deserved. Certainly one can make this point with considerable plausibility with respect to Franklin Savings, which probably did richly deserved to be shut down.

RESOLUTION PROCEDURES

The next topic we treat in depth is type of resolution procedures in use. As the book explains, but as is worth exploring with students in class, there are four main forms of resolution procedures, each with several variants.

Open Bank Assistance (pages 738-39)

The book starts with open bank assistance, which isn't quite a resolution procedure although the purposes and functions are similar. In open bank assistance the agency tries to keep the existing institution open and afloat by injecting capital and mandating changes in operations. Often, as a practical matter, in open bank assistance the former managers are booted out and new ones are brought in. This is so even though the prior management may have been quite competent.

Open bank assistance should be seen as an analogue to chapter 11 of the bankruptcy code, in that the institution is not closed, but rather is maintained as a going concern, and the incumbent managers are sometimes left in place. In both cases the hope is that the institution will return to solvency without the need for a liquidation.

It is worth exploring some of the differences between open bank assistance and chapter 11 proceedings. The most important is that in open bank assistance only the government takes an immediate financial hit. The FDIC puts money in the institution, but other creditors do not. This would seem to favor other creditors over the FDIC.

On the other hand it's not clear how this cuts. If the institution returns to solvency the FDIC will recover its investment, as will other creditors. If the institution eventually is liquidated, the FDIC will lose, but so will all the other creditors. And the FDIC will get a credit for the amount of its open bank assistance.

So one might say that open bank assistance actually disfavors private creditors of banks because they are shut out of the process. In chapter 11 the creditors committees exercise a lot of control over the process; in open bank assistance they exercise virtually none.

Liquidations *(pages 739-40)*

The simplest failure resolution procedure is the liquidation. All this means is that the receiver marshals the assets, sells them, and then distributes the sums received in the liquidation to creditors of the failed depository institution in the order of their priority. This is much like a chapter 7 bankruptcy procedure.

The key thing to note about liquidations is that *not all depositors are made whole*. Depending on the type of liquidation used, uninsured depositors—depositors with accounts over $100,000—will have to eat some loss. This means that if you have a bank with uninsured depositors who fear a liquidation, you can get a run. This happened at Continental Bank in 1984 after the FDIC had liquidated Penn Square Bank. Uninsured depositors at Continental Bank ran it and forced it into effective insolvency also.

Students should know the main types of liquidation in use today. These are the following:

Deposit payoff. The simplest type of liquidation (and the one Congress probably had in mind when it enacted the Federal Deposit Insurance Act in 1933) is the straight deposit payoff. In a deposit payoff the FDIC closes the bank and writes checks to all the insured depositors. Then there is a receivership in which the uninsured depositors and all other creditors get paid off in the order of their priority. At the close of the proceedings the institution is liquidated and all its assets and liabilities have been wrapped up.

Insured deposit transfer. A modern variant of the deposit payoff, which the FDIC favors today, is the insured deposit transfer. Under this arrangement, the insured deposits aren't paid off by the FDIC; instead they are assumed by another institution. I you are a depositor, you don't get a check from the FDIC, but rather you get a nice letter from the assuming bank saying: "we're now you bank."

We ask students why another institution would agree to assume deposits. The answer: because the FDIC pays them to do it.

We ask what the advantages of the insured deposit transfer are as compared with the straight liquidation. The answer(s): The principal difference between the insured deposit transfer and the deposit payoff is that in the insured deposit transfer the assuming institution is willing to pay something to acquire the deposit base. The assuming institution expects to earn money on the deposit accounts, and hopes that the depositors will become customers for other of the bank's products and services—home mortgage loans, etc. So the insured deposit transfer maintains some of the going-concern value of the failed institution, and the FDIC can capture some of that value when it transfers the deposits instead of paying them off. The insured deposit transfer may also provide some consumer convenience because the consumer is spared the trouble of opening a new account at another depository institution—one is opened for him or her automatically. (Note that the consumer is perfectly free to withdraw some or all his or her funds from the assuming institution and deposit them elsewhere.)

Modified Deposit Payoff. For a while the FDIC experimented with the modified deposit payoff. It works this way: at the time of failure, the FDIC pays off all the insured deposits, and makes partial payments to the uninsured depositors and other creditors of the bank based on its assessment of what the bank's assets will realize in liquidation. This way the uninsured depositors and other creditors don't have all their funds tied up indefinitely.

What happens if the amounts realized on the liquidation of the assets are different than what the FDIC thought when it made the initial distribution to the uninsured creditors? If the FDIC realizes more than it predicted, it makes a receivership dividend to the creditors in the order of their priority. If it realizes less, it eats the loss.

Although the modified deposit payoff is often portrayed as a newfangled invention, it bears a striking resemblance to the traditional method of conducting a receivership of a failed depository institution, which was to make a series of liquidating dividends to the creditors of the failed institution as the assets were sold off.

We ask students to assess the pros and cons of the modified deposit payoff. Among the pros is the fact that all creditors receive some payment up front, rather than having to wait years as the receiver liquidated the assets. Among the cons is the fact that the creditors may receive too much—more than they would receive in a straight liquidation or an insured deposit transfer. The FDIC can of course mitigate this risk by paying out in the initial dividend an amount considerably below what the agency thinks the assets of the failed institution will eventually fetch in the receivership.

Purchase and Assumption Transactions *(pages 740-43)*

As the book tells us, the FDIC has an overwhelming preference for purchase and assumption (P&A) deals. What is a P&A deal? It's one in which a solvent institution *purchases* the failed institution's assets and *assumes* the failed institution's liabilities. The P&A is basically an assisted merger. It comes in two principal forms, the whole bank and the clean bank transaction.

We treat the whole bank transaction first, because it is simpler. This is a deal in which another institution assumes *all* liabilities and purchases *all* assets of the failed institution. The FDIC kicks in cash to make the deal attractive to the acquiror.

We examine the whole bank deal from the standpoint first of the assets, then of the liabilities. On the asset side of the balance sheet, the noteworthy feature of the whole bank deal is that the acquiror takes the nonperforming as well as performing assets—half-built office buildings, failed resort developments, businesses in chapter 11 reorganization, and so on.

We ask why the acquiror would take on these bad assets. The answer is that the FDIC would like to get rid of these bad assets because if it doesn't do so it will have to acquire them itself and try to sell them off. So these agencies like the whole bank deal. From the standpoint of the acquiring institution, the assets may be a headache, but they may also pay off, and if the price is right the institution may be glad to have them.

From the standpoint of the liabilities, the noteworthy feature is that the whole bank deal involves the payment of *all* depositors, insured or uninsured. The deposit insurance ceilings don't mean anything in the whole bank deal: everyone gets paid off. In fact in a pure whole bank deal not only uninsured depositors but all creditors of the bank get paid off in full.

Contrast the whole bank deal with its opposite, the clean bank deal. In a clean bank deal the acquiring institution takes only some of the assets and some of the liabilities. So, on the asset side, the acquiring institution will purchase only the performing assets. The bad assets are left with the FDIC. This may happen because acquiring institutions don't want to be bothered with the bad assets or may not want to take on the risk that they will not perform.

On the liability side, the acquiring institution usually acquires the deposit liabilities; other liabilities are not acquired. It may even acquire only the insured liabilities, in which case the P&A looks like an insured deposit transfer linked to a sale of some assets.

The whole bank and clean bank deals represent polar ends of a continuum; there are many intermediate forms. One popular form today is the purchase and assumption with a put option. In this deal the acquiring institution takes on the dirty as well as the clean assets—or some of the dirty assets at least—but retains a put option. It has the right to return the assets to the FDIC after a period of time and get its money back if it finds that the assets are not performing as hoped. Sometimes the put option is accompanied by a "haircut" which means that the FDIC won't give all the money back, but only, let's say, 95 percent of what was paid for the asset.

We ask students to identify the pros and cons of the P&A approach. Why does the FDIC display such a distinct preference for it as opposed to other approaches? Among the pros are the fact that the P&A deal reduces transactions costs and places the liquidation of the failed institution's assets in the hands of the private sector, which may have the incentives and expertise to do a better job than the FDIC. Among the cons are the fact that linking assets and liabilities may not necessarily be the most efficient way to dispose of a failed bank. Moreover—a subtle but important point which students sometimes identify—the P&A severely limits the number of potential bidders, since the bidders must themselves be depository institutions or depository institution holding companies authorized to conduct a banking business in the location of the failed institution. By reducing the number of potential bidders, the P&A transaction probably reduces the amounts the FDIC get in the auction relative to what they could get if anyone was allowed to bid.

Bridge Banks and New Banks *(pages 743-44)*

The book describes two other relatively new mechanisms, not much used. These are basically intended as stopgap or transition measures, although in the case of new banks the reconstituted institution may continue in operation indefinitely with a restructured capital base.

Choice Among Alternative Strategies: The Cost Test *(pages 744-47)*

We discuss the impact of the cost test in 12 U.S.C. § 1823(c)(4). Before FDICIA, the cost test involved a *less-than-liquidation* requirement. The FDIC could use a non-liquidation resolution method if the cost did not exceed the estimated cost of liquidation. This requirement had almost no bite at all. The FDIC generally viewed liquidation as more costly than alternatives like purchase and assumption transactions. Moreover, the cost test did not apply if the FDIC determined that the institution's continued operation was "essential to provide adequate depository services in its community."

FDICIA significantly tightened the cost test by adopting a *least-cost* requirement, repealing the essentiality exception, and in its place adopting a narrow systemic-risk exception. The FDIC must use the resolution method "least costly to the deposit insurance fund of all possible methods" for meeting the FDIC's obligation to insured depositors. The FDIC can use a more costly resolution approach (which might, for example, involve protecting a failing bank's uninsured depositors) only in cases of systemic risk, and then only under an exacting process designed to heighten accountability for the decision. The Federal Reserve Board and the FDIC's Board of Directors must both, by two-thirds majorities, recommend the exception to the secretary of the Treasury. The secretary can then authorize the FDIC to use the more costly approach if the secretary determines, "in consultation with the President," that complying with the least-cost requirement "would have serious adverse effects on economic conditions or financial stability" and that the more costly approach would avoid or mitigate those effects.

Another provision of the cost test derived from FDICIA, § 13(c)(4)(E), sought to reinforce the least-cost resolution requirement by prohibiting the FDIC from taking any action that "would have the effect of increasing losses to any insurance fund" by protecting uninsured deposits or the claims of nondepositor creditors. But the exception for purchase and assumption transactions, adopted at the FDIC's behest, smuggles in a less-than-liquidation test and thus leaves § 1823(c)(4)(E) no stricter than the basic rule in § 1823(c)(4)(A).

MARSHALING OF ASSETS

We have covered methods of closing and resolving a depository institution. Now we consider how the assets of a failed depository institution are gathered or "marshaled" for distribution to creditors. These assets may be marshaled by the FDIC as receiver or conservator, or by an acquiring institution in a P&A deal.

We introduce this topic by pointing out that for the most part the assets of a failed institution are very easy to identify. They are loans, securities, etc. that the bank has in its portfolio. But there are a number of situations in which the assets become potentially problematic, and the book talks about three of these. In dealing with the problematic issues, however, students should not lose sight of the fact that most assets are easily identified. The problematic issues include the following:

Insurance Litigation *(page 748-52)*

One of the most important assets in any depository institution failure is the failed institution's claim against insurance carriers. If the institution has failed, usually there will be a viable claim that the failure was due to mismanagement by the institution's former officers and directors, or to fraudulent or illegal conduct by someone in the institution. These claim raise questions of coverage under two standard insurance policies maintained by depository institutions: the D&O policy and the bankers blanket bond. The D&O policy covers claims for mismanagement, but usually not for intentional or criminal misconduct. Bankers blanket bonds cover claims for intentional or criminal conduct but not for mismanagement.

These policies contain a number of standard exclusions that may or may not be implicated in a bank failure, and there is much controversy these days about whether the exclusions apply. The federal banking agencies argue that the exclusions don't apply, or that if they do apply they are void as against public policy. For example, the regulatory exclusion under the D&O policy excludes coverage for claims by regulatory agencies; this is challenged on public policy grounds.

The *American Casualty Company* case, page 748, is an important precedent interpreting the regulatory agency provision and the insured vs. insured provision. The court takes a position surprisingly hostile to the FDIC, significantly limiting the available policy proceeds in post-failure litigation.

Cross-Guarantees *(pages 752-55)*

Another big issue is the degree to which affiliates in a banking organization ought to be liable for the debts of a failed bank.

We start teaching this material by reminding students of the basic rule of limited liability. Shareholders are not generally personally liable for the debts of corporations in which they hold their shares, nor are subsidiary corporations, in general, liable for the debts of other subsidiaries of a common parent or of the parent itself (although the value of the parent's investment in the subsidiary will be reachable by the parent's creditors).

In banking law, the rules are somewhat different. One controversial rule is the Fed's source of strength policy. The Fed takes the position that the parent bank holding company ought to be liable for the debts of the subsidiary bank—ought to serve as a "source of strength" to the subsidiary. This issue came up in a series of cases involving MBank, a Texas bank holding company. The creditors of the parent holding company, which was in bankruptcy, fought the Fed's attempt to make the holding company liable for the debts of its subsidiary banks. The Fifth Circuit repudiated the Fed and found no statutory warrant for a source of strength policy. The matter went to the Supreme Court, which reversed on technical grounds leaving the basic issue unanswered.

We invite students to discuss the pros and cons of the source of strength policy. Among the pros: the fact that it provides a deep pocket to replenish the financially stressed deposit insurance funds, and that it may offer incentives to the parent holding company to monitor carefully the activities of its subsidiary banks. Among the cons is the possibility that the source of strength doctrine will deter capital formation.

The other major form of affiliate liability in banking law is the cross-guarantee rule adopted in FIRREA. Basically, under FIRREA each insured depository institution in a holding company structure is liable to the FDIC for its losses in resolving the failure of any other insured depository in the holding company structure. The FDIC's claim is junior to all other debt claims against the affiliate, but is senior to the claim of the affiliate's shareholders.

We ask students to explain why the cross guarantee rule is like the source of strength doctrine, and why it is different. The difference: the affiliated depository institution, not the parent, is made liable for the debts of a depository institution. Realistically, this places some of the parent's wealth behind the depository institution, since the FDIC's claim on the affiliate is superior to the claim of the parent as shareholder. But the FDIC has no claim on the assets of the parent aside from the value of its investment in subsidiary depository institutions, nor does it have any claim on the assets of nonbank subsidiaries of a bank holding company under the cross-guarantee rule.

Voidable Preferences and Fraudulent Transfers *(pages 755-57)*

Obviously, when a depository institution is in shaky condition and about to be closed, it is in the interest of those managing the institution to transfer its assets to themselves or to persons they want to benefit for one reason or another. In this respect depository institutions are not significantly different from other firms teetering on the brink of insolvency. This section outlines the applicable rules in the banking context to bring such transfers back into the estate of the insolvent institution for the benefit of its legitimate creditors (including the FDIC-corporate).

Claims Against Bankrupt Debtors *(pages 757-58)*

Particular problems arise when the FDIC as receiver is asserting claims against bankrupt debtors. Note that if the depository institution has failed, it is likely that a portion of its debtors will also be insolvent or will become insolvent during the period in which assets are being liquidated. The material in the book touches on the morass of complex issues that are involved when the automatic stay provision of the bankruptcy code runs up against the federal bank failure rules and policies.

DISTRIBUTION TO CREDITORS

Once assets are marshaled, the fiduciary's task is to distribute them to creditors. The general rules here are clear.

First, the fiduciary is to distribute the assets in order of priority. Thus senior debt gets paid before general debt, general debt before subordinated debt, and subordinated debt before equity. Priorities of claims are determined in the first instance by contractual agreement among the suppliers of capital to the depository institution. In addition, certain priorities are specifically set forth in legislation or administrative regulation. For example, many states have enacted depositor preference statutes which give deposits priority over other unsecured debt; federal law requires that these state priorities be respected even in the distribution of the assets of a failed national bank.

Second, the fiduciary is to make no distinctions among claimants at the same priority level. The distribution of assets is to be "ratable," meaning equal among claimants of similar priority.

While these general rules are easy to state, they are sometimes difficult to apply in practice. The reason is that when a depository institution fails, claimants try hard to enhance their priority vis-a-vis other claimants. The book explores a number of methods for enhancing priority that have proved successful, as well as some promising devices that have not worked.

Statutory Claims Procedures *(pages 758-61)*

Before addressing these questions, the book briefly treats the statutory claims procedures. This is a matter of great practical importance, and some confusion resulted from the Supreme Court's decision in *Coit Independence Joint Venture*. The Court there held that a claimant on a failed depository institution was entitled under the statute to de novo judicial determination of its claim, and that the claimant was not obligated to exhaust administrative remedies before going into court. Congress responded in FIRREA with a new claims procedure which, while anything but crystal clear, seems to provide the following:

First, Congress required exhaustion of administrative remedies. Claims not presented in the first instance to the receiver are forfeited. However, Congress also imposed a tight deadline in which the receiver is required to determine the claims—it being the absence of such deadlines that led the Supreme Court in *Coit Independence* to conclude that exhaustion of administrative remedies was not required.

Second, Congress permitted judicial review of the receiver's determinations. Although the standard of review is somewhat unclear in the statute, it would appear to be the same de novo review as under prior law interpreted in *Coit Independence*.

We ask whether review should be de novo as a matter of policy. Arguably, some weight should be given to the receiver's determinations; normal administrative practice would be to give these informal determinations a strong presumption of correctness, perhaps by limiting judicial review to the "arbitrary or capricious" standard. We ask why this wasn't done in FIRREA. The answer appears to be that Congress didn't want to raise constitutional qualms about divesting "Article III" courts of their jurisdiction over traditional matters such as determining legal claims. The opinion in *Coit Independence* expressed these qualms, although the Court did not rule directly on the issue. We think Congress probably went beyond what was strictly necessary to safeguard the judicial role under Article III of the Constitution, but that question is now moot.

It's worth asking Question 2 (page 761) after the discussion of *Coit Independence*. The point is that if the FDIC is the receiver, it has an incentive to deny private claims on the institution, since doing so will increase the FDIC's own recovery from the institution's assets to satisfy its claim as deposit insurer. This conflict of interest might well raise serious due process concerns, which are addressed to a substantial degree by a right to de novo judicial review of the receiver's determinations.

Establishment of Priorities *(pages 762-76)*

The book then turns to the question of establishing priorities of claims.

Constructive Trusts (pages 763-66)

The first issue is that of constructive trusts, addressed in the *Downriver Community Federal Credit Union* case. A credit union deposited a large amount of money in Penn Square Bank and did not get paid off in full when that institution failed. Now the credit union seeks to enhance the priority of its claim against the assets of the receivership by claiming that the court should impress a constructive trust on the amount of its deposit.

In teaching this case the first thing to do is to make sure students understand what a constructive trust is. It's an equitable remedy that sets aside assets as being impressed with a trust for the benefit of someone who has been wronged by the owner of the assets. It's called a "constructive" trust because it's essentially a fiction: no true trust is created. The rhetoric of trust law is called on to devise an equitable remedy to deal with the situation at hand.

We next try to get the student to explain why imposition of a constructive trust would have helped the Downriver Community Federal Credit Union. The answer is that if a constructive trust were imposed, the amount of the deposit in Penn Square Bank would be treated as never having passed into Penn Square's ownership. It would be treated as a trust fund held for the benefit of the credit union; and as such the credit union would have first claim on the amount of the deposit over and above all other claimants. The net effect of imposing a constructive trust is no different than giving the credit union a priority over other creditors for the amount of its deposit.

Prior law did recognize constructive trusts in the situation where a bank accepted a deposit at a time when the bank knew it was hopelessly insolvent. In the excerpted case the credit union sought to extend the principle of the constructive trust to cover a situation where it was induced to make the deposit by false representations from the bank, even though the bank was not hopelessly insolvent at the time the deposit was made (although it became hopelessly insolvent thereafter). We observe to students that this was really not an unreasonable extension of prior law.

We ask students why no constructive trust was established here. Doctrinally, the answer is that under applicable law the constructive trust is an equitable remedy to be imposed at the discretion of the court, and that the court can refuse to impose such a trust if doing so would unfairly discriminate among creditors or disrupt the orderly administration of the receivership. From the standpoint of public policy, it is evident that the court was concerned that in cases like Penn Square virtually all depositors are similarly situated, and that imposing a constructive trust on behalf of those who invested directly in the failed institution—such as the credit union—would unfairly benefit those depositors as compared with the many others who relied on the advice of deposit brokers to make a similar investment, and who therefore could not claim that they were fraudulently induced by the bank to make the deposit.

Although this case appears to shut down a broad constructive trust remedy (at least in the Tenth Circuit) there may be cases where constructive trusts will still be available. If the claimant can show some factor unique to him or her, for example, the outcome might be different. A different result might also obtain if the institution was in fact hopelessly insolvent at the time the deposit was made.

Purchase and Assumption Transactions *(pages 766-67)*

The book deals with the interaction of the ratable distribution rule with the overwhelmingly popular technique of purchase and assumption transactions as means to resolve bank failures.

Private Litigation *(pages 767-71)*

The next major topic is private litigation. We start by asking why private litigation such as that in the principal case, *Leach v. FDIC* (pages 767-70), involves priorities of claims.

Shareholders who have lost money as a result of a depository institution failure will always want to up their priority from that of equity holders—who are by definition wiped out when a depository institution fails. The best way to do this is to assert a claims against a third party who has allegedly contributed to the downfall of the institution, such as the institution's former managers or persons who advised or had dealings with the institution.

If the shareholders can successfully assert a claim against a third party, they convert their status from that of equity holders in an insolvent institution to that of judgment creditors of a (presumably) solvent third party. This is an double step-up of priority: from equity holder to creditor, and from claimant on an insolvent entity to claimant on a solvent one. Small wonder, then, that shareholders attempt this tactic.

The problem with this tactic is that the shareholders risk having their claims recharacterized as derivative rather than direct. If the claim is derivative, it is considered brought on behalf of the depository institution, and all proceeds go into the receivership where they will be used for the benefit of the institution's creditors. The shareholders will get nothing in such a case. If, on the other hand, the claim is characterized as direct and not derivative, the shareholders get the stepped up priority (provided they can win the claim).

Leach v. FDIC addresses one of the most important issues in this area, namely whether the cause of action for mismanagement under 12 U.S.C. § 93(a) is derivative or direct. The plain language of the statute seems to suggest that the shareholders have a direct claim: the directors are to be liable for damages that "the association [or] *its shareholders*" may have suffered (emphasis supplied). The statute seems to give a right of action both to the association (i.e., a derivative action) and to the shareholders (i.e., a direct action).

We ask students how the recognition of a direct right of action in shareholders for mismanagement would affect bank failure law. The answer appears rather clearly to be that it would affect bank failure law in a significant way because in virtually every bank failure the shareholders have a plausible cause of action for mismanagement against the former managers (note that § 93(a) in terms applies only to national banks).

The court here rejects the argument that § 93(a) provides a direct cause of action, in large measure because of the serious consequences that would flow from a contrary ruling. However, the student should not think that all causes of action are derivative. Shareholders may still be able to prevail with causes of action—notably ones for misrepresentation in the purchase or sale of securities under SEC Rule 10b-5—which have been interpreted as providing a direct rather than a derivative right of action. Shareholders are also sometimes successful with claims based on state law.

FDIC v. Jenkins (page 771, note 4) addresses a related but different issue. This case raises the question of whether, in cases where shareholders *do* have a direct claim, the FDIC can obtain priority vis-a-vis the shareholders over the assets of third parties against whom claim is brought. This is often an important issue these days, since the principal defendants are likely to be bankrupted by the claims and the priority of claims against the defendants is therefore going to determine whether the claimant gets any recovery in many cases.

We ask students what policy reason could support the FDIC's claim of priority. Responses include protecting the deposit insurance funds and preventing parochial state action that benefits in-state claimants at the expense of federal taxpayers. We also ask where the claim to priority comes from. Although the agency made a weak claim under the Federal Deposit Insurance Act, the basis of its assertion of priority was really federal common law. We spend a few minutes exploring how there could be a federal common law here, and, if there is one, how the court can decide what its provisions are. Federal common law, we will see, becomes very important in the context of FDIC "superpowers" which are treated at the end of this chapter.

Setoffs (pages 772-74)

The setoff is the next device for obtaining priority. This is a situation where a bank is both creditor of and debtor to another party. If there is the requisite degree of mutuality between the obligations, the party dealing with the bank may be able to claim a setoff so as to step up its priority vis-a-vis other creditors of the bank.

We ask students to explain why setoffs represent a step-up in priority. The matter can be illustrated by simple numerical examples. Assume for expository purposes that the bank in question has no deposit insurance. Say A has borrowed $10,000 from Bank, which amount has been credited to A's account at Bank. Now Bank fails, and the receiver demands that A repay the $10,000 loan. In the absence of a setoff right, A would have to pay the receiver the $10,000 and would be remitted to the status of a general creditor with respect to its claim of $10,000 against Bank. Assuming the receivership nets 50¢ on the dollar, A would receive only $5,000 in receivership dividends and would end up short $5,000.

However, A can probably utilize a setoff in this situation. A can repay the loan to Bank by setting off the amount owing to A under the deposit. Because the loan and the deposit are mutual obligations, the setoff is permitted. The result is that A will end up even rather than short $5,000. A has essentially been given a priority, vis-a-vis other creditors, with respect to A's claim of $10,000 against Bank.

We ask our students to explain the setoff right. The usual answers: the obligations at issue here are not real obligations, since they cancel each other out. In reality A owned nothing to Bank in this situation, so it would be wrong for the receiver to collect anything. Another (not necessarily inconsistent) answer: the setoff facilitates important banking transactions, such as the making of a loan by the extension of bank credit or the holding by banks of correspondent balances on one another (as in the excerpted case of *Scott v. Armstrong*).

Executory Contracts (pages 774-76)

Executory contracts are the last major topic in the area of determining the proper distribution to creditors. We start by having students explain the rationale for allowing the fiduciary to repudiate executory contracts. Basically, if the receiver were not allowed to repudiate executory contracts, the result would be to create a de facto priority for counterparties involved in favorable long term contracts with failed depository institutions. For example, suppose a bank is a lessee in a long term, above market lease with a lessor. If the receiver could not repudiate the lease obligations, the lessor would be placed in a more favorable position than other creditors.

Thus the fundamental justification for the rule permitting the receiver to repudiate executory contracts appears to be the concern for maintaining priorities among creditors. FIRREA however seems to have gone well beyond that rationale in some cases. The most onerous provision of FIRREA is the rule that if a failed bank is a lessee on an above-market lease, the receiver can repudiate the lease and the lessor's claim is limited to accrued rentals up to the point of repudiation. FIRREA appears to deprive lessors of the normal remedy available to counterparties whose contracts have been repudiated, namely a right of action for damages against the receivership, to be paid along with other claims out of the receivership assets.

We ask students whether there are constitutional problems with the FIRREA rule on leases (we think there may be). We also ask whether the long term incentives of the rule are likely to be good or bad. Arguably, the rule might have bad incentives because it will likely raise the cost of premises to depository institutions as compared with their nonbank competitors. In favor of the rule, however, it can be said that it has allowed the FDIC to avoid a large number of burdensome leases in a down real estate market at a time when the federal deposit insurance funds were themselves in desperate financial straits.

THE SIDE AGREEMENT RULE

The final topic in the area of bank failure law is the side agreement rule, often referred to as the FDIC's "superpowers." As the book observes, there are a number of ostensibly separate legal doctrines that have coalesced, as it were, into a relatively unified body of doctrine. The general thrust of this body of doctrine is to release the FDIC or its assigns from certain impediments to the assertion of rights against third parties. This could be in the form of defenses that the beneficiaries of the doctrine might have against claims by third parties, or of powers which the beneficiaries of the doctrine have as claimants to avoid defenses which third parties might have been able to assert against the failed depository institution. Because both claims and defenses are involved, the side agreement rule is treated separately from the topics of marshaling assets (i.e., claims) and distribution to creditors (i.e., defenses). We call this body of doctrine the "side agreement" rule because its purpose and effect is to insulate the FDIC and their assigns from claims or defenses based on unrecorded side agreements with the depository institution.

Sources of Authority *(pages 777-90)*

The **D'Oench, Duhme** *Doctrine (pages 777-80)*

We illustrate the basic purpose of the rule with the first excerpted case, the important decision in *D'Oench, Duhme & Co. v. FDIC* (pages 777-79). D'Oench, Duhme, a securities firm, sold some bonds to Bellevue Bank. The bonds lost value, and D'Oench, Duhme—as was the practice among securities firms on the good old days—commits to the bank to help mitigate the losses. It does so by executing demand notes to the bank that the bank can book so as not to show the bonds on its balance sheet. Proceeds of the bonds were to be credited to the notes. The receipts for the note, which were not attached to the notes, contained the bank's promise not to call the notes for payment. The apparent purpose and effect of this arrangement was to mislead the bank examiners by concealing from them the fact that the bank was holding bad paper as part of its assets.

Later the bank fails and the FDIC, as part of the resolution transaction, makes a $1,000,000 loan secured in part by the note. The FDIC proceeds against D'Oench, Duhme, the maker of the notes, and is met by the defense that the bank as payee had promised not to present the notes for payment. The Supreme Court held that as a matter of federal common law, the defense could not stand: "if the secret agreement were allowed as a defense in this case the maker of the note would be enabled to defeat the purpose of the statute by taking advantage of an undisclosed and fraudulent arrangement which the statute condemns and which the maker of the note made possible. The federal policy . . . of protecting [the FDIC] in its various functions against such arrangements is [clear and emphatic]."

We ask students to identify the policy rationale underlying this decision. A number of possible rationales are stated in note 5, page 779. It's worth exploring these in some depth. Students can often come up with other rationales as well.

Section 1823(e) (page 780-84)

The *D'Oench, Duhme* case involved an obvious fraud on bank regulators. But the opinion itself was worded broadly enough to extend to other types of secret agreements. How "secret" the arrangement has to be, and what constitutes an "agreement," are matters of much current controversy. The second excerpted case, *Langley v. FDIC*, page 780, illustrates that the side agreement rule is much broader than cases of overt fraud against the banking regulators.

Langley involved the statutory version of the *D'Oench, Duhme* doctrine, found at 12 U.S.C. § 1823(c). The Langleys borrowed $450,000 from Planters Trust to purchase land and executed a note. They defaulted, and the bank sued on the note. The Langleys counterclaimed and defended on the ground that the bank had fraudulently induced them to sign the notes with misrepresentations about the size and value of the land in question. The FDIC learned of this controversy during an examination in April 1984. The following month Planters failed and the FDIC arranged a purchase and assumption transaction as a result of which the FDIC obtained the Langleys' note. Now the FDIC renews the suit on the note and the Langleys interpose their defense.

As mentioned, at issue here is the statutory version of the side agreement rule, § 1823(e), which provides that "no agreement" which tends to diminish the right of the FDIC in an asset acquired by it in bank failure proceedings is valid against the FDIC unless it is (1) in writing; (2) executed by the bank and a person claiming an adverse interest contemporaneously with the acquisition of the asset by the bank; (3) approved by the board of directors of the bank or its loan committee, with the approval recorded in the minutes; and (4) continuously from the time of its execution an official record of the bank.

It was clear that the four-part test of § 1823(e) was not met, so the statutory issue was whether there was an "agreement" which tended to defeat the FDIC's right in the note. Justice Scalia's rather wooden opinion says that there was an agreement, because the essence of the Langleys' claim was that the bank made certain warranties regarding the size and value of the land, which the bank breached; these warranties were part of the agreement by which the loan transaction was entered into. Justice Scalia says that an agreement is an agreement and neither fraud in the inducement nor the FDIC's actual knowledge at the time it acquired the note of the existence of the Langleys' defense took this transaction outside the scope of the side agreement rule.

We criticize this opinion by eliciting sympathy for the Langleys. First they were defrauded by the bank, and then to make matters worse their defense against the fraud was eliminated by the bank's failure. Did Congress really intend to hit innocent (or ostensibly innocent) borrowers like the Langleys with such a double-whammy? We ask, moreover, whether the case fits within the *D'Oench, Duhme* rationale. In *D'Oench, Duhme* the losing party—or at least its president—was an active conspirator in a scheme to mislead bank examiners. Here the Langleys did nothing to mislead the bank examiners and indeed may themselves have been the victims of fraud.

Moreover, in *D'Oench, Duhme* the FDIC had no knowledge of the defense at the time it acquired the asset in question. Here the FDIC had express knowledge of the dispute prior to the bank's failure. And what about Justice Scalia's interpretation of the word "agreement"? Isn't it preposterous to say that someone who is being defrauded is actually "agreeing" to a contract with a warranty attached? And does this opinion represent sound social policy? In the short run it might increase recoveries for the FDIC's rather bare coffers, but what is it going to do for the banking industry in the long run given the intense competition banks now face in the market for mortgage and other loans? Won't borrowers think twice about borrowing money from a bank knowing that what happened to the Langleys might happen to them? Note that if the Langleys had had the good sense to borrow from a mortgage finance company instead of a bank they would not have found themselves in such a pickle.

The Federal Holder in Due Course Doctrine (pages 784-89)

Langley illustrates the extreme breadth of the modern side agreement rule—a rule so broad as to have drawn the epithet "superpower." The next case, *FSLIC v. Murray*, page 784, shows the third—and so far, final—way in which the FDIC or its assigns might obtain such superpower: the holder in due course doctrine. We set the stage here by briefly describing the scope of the holder in due course rule under the U.C.C. Basically, a person who qualifies as a holder in due course takes the instrument free of certain claims and defenses which would be good against the maker of the instrument. Since the FDIC's powers under the side agreement rule resemble in some respects the powers of a holder in due course, it is not surprising that the FDIC has sought, and sometimes obtained, recognition as a holder in due course.

There would be no problem if the FDIC actually qualified as a holder in due course under the U.C.C. In general, however, the FDIC does not qualify. The principal reason is that the FDIC will almost always acquire the instrument in question as part of a bulk transfer incident to a purchase and assumption transaction. Purchasers in bulk transactions not in the regular course of business do not qualify as holders in due course.

Nevertheless, some cases, such as *FSLIC v. Murray*, grant holder in due course status to the FDIC (actually it was the FSLIC in the case, but FSLIC has now been folded into the FDIC). Four married couples sign a promissory note for $3.6 million payable to Alliance Federal Savings and Loan. Alliance fails and FSLIC files suit against some of the makers of the note. The makers defend on grounds of fraud and alteration of the note. Under state law a material and fraudulent alteration of the note discharges the maker if done without his or her consent. But a subsequent holder in due course can enforce such an altered note according to its original tenor (i.e., according to what it said before the alteration).

The court here says, apparently as a matter of federal common law, that the FSLIC has at least the rights of a holder in due course even though the technical requirements for holder in due course are not met.

We ask a number of questions about this case. First, was it necessary for the court to rely on holder in due course doctrine? Given that it was operating in an area of federal common law, why not just create a rule directly out of federal common law, as the Supreme Court did in *D'Oench, Duhme*? Second, what are the implications of characterizing the FDIC as holder in due course? Are the so-called "real" defenses—such as infancy, incapacity or fraud in the factum—which are good against a holder in due course also good against the FDIC? If so, can the holder in due course rule be used by litigants against the FDIC as a way of narrowing the rights otherwise available to the FDIC or its assigns under the side agreement rule? A number of courts have recognized defenses of this sort as surviving against the FDIC, but as yet the Supreme Court has not spoken.

Relationship Among Authorities (pages 789-90)

The following material concerns the relationship among authorities. We take the position that the three sources of authority—*D'Oench, Duhme*, § 1823(e), and the federal holder in due course rule—have essentially melded into a single side agreement or superpowers rule. A number of courts agree with this, but again the Supreme Court has not spoken.

Elements of the Rule *(pages 790-98)*

The final topic in this chapter addresses certain elements of the side agreement rule. This material should be fairly self-explanatory. There are now literally hundreds of cases on the topic, although the surge has slowed to a trickle as the bank failure problem has ameliorated. Given the extraordinary complexity of doctrine in this area, it is impossible to provide any single case that provides an adequate grounding in the range of issues that are now arising under this body of law.

We have attempted to identify the main areas of doctrinal development and controversy and, by selecting interesting cases, provide the student with a brief glimpse of the enormously ramified and detailed doctrinal development that is occurring in the federal courts under the side agreement rule. To teach this material, we suggest that you pick just one note case out of each of the subject headings (beneficiaries of the rule, the requirement of an "agreement", the requirement of right, title and interest, notice, and scope of the remedy) and ask a question in class based on that case. In most cases we have provided the answer that the court gave in the actual case (we recall vividly how frustrated we were as law students in having to go look up note cases in the library). But, of course, these decisions are not gospel and many can be justly criticized.

Chapter 11: International Banking

INTRODUCTION

We generally begin this chapter with a discussion of what international banking is and why it's important. Broadly speaking, the topic of international banking can be divided into two components. The first component concerns the international activities of U.S. banks and the banking activities of U.S. citizens. The second component concerns the legal rules that affect foreign banks doing business in the United States. Foreign policy issues as well as international treaties and accords are, of course, also areas of concern for students of international banking; these affect both of these components.

International banking sounds interesting, and students generally do not need much encouragement to engage their enthusiasm for the subject. However, we do find it useful to catalogue precisely why we think the topic is important. We usually mention the following items in particular:

1. It is commonplace to say that economic markets are becoming increasingly global. As more and more businesses—even small businesses—become involved in world trade, their banks must develop international expertise to keep up.

2. The financial markets have become global at an even faster pace than other areas of the economy. This is because money is the world's most easily transportable commodity. Billions of dollars can be transferred virtually instantaneously via wire transfer. This cresates two sorts of legal issues. The first concerns the need for simple monitoring and oversight of money movements for tax, drug enforcement and related regulatory issues pertaining to bank clients. The second concerns issues more directly related to regulating the banks themselves. As became apparent in the wake of the BCCI scandal, banks can, to some extent, avoid regulation by dealing in international markets. Since there is no international regulator, bankers can act strategically to avoid domestic regulation. Similarly, there is a danger that banks will locate their activities in those countries with the least amount of regulation. This is a particular concern to the extent that U.S. deposit insurance applies to deposits in foreign banks doing business in the United States. Finally, even banks that are firmly located in the United States can operate in overseas markets and have those activities off-balance sheet, which creates difficulties for U.S regulators.

3. Another reason why international banking issues are important is that regulators and politicians recognize that, to some extent, helping international banks do well internationally will help domestic manufacturing firms improve their international sales. This, in turn, may increase U.S. exports and improve the balance of trade.

FOREIGN BANKS IN THE UNITED STATES

The chapter opens with a list of possible regulatory regulatory approaches to international banking regulation. We encourage you to explore these with students at some length, since they outline, albeit in highly abstract and idealized form, the major regulatory approachs that are used, or proposed to be used, throughout the world. Which do your students think are the best approaches, and why?

The book treats the evolution of U.S. regulation of the activities of foreign banks operating in U.S. markets. As can easily be seen, the regulatory approach has gone from a system with some features of the special dispensation model to one primarily based on a national treatment model but also with elements of special control.

The legal regulation of foreign banks in the United States can best be understood in its historical context, since the statutes tend to respond to perceived pressures and crises rather than to any systematic analysis of the problem. The FBSEA, in particular, is a response to the BCCI affair. The selection from the Kerry-Brown report (pages 803-07), which we have supplemented with information from other sources, should be interesting and entertaining. The personalities involved are compelling, and the events have elements of high drama and tragedy, mixed in with no small dose of farce. Ultimately, few people in the United States were hurt by BCCI, and even the individuals accused of being the principal domestic culprits have so far avoided either criminal or civil liability. However, many people lost money in other countries, and BCCI itself became the focal point for efforts to strengthen supervision of foreign banks doing business in the United States

You might spend some time on the question of how U.S. authorities are to administer the requirement of "comprehensive supervision or regulation on a consolidated basis." Doesn't this involve the Fed in U.S. foreign relations? Think of the consequences, for example, if the Fed were to determine that Japan did not offer sufficiently comprehensive supervision. On the other hand, the Fed has been astute in its international activities, and the Fed chair is a member of the diplomatic teams which deal with issues of international economic policy at the highest levels. Perhaps the Fed is exactly the agency that should be charged with making the FBSEA determination. And isn't it true that some comprehensive regulation requirement is the only way to avoid a repetition of BCCI-type multinational fraud?

The *Daiwa Bank* order (pages 812-13) deals with another highly publicized scandal involving a foreign bank doing business in the United States. Here a top official of Daiwa's New York branch lost more than a billion dollars in trading in U.S. Treasury securities and, amazingly, managed to cover up the losses for over ten years. The Fed took the unprecedented step of expelling this major foreign bank from U.S. operations.

Especially noteworthy is the apparent lack of cooperation and communication that characterized the Japanese authorities' initial response to Mr. Iguchi's confession: the Ministry of Finance did not promptly inform the Fed of the problem at the New York branch.

As noted in to book, Fed Chairman Greenspan sharply criticized the MoF for this lapse (at least, in the superpolite terminology of international economic diplomacy), calling the action "regrettable".

You might ask your students why the United States should care if a rogue trader at a New York branch of a Japanese bank loses a billion dollars in the Treasury securities market. Wasn't this essentially a gift of a billion dollars to the counterparties to the trades, most of whom were probably American citizens? Shouldn't Americans thank Daiwa and urge it to stay, rather than throwing it out on its ear?

INTERNATIONAL ACTIVITIES OF U.S. BANKS

Regulation by the Federal Reserve Board *(pages 815-17)*

U.S. banks doing business abroad must pay attention to both the relevant portions of U.S. law that affect their activities, as well as to the banking laws of the foreign countries in which they wish to do business. We begin this section of the chapter with a description of the regulators that have jurisdiction over international banking issues.

The Fed is the primary regulator of domestic banks' international activities. The Fed approves the establishment of foreign branches by member banks and also regulates banks' foreign investments. The Comptroller does the hands-on regulation of overseas banking by national banks, including on-site examinations. The Commerce Department issues licenses to exporters and bankers financing international trade who must be aware of the regulations concerning exports of sensitive material and of the antiboycott laws. The Treasury Department conducts negotiations for the U.S. on international trade and represents the U.S. in its dealing with international financial organizations such as the International Monetary Fund (IMF).

U.S. banks can do business abroad through a variety of legal forms, including the following:

Member Banks (page 815): The first way that a U.S. bank enters international markets is by opening a *branch* in a foreign country. Banks with capital in excess of $1 million are eligible to do this. Banks doing business abroad through overseas branches must keep separate accounts for their overseas branches.

Export Trading Companies (pages 815-16): The second way U.S. banks can engage in overseas activities is by establishing an "export trading company." These are companies that specialize in financing and otherwise facilitating the export of goods and services abroad. Export trading companies market and advertise overseas, secure orders for U.S. goods, and work with domestic producers to facilitate importing and exporting operations, all for the purpose of improving international trade. There doesn't seem to be much demand for these companies, and they have not played an important role in international banking.

Edge Act Corporations (page 816): A third avenue by which U.S. banks can involve themselves in overseas activities is by forming so-called Edge Act corporations. The reason Edge Act corporations became popular was because they are not considered banks, and thus state law restrictions on interstate banking do not affect them. Banks have been establishing Edge Act corporations since the Edge Act was passed in 1926 as a means of avoiding state law restrictions on interstate expansion. The demise of most such restrictions (pages 32-33 and 358) has largely removed this regulatory advantage. Mention should also be made of Agreement corporations, established under state law, which have powers similar to Edge Act corporations.

International Banking Facilities (pages 816-17). An international banking facility is a corporate form created by the International Banking Act of 1978 as a way of booking international loans and taking international deposits while avoiding U.S regulations such as reserve requirements and certain taxes. We ask why the United States would pass a law that makes it easier for U.S. banks to avoid requirements of U.S. law. The answer, of course, is that U.S. banks were successful in their efforts to persuade Congress that these changes were needed in order to permit U.S. banks to compete successfully with foreign banks not subject to U.S. law.

Home Bank Liability for Foreign Branch Deposits *(pages 819-36)*

FDICIA makes it clear that deposits in U.S. banks' foreign branches are not protected by deposit insurance, and banks do not pay FDIC insurance premiums for such deposits. The law dealing with the liability of solvent banks for the deposits made in its foreign branches is surprisingly complicated. One's instincts suggest that the legal problems in this area should be a matter of basic contract principles, and that the inquiries should revolve around whether the depositor and the bank had an explicit agreement, and if not what the nature of the default rule is. But, as the cases point out, the law is not so simple.

The Deposit Contract in International Banking (pages 819-24)

Citibank v. Wells Fargo Asia (pages 820-22): Citibank had a branch in the Philippines. Wells Fargo Asia Limited (WFAL) was a Singapore-chartered bank, wholly owned by Wells Fargo Bank, a U.S. bank. WFAL made two $1 million time deposits with Citibank/Manila. The interest rate was 10% and the deposits were to be repaid on 12/9 and 12/10.

After these deposits had been made, Citibank's Philippines branch was prohibited from repaying WFAL without the approval of the Central Bank of the Philippines. This regulation reflected an effort by Philippine government to keep money from being repatriated out of the country in the midst of the political upheaval surrounding the collapse of the Marcos dictatorship.

WFAL turned to Citibank/NY for repayment. One question we ask is whether the Philippine decree prevented Citibank from repaying the money in NY and thereby barred

WFAL from collecting in NY. The answer to this is no. The Philippine government's decree only prevented repayment with Philippine assets. Citibank would not have violated Philippine law by choosing to repay the deposits in New York.

A second question concerns theories of recovery. Was there an implied agreement between the parties allowing WFAL to collect in NY, and if not, is there a duty to pay in NY created by the law as a default rule in the contract between WFAL and Citibank?

The district court distinguished agreements respecting *repayment* (which concerns where a depositor can go to get money) and *collection* (which concerns where assets may be taken to satisfy claims). Repayment was to occur in New York. But the trial court found that there was no agreement as to where collection would occur.

We ask students whether this makes sense, or whether the Court of Appeals' argument that it is reasonable to infer that collection and repayment should be at the same place unless there is an explicit agreement to the contrary represents the better view. Moreover, as a matter of corporate law, aren't branches just extensions of banks, much as divisions within a single corporation generally are considered extensions of that corporation. If you have money deposited at the downtown branch of a bank and you go to an uptown bank, don't you expect to be able to make deposits and withdrawals?

What about the testimony of the expert witnesses? We spend a bit of time on this. Both sides had expert witnesses testifying that the interest rates on the deposits provided support for their positions. The interest rates on these deposits were higher than the interest rates on similar accounts in U.S. branches of Citibank. Citibank's experts testified that the interest rate differential was due to the fact that the costs of administering these foreign deposit accounts is lower due to the lack of reserve requirements for these deposits, and the fact that deposit insurance premiums did not have to be paid. But the WFAL experts seeme to have the better argument, namely that the fact that identical interest rates being offered in Manila and in London despite the differences in sovereign risk suggest that the home branch would be liable if the foreign branch was unable to repay. On the other hand, perhaps WFAL had some reason for making this deposit in the Manila branch, such as a desire to curry favor with Philippine governmental or business interests.

The note cases that follow (pages 823-24) provide an interesting foil for *Wells Fargo Asia*. In *Garcia* there appears to have been a specific agreement among the parties, while in *Perez*, there was dispute about whether the money on deposit actually belonged to the depositor or to the Cuban government under Cuban law. The Cuban government took the position that deposits, which came from the wife of a former high-ranking official in the Batista regime, actually belonged to the Cuban government. We note that the court seems to have found the fact that Chase Manhattan bank paid the amount owing to the plaintiff to the new Cuban government a persuasive element on the bank's behalf. But should this be the case? If the depositor had shifted the risks associated with revolution and nationalization to the bank, then she still should be entitled to repayment, right?

Transfer Risk, the Act of State Doctrine, and Sovereign Immunity *(pages 824-36)*

The cases in this section differ fundamentally from those in the previous section, in which the banks involved could repay the depositors without violating the domestic laws of the countries in which their foreign branches were located. By contrast, in the cases that follow involving the Act of State Doctrine and sovereign immunity, the banks involved could not repay the deposits without violating the laws of a foreign sovereign. This puts the banks on firmer legal footing.

Callejo v. Bancomer (pages 825-31): Mexico instituted exchange control regulations requiring that all deposits in Mexico's banks, however denominated, be repaid in Mexican pesos at specified rates of exchange. The rate of exchange was set below the market rate. Someone depositing US$100,000 expecting to get back US$100,000 plus interest would get only, say 1,000,000 pesos worth about US$50,000.

The plaintiffs were U.S. citizens who bought certificates of deposit in private Mexican banks, which, along with other Mexican banks, were later nationalized. The plaintiffs filed suit in the United States against the banks to prevent them from repaying the certificates of deposit in pesos at low rates of exchange. Plaintiffs wanted either rescission of the initial agreement or money damages.

Astonishingly, the district court held that the suit was not based on the bank's commercial activities, and that the bank, as an instrumentality of the Mexican government, was entitled to sovereign immunity. The Court of Appeals held that there was no sovereign immunity because of the specific exception in the statute for suits based on commercial activities.

In essence, the bank was required by Mexican law to breach its contractual obligations to U.S. depositors; still, the commercial activity exception to sovereign immunity applies. The harder question concerns the jurisdictional issue. Under the relevant statute, 12 U.S.C. § 1605(a), U.S. courts will have jurisdiction over (1) commercial activity carried on in the United States; (2) commercial activity carried on outside the United States with acts performed in the United States in connection with that activity; and (3) commercial activity carried on outside the United States that has direct effects in the United States. Which part of § 1605(a) applies? The court rejects the plaintiffs' argument that (1) applies, but accepts the argument that (3) applies on the grounds that it was foreseeable that the banks's activities would have effects within the United States

The final issue concerns the Act of State Doctrine, which holds that courts in one country will not invalidate the acts of independent sovereigns. Plaintiffs have three arguments against the application of the doctrine:

(1) *Commercial activity exception.* Because Mexico's acts were sovereign and not commercial in nature a court could only get the bank to comply with contract by disregarding the regulations. This exception did not apply.

(2) *Treaty exception.* Here the court says the Act of State Doctrine is based on a pessimism about the competence of courts to ascertain norms of international law. The IMF opined that the Mexican government's actions were not inconsistent with IMF rules to which the United States was a signatory. The IMF rules did permit repayment in pesos but said nothing about the rate of exchange. Mexico's actions seemed to have violated IMF rules, because the IMF prohibited exchange control regulations on current international transactions (i.e. any exchange controls must operate prospectively, not retroactively as was done here). But the court went out of its way to avoid this issue.

(3) *Situs of the certificates.* This was a weak argument for the plaintiffs. The remittances were in Texas, but the situs of the certificates was Mexico.

For all these reasons, which basically can be boiled down to a desire on the part of the court to avoid a conflict with the Mexican government's desire to confiscate the assets of American depositors, the plaintiffs lose.